How To Be Green

Friends of the Earth

How To Be Green

John Button

CENTURY

London   Sydney   Auckland   Johannesburg

Published by Century Hutchinson Ltd
Brookmount House, 62–65 Chandos Place, Covent Garden,
London WC2N 4NW

Century Hutchinson Australia (Pty) Ltd
88–91 Albion Street, Surry Hills, NSW 2010, Australia

Century Hutchinson New Zealand Ltd
PO Box 40–086, 32–34 View Road, Glenfield, Auckland 10,
New Zealand

Century Hutchinson South Africa (Pty) Ltd,
PO Box 337, Bergvlei, 2012, South Africa

First published 1989
Reprinted 1989 (twice)

Set in Linotron Palatino by Deltatype, Ellesmere Port

Printed and bound in Great Britain by
The Guernsey Press Co. Ltd., Guernsey, Channel Islands.

British Library Cataloguing in Publication Data
Button, John, 1949–
    How to be green
    1. Environment. Conservation
    I. Title
    333.7'2

    ISBN 0-7126-3543-2

Acknowledgements

Another green book, and more people to thank for their tireless help with facts, suggestions, photocopied articles, checking and proofreading. At Friends of the Earth it would have been almost impossible to complete this project without the help and support of Chris Church, Pippa Hyam, Liz Peltz, Jonathon Porritt, Charles Secrett, Jeremy Vanke, and especially Jan McHarry. Assistance with and scrutiny of particular sections came from Karen Christensen on home and children, Margaret Elphinstone on gardening, Eric Brunner and Riva Joffe on food, and James Hawkins and Clare Hill on health. Marion Paul read nearly all of the manuscript and made many useful suggestions.

A 1 per cent share of the price you pay for this book goes directly to support the campaigning work of Friends of the Earth.

Contents

6 CONTENTS

FOREWORD

Living is polluting. Our very presence on the planet makes us all exploiters of its natural wealth and contributors to the vast volume of waste we collectively spew out into earth, air and sea. In essence, *we* have created today's ecological crisis, not industry or government. After all, it is we who demand industry's products and continue to condone the government's environmentally damaging policies. This is why the notion of individual responsibility is central to the business of cleaning up the planet and developing sustainable ways of creating wealth in the future. It's down to each and every one of us to do our bit for the future by learning to tread more lightly on the planet *right now*.

Awareness of just how much we can do is greater than ever before. The last 12 months have witnessed a veritable explosion in 'green concerns' and it is becoming harder and harder for people to go on claiming that there is nothing they can do. That thin line between feelings of genuine powerlessness and good old-fashioned laziness has been exposed to a far more rigorous scrutiny!

But millions of people still feel they lack the basic information they need to change their lifestyle. *How To Be Green* fills that gap in a no-nonsense, highly practical way. Indeed, as far as our current understanding of green issues goes, it is the definitive guide on how each and every one of us can do our bit for the maintenance of Planet Earth.

There is little point in preaching at people unless they have the wherewithal to make practical changes. Knowledge, after all, is power. Be it in the home or garden, at work or on holiday, there are a multitude of challenges to be met on a daily basis. However small and insignificant these everyday actions may sometimes seem, they are the individual bricks and mortar needed to build a more caring, responsible society.

'Green consumerism' has suddenly become all the rage, and many businesses are making quite genuine efforts to operate in a more environmentally sensitive way. But bandwagons are an alluring means of transport. So we need to beware of those companies and industries that are out to earn a few cheap 'greenie points' simply by making a couple of cosmetic changes in their product ranges or production processes.

By the same token, green consumerism really means a great deal more than simply changing over from an earth-bashing product to a slightly more environmentally sensitive one. It means questioning both the nature and the volume of our consumption. It means reassessing our role as individuals in reinforcing or transforming the fundamental inequalities in today's world economy. And it means challenging politicians to create a policy framework that will encourage more people to adopt a greener lifestyle.

There are some who still find it easier to blame it all on 'the system', on the wicked multinationals, or on this or that political ideology. But in allocating responsibility for the parlous state of the Earth today – let alone for the enormous and continuing human suffering in the poorer countries of the world – we do well to start with ourselves and our own role in perpetuating those wrongs. Of course it is absolutely true to argue that the world will not be saved just because you or I choose to eat organic produce or recycle our daily newspaper, but neither will the world be saved *unless* we make such choices.

A much-loved saying, often quoted by the Quakers, puts it like this: 'It is better to light one small candle than to curse the darkness.' That is the philosophy which has guided Friends of the Earth over the last 20 years. I profoundly hope that this book will now light any number of very practical, small candles for thousands and thousands of people. Ultimately, there is no other way of lightening the ecological darkness that otherwise threatens to engulf us.

Like all good books, the message of this one is remarkably simple. It tells us that seeing, living and being green is a form of self-empowerment; a practical, unpretentious commitment to the dispossessed, to future generations, and to the Earth itself.

Jonathon Porritt
20 March 1989

INTRODUCTION

Overnight, it seems, Britain has turned green. Supermarket chains and disposable nappy manufacturers are falling over each other to be seen as environment-friendly. Television advertisements for fast cars show them carefully avoiding wildlife, and power stations are said to enhance the landscape. Heinz are guardians of the countryside and BP are partners in conservation. Government agencies are promoting green policies and green initiatives. Ministers appear on television explaining how worried they are about global warming, the Prime Minister has claimed the title of 'Friend of the Earth', and 'Her Majesty the Green' (as one daily paper dubbed her) has changed to unleaded petrol.

Never before have so many people been so concerned about the environment. Recent polls show that 94 per cent of us are worried about water pollution and 90 per cent see nuclear waste as a real hazard. The good news is that we are prepared to do something about it, with a bit of encouragement. One survey showed that 94 per cent of households would be prepared to sort their rubbish out at home if councils were to give them some practical support. We are just as concerned about our own health, and that of the people we care about. Four out of five adults have made improvements in their diet in the last four years. And one in five has tried a form of 'natural medicine' rather than relying solely on the drugs routinely handed out by doctors.

You might think that such a level of concern would quickly lead to change. But at this stage there are only small and localised glimmers. Nationally and globally, there is hardly a single indicator of human or environmental well-being which is currently improving. Until very recently, the overwhelming preoccupations of the age have been 'progress', 'growth' and 'expansion'. And cash value has been the only way of measuring the relative advantages of change. While there are still many people for whom cash value is the only one that really counts, more and more of us are growing uneasy about the state of the world. Money can buy many things, including the basics to which every human being on the planet has a right, but there are lots of things it can't guarantee. Money alone can't guarantee our health and fulfilment, nor can it guarantee the future of the giant panda or the Bengal tiger, the fish in the sea or the quality of our drinking water.

Many things have to change if we are to ensure that life – both for us and for all the planet's inhabitants – remains worth living. And the most fundamental step is to change our values. We need to stop seeing the planet's resources as something that human beings have a right to exploit, regardless of the damage which is done in the process. We have to stop believing that what we can take from the planet is limitless; that there will always be more. There are no new places to look for vast untapped resources.

In practical terms, this means using resources as carefully and sparingly as possible. Whether we choose to acknowledge it or not, the wasteful use of resources – whether energy, food or materials – hurts other people and damages the environment. If we really care about other people and about the health of the planet, it's impossible to ignore the gnawing hunger suffered by a tenth of the world's population, or the tragic loss of nearly half the world's rainforests in the last half-century.

Hunger in the Third World and the loss of the rainforest (not to mention inner-city malnutrition and trees stunted by acid rain in Britain) are not just unfortunate, isolated events which happen somewhere else, and about which we can do nothing. Thinking and acting in a green way is about accepting joint responsibility for these things, and then doing something about them. If human beings didn't take more than their fair share, we wouldn't have chronic pollution and starvation. Left to its own devices, nature will not tolerate lasting imbalances. Long-lasting and far-reaching global imbalance such as currently exists is a uniquely human phenomenon.

Luckily, the chance of solving this dilemma is also in human hands. But we must act decisively, and act now. When faced with impending disaster, psychologists tell us, many people are able to continue functioning only by denying the all-too-obvious signs of catastrophe. Part of the denial process is becoming numbed into a state of apathetic acquiescence, into a state where people believe that even though things aren't going as well as they should be, there is little they can do about it.

In fact nothing could be further from the truth. And many of us are beginning to recognise that every action we take can affect the well-being of the planet. Some things we can do on our own whereas others require groups of like-minded people. Still others need pressure to be exerted on those who hold power in our society. But there is no end to the things we can do. And of course they don't all have to be done at once. You can begin in small ways, taking it one step at a time.

For example, most people would find it easy to stop buying aerosols, and start buying more fresh produce rather than packets and tins. Another simple but important step is to take a bag when you go shopping instead of getting new plastic carrier bags every time. And for short journeys, it only takes a bit of planning to leave yourself enough time to walk rather than drive. Once you start, you may find yourself wanting to change every aspect of your life, but you'll soon find the right balance. And there is no doubt that an excess of enthusiasm is always preferable to an excess of apathy.

How To Be Green suggests what you can do at the personal level, in the everyday choices you make about what to eat, what to wear, how to travel, and so on. You may sometimes feel that one person's actions won't make much difference, but when many individuals make the same decisions about their own health and the planet's well-being, then changes start to happen at the next level. Why else would supermarkets have started stocking additive-free lines, or politicians waxing lyrical about rare birds?

Industrialists and shopkeepers would like us to believe that we can save the planet simply by buying a different range of products – ones that don't contain nasty ozone gases or coal tar dyes. But this is only part of the story. 'Green consuming' will certainly help both us and our environment, but it is still consuming. And the blunt truth is that we must learn to consume a lot less. This isn't really a penance. Not only does consuming less save us money; in many cases it is healthier and less stressful too. The American author Duane Elgin calls it 'voluntary simplicity' and describes it as 'a manner of living which is outwardly more simple and inwardly more rich'. It is certainly not ascetic and joyless – in fact quite the reverse.

Though Westminster and Strasbourg may seem far removed from your own living room, you can actually do a great deal about changing things at the highest levels, especially at a time when politicians are falling over themselves to be seen as green. Representatives from campaigning organisations and green-tinted interest groups are suddenly in demand. You too can be part of this growing movement, not by becoming a martyr to the green cause, but simply by saying, 'No, I'm not going to remain blind to the damage we are doing to ourselves and our planet. Yes, I'm going to start doing something about it – today.'

How to use this book

We have tried to make *How To be Green* as easy and practical to use as possible. Under the 'What you can do' headings on each right-hand page, the first steps that you can take have a • symbol against them, followed by a paragraph giving details of books and organisations that you can follow up if you want to look more deeply into a subject.

If you wish to contact any of the organisations or suppliers mentioned, you will find their addresses listed on pages 223–229.

THE ENERGY EQUATION

THE FACTS

The warming of the Earth's atmosphere as a result of the blanketing effect of sulphur, carbon and other polluting gases (often known as the greenhouse effect) is now being taken seriously by scientists and politicians. Although there are other reasons, like deforestation and the chlorofluorocarbons (CFCs) used in fridges and aerosols, the problem is caused mainly by the burning of fossil fuels. Some people think that nuclear power is the answer. But apart from the very serious radiation risks, at today's levels of consumption nuclear power stations cannot be built quickly and cheaply enough to replace fossil fuel energy. Nuclear power produces less than 5 per cent of the energy we use, all as electricity, and increasing the use of nuclear power would have no effect on the fossil fuels used in cars, ships and aeroplanes.

The amount of energy used in Britain has been rising by about 2 per cent every year for the last decade. Sixty-one per cent of all the energy we harness is still lost transporting it round the country, converting it from one sort of energy to another, and using it inefficiently. About 40 per cent of Britain's energy is used in private houses, and two-thirds of that is for space and water heating. Official estimates suggest that this figure could be reduced by about 2 per cent annually fairly easily, though many architects believe that a 20 per cent saving is not unrealistic if existing houses are heated efficiently and insulated, while specially designed houses can cut energy costs by up to 75 per cent.

Taking dwindling resources and the greenhouse effect into account, the answer must be energy efficiency and conservation. This is one area where it is easy to maintain standards of living while consuming less. Solving the equation any other way would be madness.

WHAT NEEDS TO CHANGE

Britain needs a coherent and integrated energy policy which supports energy efficiency and conservation and promotes less polluting ways of generating energy. Energy generating companies should be held responsible both for their own pollution and for encouraging energy efficiency among their customers.

WHAT YOU CAN DO

- Use as little energy as you comfortably can, and use it as efficiently as possible.
- Ask yourself whether you really need all the appliances you have (see page 22), and dispose of the ones you don't need.
- When you buy a new electrical appliance, check its wattage, and take this into account when choosing.
- Try very hard to turn things off when you're not using them.
- Use your car as little as possible (see page 180).
- Find out whether your council runs an energy advice centre and pick up their literature. They may be able to help you with a 'domestic energy audit', and so reduce your fuel bills.

Write to the government's Energy Efficiency Office for their free literature. They can also send you (on request) a copy of their *Network Energy Directory* listing local organisations specialising in domestic energy efficiency. If the subject really interests you, why not subscribe to SCRAM's bi-monthly magazine *The Safe Energy Journal*?

UNDERSTANDING THE ENERGY EQUATION – WHO BENEFITS?

You

The main way in which you benefit immediately from energy efficiency is by spending less, or at least by getting more usable energy for your money.

Other people

Several studies have shown that energy efficiency and conservation projects provide far more employment than high-tech energy generation like nuclear power. Because the skills involved (such as carpentry and plumbing) can be used in other fields, it is also very useful training, especially for young people.

The environment

Less energy generation means reduced emission of the greenhouse gases responsible for over-warming the atmosphere. Fewer power stations, and less waste heat from existing power stations, means less environmental damage.

HOME INSULATION

THE FACTS

Traditionally, buildings in Britain are quite badly insulated. In a typical house as much as half the heat is effectively lost, 15 per cent of it through the roof and 12 per cent through the walls. Lack of insulation is not only costly in terms of energy. Warm air cooling quickly on cold walls creates uncomfortable floor-level downdraughts, and the condensation of water vapour can lead to severe problems of dampness and mould.

As a result of energy conservation campaigns and the availability of special grants, insulation is now acknowledged to be a vital part of the planning, construction and overhaul of buildings. Almost all new houses incorporate reasonably high levels of insulation. A recent survey showed that 92 per cent of hot water tanks are now properly lagged, and 81 per cent of houses have some loft insulation. Draught-proofing is another cheap and important way of conserving energy: about 180,000 houses are currently being surveyed and treated each year.

Despite continuing local and national campaigns, there is still a lot of confusion about the relative benefits of different sorts of home insulation. Surveys have shown quite conclusively that reasonably cheap and simple measures (like draught-proofing and loft and cavity wall insulation) pay for themselves within four years. Double glazing, on the other hand, unless it is installed when the house is built or when the windows need replacing, can take a lifetime to become cost-effective. If buildings are well insulated when they are first built, energy and cost savings can be dramatic.

WHAT NEEDS TO CHANGE

The proper insulation of buildings ought to be an integral part of the specification and design process. High insulation standards should be demanded by house-buyers, and independent random inspection should be used to check that standards are being maintained. Financial help with home insulation needs to be maintained at the present level at least, and local energy initiatives should be encouraged.

WHAT YOU CAN DO

- Insulate yourself by wearing warm clothes, the cheapest way of saving energy.
- Fit draught-excluders to the bottom of your doors, or at least lay 'sausage' cushions against them.
- Check all air leaks from badly fitting windows and doors.
- Carpeting reduces heat loss through the floor, and thick curtains are far more cost-effective than double glazing. Draw them at dusk, behind radiators rather than in front.
- Make sure your hot water tank is properly lagged.
- Check that you have 4 inches (10 cm) of insulation in your roof space, specifying mineral fibre or expanded polystyrene rather than CFC-containing polyurethane or extruded polystyrene. When installing insulation, it is important to allow for proper ventilation or you could find yourself with pollution problems from gas appliances and a high level of carbon dioxide, making you feel lethargic.

The government's Energy Efficiency Office has a range of free leaflets. *Which?* magazine have produced the useful *Energy Savings with Home Improvements* (Hodder and Stoughton, 1987). *The Heating Advice Handbook* (see page 19) contains a very helpful and practical chapter on home insulation.

HOME INSULATION – WHO BENEFITS?

You

You and your household will keep warmer, and you can cut your fuel bills by as much as a quarter simply by insulating your house effectively.

Other people

Council-sponsored local energy schemes help the less well-off to keep warm too. Old people are particularly at risk, with 1,000 people dying of hypothermia each year.

The environment

Coal mines, oil wells and power stations will not have to produce fuel whose energy is then largely wasted, and this will help reduce the greenhouse effect. A reduction in fuel consumption will also cut down on the problems of oil slicks, nuclear accidents and acid rain.

HEATING YOUR HOME EFFICIENTLY

THE FACTS

Between 80 and 90 per cent of the fuel used in Britain's houses is used for space and water heating, yet we still have some of the coldest houses in Europe. By insulating our houses properly and heating them efficiently, we could save £7 billion a year on our annual fuel bill. Efficient energy use is also cost-effective: energy conservation measures cost between 5p and 40p per therm (unit of heat) saved. Investment in energy generation is much more expensive. Building coal-fired power stations costs about 60p per therm gained, and nuclear electricity generation between 80p and £1 per therm.

A lot of energy is wasted keeping water and rooms hotter than necessary, and by maintaining inefficient and inflexible systems. A 1°C temperature reduction on your central heating thermostat, for example, can reduce your fuel bill by between 5 and 8 per cent. Modern boilers are often 35 per cent more efficient than those put into houses 10 years ago. Another recent development is the use of direct solar energy to help heat houses.

With all the competing claims of the energy supply industries, it is difficult to assess which fuels and systems are the safest and most cost-effective. In fact there is relatively little difference between the various fuels if they are used efficiently. Gas produces the least carbon dioxide. Oil and solid fuel are next best, usually being slightly cheaper and creating relatively little pollution *en route*. Electricity is the most expensive and most wasteful, though off-peak heating evens out energy demand and electric heating is the easiest to install. Small electric heaters, radiators blocked by furniture, and the heating of unused spaces are most definitely inefficient.

WHAT NEEDS TO CHANGE

Efficient domestic heating should always be taken into account when planning or renovating buildings. Local councils should offer a heating advice service, and explore the potential for community-wide heating like combined heat and power (CHP) stations, district heating schemes and creating warmth from the burning of domestic refuse.

WHAT YOU CAN DO

- Turn the thermostat on your hot water tank down to 60°C, and mend any leaking hot water taps.
- Think about fitting a shower: a shower uses about half as much hot water as a bath.
- When you wash yourself or the dishes, put the plug in or use a bowl.
- Set central heating thermostats relatively low and only turn them up if it is uncomfortable.
- Don't block radiators with furniture; and put foil behind radiators on outside walls to reflect heat back into the room.
- Keep the use of fan heaters, bar fires and portable gas heaters to a minimum.

See what information is available from your gas and electricity showrooms: some now have energy advice centres. The *Heating Advice Handbook*, published by the London Energy and Employment Network and distributed by ECSC, gives full details of all the alternatives, together with pros, cons and costings. If you are interested in solar heating, which offers real potential for reducing domestic energy needs, ask The Solar Trade Association for their literature.

HEATING YOUR HOME EFFICIENTLY – WHO BENEFITS?

You

Using energy efficiently can cut your fuel bills considerably or, if your house is a cold one, make it warmer for the same financial outlay.

Other people

Insufficient heating and the associated problems of dampness are thought to contribute to the deaths of as many as 50,000 people a year. Community energy-saving schemes can help everybody by sharing experience and skills.

The environment

Efficient heating means that less energy is needed. This in turn reduces the consumption of natural resources and alleviates a wide range of pollution problems, from the poisoning of our forests to the disposal of nuclear waste.

SAVING WATER

THE FACTS

The current debate about the state of Britain's water supply usually hinges on whether a limitless supply of fresh clean water to every home in the country is an inalienable right. The opposing argument is that consumers should be made aware of the true cost of providing that supply by being charged an economic rate for every drop used. The debate continues, but there is no doubt that we are profligate wasters of this important resource. We flush a third of our drinking-quality water down the toilet, bathe in a further 17 per cent and put another 12 per cent through our washing machines and dishwashers. Only 0.008 per cent of drinkable tap water is actually drunk.

Because there is little incentive *not* to use water, the average Briton uses around 10,000 gallons (45,500 litres) of water each year compared with the 2,000 gallons (9,000 litres) used by the average Indian. A few households have already chosen to install a water meter to ensure that they pay only for what they use; such meters are expected to become commonplace as our water is increasingly supplied by commercial companies. After 20 years in which our water consumption has increased by 2 to 3 per cent a year, demand is now levelling out. However, many of the environmental problems associated with water and sewage services are becoming increasingly complex and costly (see page 100). In some areas the true cost of supplying clean water is expected to double in the next five years.

Industry has often led the way in saving water, with water for cooling and cleaning sometimes being recycled 10 times or more before becoming effluent. Domestic water efficiency, on the other hand, has hardly begun as yet.

WHAT NEEDS TO CHANGE

The environmental and health reasons for water conservation policies need to be stressed, and both the public and industry should be educated in simple water conservation measures. Water should be metered to consumers at a fair and equitable cost. Water quality needs to be guaranteed, and safeguarded by independent monitoring bodies. Experimental water conservation projects should be supported and encouraged.

WHAT YOU CAN DO

- Be aware that using water in the way you do, and certainly in the quantity you do, has environmental and health implications. The less you use, the fewer reservoirs are needed and the less sewage is created.
- Mend any leaking taps.
- Put the plug in or use a bowl in the sink when you run water.
- Shower rather than bathe whenever possible.
- Use the minimum flush on dual-flush toilets.
- Only run washing machines and dishwashers with full loads.
- Collect water in a water butt for outdoor use in preference to tap water; dirty washing-up water is fine for the garden.
- Don't wash your car more than once a month. This is usually quite adequate.

Choose water-efficient appliances, especially washing machines – *The Green Consumer Guide* (Gollancz, 1988) contains a detailed listing of the models available. Install a low-volume or dual-flush cistern in your toilet.

CONSERVING WATER – WHO BENEFITS?

You

When water is metered you can quite easily save as much as 25 per cent of your water bill simply by cutting down on wasted water. Less water in the public supply system also prevents sewage works from being overloaded and leaking, with the attendant health hazards.

Other people

The health risks of old and overloaded sewage systems are particularly acute for young children, who play near ground level and constantly have their fingers in their mouths.

The environment

Wildlife and natural beauty suffer when dams and sewage works are built. Overloaded sewage works (currently about 1,800 of the country's 6,000) are a constant pollution threat.

LABOUR SAVERS OR MILLSTONES?

THE FACTS

The average British house contains 23 electrical and four gas appliances, six battery-driven items, 18 electric lights and a miscellaneous collection of hand tools and gadgets. Yet a recent survey showed that the amount of time spent doing housework has hardly changed since 1950 (neither, incidentally, has the share of housework done by men). Whereas clothes washing used to be done once a week, 60 per cent of automatic washing machines are now used at least five times a week. More than 95 per cent of the people who buy multi-attachment hoovers, food-processors and sewing machines never use all the special attachments.

Though some appliances and gadgets make our lives easier and pleasanter, the benefits offered by most manufacturers are questionable. A well-known chef recently explained why he had given away his food-processor. Christina Hardyment, author of a history of household machinery, believes that 'efficient' machines have created impossible standards for the homemaker.

These appliances and gadgets not only clutter up our lives, they also use large quantities of resources and energy, and many pose specific and severe environmental and health risks. Most batteries, and all 'button cells' used in cameras and hearing aids, contain toxic heavy metals such as mercury and cadmium. Most fluorescent lights contain small quantities of mercury compounds, and old ones also use poisonous polychlorinated biphenyls. Nearly all refrigerators contain ozone-destroying chlorofluorocarbons (CFCs), and even the aluminium in the homely saucepan has been linked with Alzheimer's disease.

WHAT NEEDS TO CHANGE

We should question the apparent benefits of all but the most essential appliances and gadgets. We need to change our attitudes towards physical tasks, seeing both the pros and cons of 'labour-saving' devices. And we must get beyond the idea that ever more sophisticated machinery and equipment is necessarily a good thing. More emphasis should be put on usefulness, flexibility, mendability, reliability and environment-friendliness.

WHAT YOU CAN DO

- Look at the household machinery you have and ask yourself whether you really need it all. Sell or give away what you don't need.
- Think about borrowing, renting or sharing things you don't use very often, or buy them second-hand.
- Only buy a new machine when you really must. Check the relevant report in *Which?* magazine, though remember that they won't take things like repairability and environmental impact into account.
- Try appliances and gadgets out at a friend's house before you buy them; see if they really do save time and effort.
- Choose simple, sturdy hand tools rather than complex electrical versions (a good example is the Mouli hand-grater, which is cheap, versatile and silent in operation).
- When you buy batteries, buy the new non-toxic ones.
- Buy long-life lightbulbs.
- If you're buying a large appliance, choose an energy-efficient 'environment-friendly' one.

Read Christina Hardyment's study of appliances, *From Mangle to Microwave* (Polity, 1987) and Doris Longacre's *Living More With Less* (Hodder and Stoughton, 1980).

UNDERSTANDING GADGETS AND APPLIANCES – WHO BENEFITS?

You
With fewer gadgets around the house you will have more space and get more exercise. You will reduce stress, noise and clutter. And you will save money, both on buying things and on getting them repaired when they go wrong.

Other People
Buying only useful, environment-friendly appliances encourages the businesses – which are often small and green-tinted – that make them.

The environment
Every additional gadget you buy uses up resources, most of them non-renewable; many also create toxic pollution. Most household machinery runs on electricity, thus using yet more resources as well as contributing to global warming.

CLEARING CLUTTER

THE FACTS

The veteran green campaigner John Seymour wrote recently: 'Slowly and steadily I am ridding my home, so far as I can, of mass-produced rubbish, and either learning to do without certain things or replacing them with articles made out of honest materials by people who enjoyed making them.'

Though nobody has ever been able to quantify the problem, the vast majority of British homes are stuffed full of things that are rarely or never used, creating vast amounts of cleaning, anxiety and guilt. The American author and cleaning consultant Don Aslett, coiner of the word 'junkosis', reckons that 80 per cent of what we own is more or less redundant, the real usefulness and pleasure coming from the remaining 20 per cent. He tells of the cupboard in the house of a well-off but fairly ordinary 55-year-old woman which yielded five cigarette lighters, 47 pairs of shoes, a box of 1920s magazines, several tennis racquets, 14 boxes of Christmas cards, six poodle collars and a side-saddle. Another household 'dejunked' three lorry-loads of useless clutter and was much happier as a result. Everything we keep and store but never use takes resources out of circulation, and provides us with extra work and worry.

Meanwhile manufacturers and advertisers exhort us to buy more and replace what we have more often. The relative importance of owning things appears to have increased dramatically in recent years: in real terms we spend 29 per cent more on household durables than we did in 1976. A recent 'bride's list' from a major London store contained more than 450 items 'essential to the setting up of a new home'.

WHAT NEEDS TO CHANGE

We ought to think carefully before we add to what we own, whether it is bought, borrowed or given, and learn to live more simply and elegantly. We need to rethink the concept of home being a place full of things, and resist the pressure to 'keep up with' fashion and design trends. As much as possible we need to reduce our dependence on material possessions and place a renewed emphasis on quality rather than quantity.

WHAT YOU CAN DO

- Don't take into your life or your home anything you don't need; if you do, get it out again as soon as possible.
- Don't buy anything (except necessities like fuse wire and sticking plasters) that you 'just might need one day'. This applies even to bargains and free offers.
- Learn to say no when friends offer you things you don't need.
- Spring clean: throw out (into the appropriate recycling containers where possible) anything that is broken, ugly, useless or mouldy; take anything that still has life in it to the local charity shop or offer it to a friend; sort out everything that's left and put it neatly where you can find it again easily. Nothing – not even books, tapes, antiques, crockery and gifts from loving relatives – is automatically junk-proof.

Read Don Aslett's useful and revealing book *Freedom From Clutter* (Exley, 1985), which is full of useful advice.

CLEARING CLUTTER – WHO BENEFITS?

You

Being the less-than-proud owner of a hidden mountain of clutter can be very stressful. Getting rid of clutter makes it much easier to keep your home clean and tidy, and gives you more room to live in instead of using the space to store things you don't really need.

Other people

A cluttered home is a dangerous home, especially for children and old people. The recipients of your hand-me-downs will benefit, as will the makers of the useful and beautiful things you buy to replace the junk.

The environment

The clearing of clutter reduces the resources which are otherwise kept out of circulation. The lower consumption that goes with aware ownership conserves resources and energy and reduces pollution.

RECYCLING USEFUL BITS AND PIECES

THE FACTS

Too often, it seems, our lives turn into an endless round of things breaking down and falling to pieces. We reorganise ourselves around temporarily useless objects and machinery, and move assorted remnants from place to place, waiting for 'someone to come and mend them', or until we can remember to find out the address of 'that place where they might be able to do something with it'.

Living with so many possessions, and hanging on to them whether or not we really need them, is a recent development, and one which is common only in the affluent West. If we don't leave things rotting in cupboards and sheds, we throw them into dustbins and skips. But in countries like China and India there is a thriving market in a wide range of second-hand parts and materials. This trade in recycling and repair supports thousands of small craft businesses, and keeps both skills and money within the local community.

In Britain 30 years ago every town and village had shops and workshops where you could take things to be mended, usually on the premises. Such businesses are now more difficult to find. These days you will probably be told that something simply can't be mended and that you'll have to buy a new one. Yet it is still possible to find efficient and reliable businesses dealing with repair and refurbishment. For example, there are firms in London which specialise in refilling duvets, repairing cane chairs, retinning pots and pans, and repairing and reglazing casserole dishes; while a Newcastle tailor's speciality is replacing worn cuffs and collars on favourite old shirts.

WHAT NEEDS TO CHANGE

We need to rely more on things which last a long time and can be repaired easily, rather than always going for the latest and most up-to-date version. We should demand products which are well made and reliable, since although the situation is improving, built-in obsolescence is still the rule rather than the exception. We ought to pass on the things we don't need, and be willing to repair broken items and buy second-hand whenever possible.

WHAT YOU CAN DO

- When you buy things which you hope will last a long time (from toys and tools to furniture and machinery) choose items which are well made and can be repaired – preferably by you.
- Make things last; don't buy new just for the sake of it.
- Have things repaired, even if it means taking a little trouble to find somebody to mend them for you. Shop windows, adverts in local papers and friends' recommendations can be helpful. If you ask them, the manufacturers may be willing to send you a service manual.
- Pass on the things you don't need any more to a jumble sale or recycling workshop. The Bristol-based organisation Resource will be able to tell you where your nearest one is.
- Try buying things second-hand .from sale-rooms and auctions; you might be surprised at the bargains available.

Tools for Self-Reliance is a nationwide network of people who refurbish hand tools and sewing machines for use in Third World countries. See what you have in your shed or cupboards which might be of use to them, and let them know.

RECYCLING USEFUL BITS AND PIECES – WHO BENEFITS?

You

Recycling things keeps your house free from unwanted clutter, and gives it an individuality which is hard to achieve if everything in it is new. Long-lasting and reliable products save you a lot of bother and frustration, and also save you money in the long run.

Other people

There is a great deal of potential employment in the repair and refurbishing fields. Passing on unwanted items makes it easier for other people to find what they need cheaply.

The environment

The more things that are recycled, the less new raw materials and energy have to be used. In addition, reducing the amount of rubbish we throw away lessens waste and pollution problems at disposal sites.

SQUEAKY CLEAN OR ECOCLEAN?

THE FACTS

Where cleaning products are concerned the market is hogged by a couple of companies: to all intents and purposes the detergent business *is* Unilever and Procter and Gamble. Persil, Surf, Drive, Lux, Comfort, Squeezy, Vim, Sunlight, Lifebuoy, Shield and Domestos are among the two dozen household brands made by the giant Unilever group (who also own Brooke Bond, Oxo and Birds Eye Wall's). Detergents are also among the most highly advertised products in everyday use.

Our passion for cleaning has serious environmental repercussions. The manufacturers of cleaning products are always exhorting us to use 'more and better', so we regularly use two or three times as much as we actually need to get things clean. Though most cleaning products biodegrade within a couple of weeks, many of the ingredients used in them do considerable harm in the process. As much as 30 per cent of most washing powders consists of phosphates, which soften the water and break up dirt. They also over-enrich standing water, contributing to the slimy coating of algae often found on lakes and slow rivers. Chlorine bleaches can produce toxic organochlorines, while many of the synthetic perfumes and colourings used in these products do not degrade easily. In addition, most cleaning products have been tested on animals (see page 34).

In most European countries, phosphate-free natural ingredient cleaning products are widely available, and environment-friendly ranges are now appearing on supermarket shelves as well as in wholefood shops. The detergent tide is beginning to turn.

WHAT NEEDS TO CHANGE

Stringent non-animal tests must ensure that all ingredients used in cleaning products are safe. Phosphates and chlorine bleaches should be phased out in Britain, as in other European countries. Cleaning products should have labels carrying a list of ingredients and describing any health or environmental risks associated with them. Water boards should inform customers about local water hardness so that new 'component' cleaning products can be matched accurately to water quality.

WHAT CAN YOU DO

- Inform yourself about cleaning products, what they contain, and what they do to you and the environment. Ecover produces a useful *Information Handbook* on the subject.
- Use environment-friendly products whenever possible, and always use the minimum amount – try starting with one-third of the recommended amount.
- Avoid detergents as much as you can. A weak vinegar solution makes a good window and ceramic cleaner, and ordinary hot water will deal with most washing up.
- Avoid bleaches as far as possible, and don't pour them down plug holes and lavatories as a matter of course; use hot water and a mild cleaner like Ecover instead.
- Use a warm washing soda solution to clean your oven rather than caustic soda cleaners. If something spills in the oven, sprinkle salt on while it is still warm – it will be easier to clean when cool. Most stains only need a warm detergent solution.

Mike Birkin and Brian Price's *C For Chemicals* (Green Print, 1989) contains full details of the chemical constituents of every type of household cleaning product.

KEEPING THINGS ECOCLEAN – WHO BENEFITS?

You

Using a minimal quantity of environment-friendly cleaning products protects your skin from harmful chemicals. It also keeps your surroundings clean without any health risks, and saves you money in the process.

Other people

The incidence of allergic reactions in children has increased twenty-fold in the last 30 years. This is due largely to the increased use of household chemicals, especially 'biological' detergents. Using as few as possible helps to protect your family.

The environment

Using fewer chemical cleaners reduces the demand for non-renewable resources and minimises water pollution.

HOUSEHOLD PEST CONTROL

THE FACTS

We share our homes with thousands of other living things, many of them too small to see and most of them causing us no harm at all. Some are actively beneficial, like spiders, which eat other insects such as houseflies, earwigs, cockroaches and silverfish, or bats which can eat 3,000 midges in one evening. The larger animals, often quite unfairly, tend to be seen collectively as 'vermin', but many of them only create a health hazard because of the way we dispose of our rubbish.

Almost any animals that share our homes tend to be seen as pests, to be attacked by any means possible, which these days tends to be poison rather than traps. Many of these poisons are toxic to human beings and create acute environmental pollution. A large number of lice, flea, wasp and fly killers, as well as most woodworm treatments, are based on lindane and dichlorvos, both known to cause cancer and listed as 'highly hazardous'. They should never be sprayed indiscriminately indoors, though they often are. Insect repellents designed to be applied to the skin commonly use diethyl toluamide, which is highly toxic if licked or swallowed, and has been known to cause acute poisoning and death. Poisons most commonly used to kill rats and mice – brodifacoum, difenacoum and bromadiolone – have killed many pets and poisoned human beings. The rare and threatened barn owl is particularly at risk from eating poisoned prey.

We kill many animals which are not really pests at all, and even when action is necessary there are always safe alternatives. By playing at chemical warfare we put our own health and the health of the environment at grave risk.

WHAT NEEDS TO CHANGE

We need to learn about the wildlife that shares our houses, to understand which animals and insects are beneficial and which are not. The use of hazardous chemical pesticides for domestic purposes should be severely restricted, and safer alternatives should be widely available. Hazardous pesticides ought to carry a detailed health warning, listing the risks to both the user and the environment.

WHAT YOU CAN DO

- When you see an insect or hear scrabbling in the kitchen cupboard, don't automatically reach for the poison. Spiders and silverfish, for example, do no harm at all and should be left alone, though the presence of silverfish may indicate damp problems.
- It is illegal to kill bats. If you want them moved, contact your local Nature Conservation Trust.
- Keeping food covered and your kitchen clean is the best way to avoid flies and mice.
- Keeping your pets' coats and bedding clean and aired will discourage fleas and lice.
- Mice can be caught in humane mousetraps and released outside.
- If you must use pesticides, use the least harmful ones (like methoprene for lice and fleas and one of the pyrethroids for flies) but remember that swatting flies works just as well.

Michael Allaby's *Conservation at Home* (Unwin Hyman, 1988) is full of information about household wildlife. If you are thinking of having the woodwork in your house treated with pesticides, first read the *Toxic Treatments* report from the London Hazards Centre. It may change your mind about what to do.

UNDERSTANDING HOUSEHOLD PESTS – WHO BENEFITS?

You

You will not be filling your house with chemicals which are well known to be health hazards. By sharing your home with beneficial creatures like spiders you will not need to kill all the flies yourself.

Other people

As with all household chemicals, children are particularly at risk from household pesticides, so using less and using safer alternatives protects them too.

The environment

Many household pesticides are dangerous and persistent environmental pollutants, since they do not stop killing once they have knocked out your chosen victim. The poisons get into the food chain, and end up endangering many other species.

BATHROOM CHEMICALS

THE FACTS

Most bathrooms house a potent mixture of detergents, disinfectants, medicines and personal care products. Despite the pictures of fresh-looking ingredients, they often contain chemical cocktails which are proven health risks.

The lemon smell in your cleaning liquid is usually created with limonene, a possible carcinogen; and the air freshener block in the toilet probably contains paradichlorobenzine, which can cause cancer and liver failure. The descaler you use to clean the bath may well contain phosphoric acid, which could cause serious eye and skin injuries; while sodium hydrogen sulphate, the commonest active ingredient of toilet cleaner, is a powerful skin irritant. The foam bath may contain dangerous levels of formaldehyde, and the toilet paper unacceptable levels of dioxins.

Even cosmetics are not exempt from potential health risks. The cancer-causing lead and mercury with which eighteenth-century upper-class women painted their faces may be a thing of the past, yet imported cosmetics do still occasionally include pigments of these heavy metals. The ammonium thioglycollate commonly found in home perm kits sometimes causes dermatitis in people with sensitive skin, and several anti-dandruff shampoos contain selenium sulphide, a known carcinogen which can be absorbed through the skin and has been implicated in premature aging.

A wide range of 'environment friendly' bathroom products is now available, but many of our bathrooms still contain a large number of chemicals which pose a considerable risk for us and the environment.

WHAT NEEDS TO CHANGE

All bathroom chemicals should carry an ingredients list. Information about the possible health risks of personal care products should be more widely available, especially about what happens when they are combined. Research needs to be done into safe and effective alternatives, ideally using natural renewable resources instead of artificial chemical ingredients.

WHAT YOU CAN DO

- Always think carefully before you buy chemicals for the bathroom. Buy environment-friendly, cruelty-free personal care products (see page 34).
- Avoid chemical 'fresheners': use natural fragrances like lavender or mint leaves instead. Grow a scented plant in the bathroom, or simply open the window.
- Avoid overdosing with bleaches: they don't make your bathroom healthier, and they kill the bacteria which help to decompose sewage.
- Use environment-friendly bathroom cleaning products such as the range marketed by Ecover, which includes cream cleanser and toilet cleaner.

The best source of information about household chemicals is Mike Birkin and Brian Price's *C For Chemicals* (Green Print, 1989); it also suggests safer choices for most purposes. *The Body Shop Book* (Macdonald, 1987) explains why many chemical personal care products are harmful, and gives plenty of natural and commonsense alternatives.

UNDERSTANDING BATHROOM CHEMICALS – WHO BENEFITS?

You

Your health, and your complexion, will almost certainly benefit by shifting away from harsher chemicals to gentler, natural alternatives. You will probably also find that you need fewer bathroom products, which will save you money and space.

Other people

Children are particularly susceptible to chemicals. Water and natural-ingredient soap and toothpaste are all they need in the bathroom.

The environment

The chemicals used in bathroom cleaners and personal care products create a wide range of environmental problems, both in their manufacture and in their disposal. Rivers and ground-water, in particular, will benefit from less chemical dumping, as will our wildlife.

BEAUTY WITHOUT CRUELTY

THE FACTS

Each year the British spend £1.5 billion on cosmetics and toiletries, and until recently most of them were routinely tested on animals, supposedly to see if they would do any harm to human beings. In the last five years the situation has changed quite radically, and now more than 100 companies, including chains like Boots and Tesco, sell 'cruelty-free' products.

Yet many cosmetics and toiletries are still tested on animals. Every year in Britain over 21,000 animals are used to test such products, and thousands more are killed in other countries – 100,000 a year in the USA, for example – for the same reason. Routine tests include the Draize eye and skin tests, where a chemical is dripped into an animal's eyes or applied to their shaved, scratched skin. In the Lethal Dose 50 per cent test, a crude toxicity test, a group of animals is slowly poisoned to death. In one such experiment, rats were force-fed the human equivalent of 4½ lb (2 kg) of lipstick.

The main animals used are rabbits, rats, mice and guinea pigs, though monkeys and dogs are regular victims. Pregnant monkeys have been injected with talcum powder preservative, and dogs fed with toothpaste for over seven years. Animals are also widely used as ingredients for cosmetics – including foetal cells in moisturisers and deer musk in perfumes – despite the fact that there are perfectly good synthetic substitutes available. And there is no evidence that animal testing proves that products are safe for human beings. Indeed, a recent report showed that one in eight users of cosmetics suffer adverse reactions to them, despite the animal suffering which is supposed to protect the user.

WHAT NEEDS TO CHANGE

Manufacturers should be required to list the ingredients of their products, and to indicate whether any of the ingredients have been tested on animals. Information about the cruelty-free alternatives to animal ingredients should be more widely available. A complete ban on the use of animal testing and animal products in the cosmetics industry ought to be implemented as soon as possible.

WHAT YOU CAN DO

- Think carefully before you buy cosmetics and toiletries. Even the most natural and cruelty-free ones usually come in small quantities and complex packaging, which make them quite expensive and wasteful of resources.
- Remember that nothing will keep you more youthful, healthy and attractive than a good diet, fresh air, clean water and a minimum of stress.
- When you do buy toiletries and cosmetics, make sure that you buy 'cruelty-free'. Look out for the 'Choose Cruelty-Free: Not Tested on Animals' rabbit logo.
- The British Union for the Abolition of Vivisection (BUAV) lists 100 cruelty-free companies in their free *Approved Product Guide*: buy the products you need from these companies (many do mail order) and tell your friends about them.

Ask BUAV for a copy of their cruelty-free guidelines, so you understand what makes products truly cruelty-free. The Vegan Society produces a more detailed guide called *The Cruelty-Free Shopper* (including lists of food and clothing which are free of animal products).

BEAUTY WITHOUT CRUELTY – WHO BENEFITS?

You
Many chemical-based cosmetics and toiletries (and a few natural ones too) are known to cause allergic reactions. Using natural alternatives will usually help you to avoid doing damage to your health, particularly to your skin, and help you to learn about the properties of the different natural ingredients.

Other people
Young people are especially susceptible to harmful chemicals in cosmetics, and will benefit from changing to natural alternatives (used as sparingly as possible).

The environment
The main beneficiaries of a shift to cruelty-free products are the animals which are at present bred to suffer torture and distress. A change to products using natural ingredients also reduces pollution around chemical factories.

SAFETY IN THE HOME

THE FACTS

More than three million people a year – one in 20 of us – injure ourselves in our homes badly enough to require hospital or surgery treatment. In 1987, 4,500 people died in home accidents, about half of them involving falls. The cost to the National Health Service of treating home accidents has been estimated at £325 million a year, with another £1.5 billion in lost production and the cost of operating emergency services.

Though home safety may not seem to be a particularly 'green' concern, the main causes of accidents in the home all have an environmental dimension. Many 'impact' accidents, which account for 65 per cent of domestic accidents, are the result of collision with sharp edges and hard surfaces. 'Heat' accidents (including fires) are often associated with inefficient heating systems and soft furnishings which give off toxic fumes when they burn. And 'through the mouth' accidents include a large number of poisonings by household chemicals: nearly 8 per cent of all home accidents in Britain involving under-5s are 'accidental poisonings'.

There are strict safety codes for many items used in the home (including toys, electrical goods and furniture) but products incorporating toxic paints, highly flammable materials and dangerous sharp edges still regularly come on to the market. Some household chemicals now come in tamper-proof containers and have bitter-tasting flavours added to deter children from drinking them. But the simple fact is that our homes contain far too many chemicals which put us, our children and our environment at risk (see pages 28–33).

WHAT NEEDS TO CHANGE

Home health and safety should be essential elements in the education of both children and adults. Trading standards relating to health and safety need to be strictly monitored, and constantly updated in the light of new evidence. Manufacturers of household products should see safety as one of their primary concerns, and ought to be at least partially responsible for educating people about the safety aspects of their products.

WHAT YOU CAN DO

- Educate yourself and your children about safety in the home. The easiest way to do this is to write to the Royal Society for the Prevention of Accidents (RoSPA) for a copy of the *Home Safety Book*, a 16-page illustrated booklet.
- Many of the precautions you can take come down to common sense. Keeping furniture simple and uncluttered helps, as does making sure that floor-coverings won't slip or trip you up.
- Have potentially dangerous electrical equipment checked and mended.
- Keep children's playthings simple and safe.
- Keep household chemicals, especially dangerous ones, to a minimum (see pages 28–33).

RoSPA produces a wide range of useful material apart from their home safety booklet. Ask for a copy of their publications list. Karen Christensen's *Home Ecology* (Arlington, 1989) includes many suggestions for safer, more ecological homes, while anybody interested in people-friendly home design will find a wealth of ideas in Christopher Alexander's *A Pattern Language* (Oxford, 1977).

HOME SAFETY – WHO BENEFITS?

You

A safer and more 'user-friendly' home will save your health and put your mind at rest. A safer house is also likely to be more comfortable and efficient.

Other people

Nearly 40 per cent of all domestic accidents happen to children under 15. Making your home a safer place helps to safeguard their health and their future.

The environment

Safer houses are usually more environment-friendly too. They contain fewer poisonous chemicals, use fewer items made from non-renewable resources, and contain less wasteful junk.

FURNITURE

THE FACTS

Fashions in furniture come and go, but the basic function of chairs, tables, cupboards and drawers has remained unchanged over the decades. This, coupled with the long life of good furniture, explains why the market in second-hand furniture is rapidly expanding. Yet at the same time, demand for new furniture (a market currently worth £2 billion a year) is also increasing. Britain's population has virtually stopped growing, so this suggests that a great deal of furniture is being thrown away.

Until about 40 years ago, most furniture was made of natural materials like wood, leather and horsehair. Wood is still the most popular material, though there is now considerable concern that many of the hardwoods used in furniture are coming from forests which are not being properly managed and replaced. Britain is one of the largest consumers of hardwoods in the world. More than 60 per cent of our hardwoods come from the tropics, 99 per cent of them from badly managed and unsustainable sources (see page 40).

Today a wide range of materials is used in furniture, including plastics, fibreglass, and reconstituted wood products. Several of these materials have proved to be considerable fire and health hazards, especially the polyurethane foam used in soft furnishings such as sofas. This foam creates dense black, acrid, toxic smoke when it burns. Formaldehyde – a known carcinogen – is used in chipboard, and the PVC used in some upholstery gives off toxic dioxins as it burns. Although safer alternatives are now being introduced, there is still a lot of furniture in daily use which puts its owners at risk, not to mention the eventual problem of disposing of it safely.

WHAT NEEDS TO CHANGE

We should have a comprehensive system, like the Friends of the Earth *Good Wood Guide* (see next page), to monitor the hardwoods used in furniture. Customers should be able to ask for, and be sure of getting, timber products from well-managed plantations. The renovation and re-use of durable basic furniture should be encouraged.

WHAT YOU CAN DO

- Buy furniture wisely, and look after it.
- Choose furniture made from natural materials whenever possible; avoid plastics and plastic-laminated board.
- Don't buy new furniture made from tropical hardwoods like mahogany and teak.
- Avoid untreated foam furniture and PVC.
- Think carefully about buying second-hand, especially for basics like tables, chairs and bedsteads – you will almost certainly get better value.
- Find a good home for your unwanted furniture, like a member organisation of the Community Furniture Network.

Friends of the Earth have produced a *Good Wood Guide*, which gives full details of furniture manufacturers and retailers who use only certified or recycled hardwoods. The 'home' section of *Green Pages* (Optima, 1988) contains sections on ecologically sound, health-enhancing beds and chairs, including futons and special 'back chairs'.

THINKING ABOUT FURNITURE – WHO BENEFITS?

You

Choosing your furniture carefully can make an enormous difference to your comfort and posture, as well as eliminating fire and health hazards from your home. Buying wisely, especially if you buy second-hand, can also ease the pressure on your finances.

Other people

Buying ecologically sound furniture creates employment in small furniture workshops, and helps to save the rainforest for the indigenous people who depend on the forest for their survival.

The environment

The main beneficiary of wise furniture-buying is the tropical rainforest, though home-grown trees also benefit from careful management. Cutting down on dangerous plastics reduces harmful toxins in the atmosphere and in groundwater.

GOOD WOOD

THE FACTS

Because our demand for timber exceeds the amount we can grow on a sustainable basis in the Western world, timber harvesting is now a major cause of Third World forest clearance. At least 100 acres (40 hectares) of rainforest are currently being cleared every minute, mostly in order to extract the valuable timber. Although only one tree in 10 is actually used, the destruction is usually total, causing massive ecological and social upheaval. Native peoples are forcibly resettled, and an estimated 50 species of wildlife become extinct every day as a result of the felling. Already more than 30 tropical countries have reached a critical level of forest destruction – and one-time exporters like Nigeria and Thailand now have to import timber. If the felling goes on unchecked, less than a third of the remaining rainforest will still be standing by the year 2000.

About a sixth of Britain's imported hardwood comes from tropical countries, and one-third of that consists of valuable tropical hardwoods like teak, mahogany, ramin and iroko. Over 40 per cent of our plywood comes from the tropics, and we import over two million hardwood doors from tropical countries every year. Less than one-eighth of 1 per cent of our tropical hardwood imports come from properly managed plantations.

In 1988 Friends of the Earth, in conjunction with the National Association of Retail Furnishers, launched a nationwide Good Wood campaign, which aims to provide timber users with information about importers, manufacturers, retailers and designers who use hardwoods from ecologically sound sources. Already over 100 companies and organisations, including a major retail chain, have received a 'seal of approval'.

WHAT NEEDS TO CHANGE

All imported hardwoods, and the products made from them, should indicate their country of origin and whether they have come from a managed plantation. Building firms and local authorities should be encouraged to adopt a 'no tropical hardwoods' policy, and timber and do-it-yourself shops should offer their customers ecologically sound hardwoods.

WHAT YOU CAN DO

- When buying timber, or products made from wood, choose relatively fast-growing softwoods like pine, larch and spruce.
- If you really need to use a hardwood, use temperate beech, elm or oak in preference to tropical woods.
- If you must use a tropical hardwood – though unless you are matching existing timber this should never be necessary – then make sure it is plantation-grown timber which carries a Friends of the Earth Good Wood seal of approval.
- Write to Friends of the Earth for a copy of *The Good Wood Guide*, which gives full details of sources for ecologically sound hardwoods in Britain.

If you have any influence on buying policy for a company or organisation, urge them to adopt a 'no tropical hardwoods' policy. Encourage your local council to follow suit; several already have. Read Catherine Caufield's eloquent plea for the trees, *In The Rainforest* (Heinemann, 1985), in which she says, 'The loss of tropical rainforests is the most crucial ecological issue of our time.'

GOOD WOOD – WHO BENEFITS?

You

The forests of the tropics have given us medicines, rubber, fibres, coffee, tea, sugar, rice, maize, peanuts, oranges and lemons. Nobody knows what other resources they might yet provide. Do we not owe them something in return?

Other people

Native peoples, particularly those of the Amazon Basin and South-East Asia, have been decimated in the race to cash in on forest resources. Stopping the destruction will give them and their children a chance of survival.

The environment

Many ecologists believe that the tropical rainforests hold the key to the climatic balance of the whole planet, as well as protecting fragile soils and preventing desertification. Further destruction of these forests could spell ecological disaster.

DOING IT YOURSELF

THE FACTS

Self-help and self-reliance are important green ideas; nobody knows more about what we need and how we would like our surroundings to be than we do ourselves. The boom in 'do it yourself' (or DIY) over the last 20 years reflects a trend towards creative self-expression. And the ability to use tools and understand building materials puts power, often quite literally, in the hands of the individual householder. Doing it yourself opens up enormous possibilities, but it is also important to recognise and avoid the pitfalls.

Whether we make things ourselves or have them delivered and installed, it is easy to end up following fashion slavishly. DIY projects are more often dictated by the experts who write the manuals than by the builder's individual needs. And DIY materials are too often shoddy, second-rate and ecologically disastrous: a recently published book describes the local DIY shop as 'one of the most comprehensive sources of hazardous materials available without prescription or special licence'. In most DIY projects convenience reigns supreme. This means that traditional construction techniques that have stood the test of time are given up in favour of plastic clips and plywood veneer.

Many DIY techniques involve health hazards too, especially those which use toxic chemicals like wood treatments and solvents. DIY power tools cause 11,000 serious accidents each year. But if you use ecologically sound materials, learn to use tools safely and take proper precautions (such as wearing goggles and ear plugs when necessary), doing it yourself will enable you to create the surroundings you want, and give you a great deal of pleasure in the process.

WHAT NEEDS TO CHANGE

What the do-it-yourself enthusiast needs is full and accurate information about the products and techniques on offer. All DIY chemicals should be labelled with detailed lists of ingredients, safety instructions, and health and environmental risks (see also page 31). Safer alternatives should be developed, and householders encouraged to use them.

WHAT YOU CAN DO

- Learn about basic DIY safety precautions (how to use tools properly, protective clothing, proper ventilation and fire hazards). The Royal Society for the Prevention of Accidents can provide literature.
- If you want to learn DIY, ask your local education department about evening classes.
- Before you start a DIY project, think carefully about the end result. Is it what you really want, or is it what the designer or manufacturer wants?
- Try to use healthy, environment-friendly materials and techniques: natural materials, and mechanical rather than chemical techniques. Use only 'good wood' (see page 40).
- Use chemicals sparingly and appropriately, especially solvents and wood treatments. Check, for example, that you have live woodworm (look for sawdust round the holes) before using highly toxic chemicals.
- Remember that you can now hire many tools rather than buying them.

The Green Consumer Guide (Gollancz, 1988) has a useful chapter on safer DIY products, while Mike Birkin and Brian Price's *C For Chemicals* (Green Print, 1989) gives full details of the risks of specific DIY products.

DOING IT YOURSELF – WHO BENEFITS?

You

Ecologically safe DIY allows you to create the small-scale environments you want while saving you money. Avoiding dangerous chemicals protects your health.

Other people

Children are particularly at risk from DIY chemicals used in the home, often for long periods at a time. Careful use of safe products protects their future.

The environment

Creating your own small-scale environment, especially if you use local materials and the minimum of dangerous chemicals, can reduce environmental damage and pollution.

ORGANISING YOUR SPACE

THE FACTS

There are as many ways of using the private space we occupy as there are people. Yet despite the immense variety of possibilities, we tend to furnish our rooms and plan our gardens according to how we are told they should look, rather than how we might really like them. As a result they become very predictable and generally extremely unecological. The similarity arises because it is not we who choose how to organise our space, it is the 'experts': the kitchen designer, the garden planner, the architect.

It is only quite recently that we gave away so much of our ability to design and create unique and individual spaces. Three hundred years ago most families, with help, built their own houses, and what little furniture they had was home-made. Houses were built from local materials, and had a character which today's designers often strive for in vain. Living spaces were more adaptable than they are now and, though built by hand, tended to last longer. Because the designer was also the person living in the building, there was little chance of such gross miscalculations about what people want as today's tower blocks and concrete slabs.

In the last 10 years the self-build housing and community architecture movements have started to put design decisions back into the hands of the consumers of housing, and this impetus is trickling into interior and garden design too. In 1987 more than 10,000 houses, including some highly attractive and innovative dwellings, were built by their owners. Not only are they better built, there is also an average 40 per cent saving in cost.

WHAT NEEDS TO CHANGE

It needs to be accepted that the people who actually inhabit spaces should as far as possible be involved in designing them. Community planning and building projects ought to be encouraged, and it should be made easier for the public to participate in the design process. Building and planning law should be flexible enough to allow for innovative environment-friendly design, and small-scale experimental 'green' design projects encouraged and supported.

WHAT YOU CAN DO

- Look carefully at the spaces you live in. See what could be done to make them more attractive and maintenance-free.
- Make things as simple as possible by reducing furniture – and thus cleaning – to a minimum (see page 38).
- Introduce as much natural light as possible, and spend as much time as you can in the lightest rooms. Daylight is much better for you (and cheaper) than artificial light. Make sure that curtains are drawn right back from the windows during the day.
- Mirrors can be used effectively to increase natural light.
- Having plants in a room softens the edges and cleans the air; aromatic plants provide a natural perfume too.

Let your imagination go, and think how your space could best be used: it's much easier to adapt than move house. Carol Venolia's *Healing Environments* (Celestial Arts, 1988) is a treasure trove of ideas, as is David Pearson's *The Natural House Book* (Conran Octopus, 1989). Nick Wates and Charles Knevitt's *Community Architecture* (Penguin, 1987) puts the issues in a wider context.

ORGANISING YOUR SPACE – WHO BENEFITS?

You

Considering how much time you spend at home, including most of your leisure time, think of the benefits to you if that space is beautiful, restful and as simple as possible to look after. Having the minimum of clutter prevents accidents, saves cash and may spare you the bother of looking for a new home when your needs change.

Other people

Visitors will enjoy coming to see you if your home is interestingly and comfortably different from the mass-market designer's dream.

The environment

A well-organised and easily maintained house is usually a more environment-friendly house, using fewer resources and creating less pollution. It is almost certainly more beautiful.

NOISE

THE FACTS

Most of us live in noisy surroundings, places where high levels of unwanted sound reach our ears nearly all the time – traffic, aircraft, factories, construction sites, other people's music and conversation. Our brains have a mechanism for shutting out what we don't want to hear, but noise continues to affect our hearing and our health even when we are not aware of it. Noise is one of the most pervasive forms of pollution. Our attention cannot be averted from it as with visual ugliness, it is very widespread and, because it is rarely considered to be true pollution, little is done to reduce it.

Noise is a little-acknowledged but potent health hazard: 80 decibels (the noise level of an alarm clock or a busy office) is the level at which continued exposure can damage hearing, but many everyday noises are louder than this. Jets taking off are permitted to make 110 decibels, while an MOT-approved lorry passing 12 feet (3.6 m) away makes 100 decibels, as does the average food blender at 2 feet (0.6 m). The average noise level of the London Underground is 90 decibels. In the Western world we assume that hearing ability naturally decreases with age, though there is no medical evidence to suggest that deterioration is inevitable.

Though we tend to take noise for granted, 18 per cent of Britons say they are frequently bothered by traffic noise and 20 per cent by neighbours' noise; 8 to 10 per cent of industrial illnesses are exacerbated by noise. In recent years considerable effort has been put into noise reduction and insulation by appliance and car manufacturers and by house-builders, but there is still a long way to go.

WHAT NEEDS TO CHANGE

Annoying noise levels should not be accepted as unavoidable, and noise reduction needs to be taken into account in all building design and planning decisions. Noise levels should be printed on all electrical appliances, and interior and exterior noise levels given with other specifications for cars. Product standards ought to include maximum acceptable noise levels. Offences under noise abatement legislation should be dealt with promptly and thoroughly.

WHAT YOU CAN DO

- Be aware of how much noise you make, and how appropriate it is to the place you are in. Find suitable places for making loud noises, but keep sound levels down in quiet places.
- Be aware of where the noises you don't like are coming from. Asking someone to reduce the volume of whatever is bothering you will often improve things – ask politely rather than suffering in non-silence.
- Avoid loud noises whenever you can, especially prolonged loud noise.
- Ask your local Citizens Advice Bureau for a copy of the official booklet *A Guide to Noise Complaints Procedure*, to check what you can do when noise becomes a real problem.

Check the noise level of an appliance before you buy it, and imagine living with that extra volume. Similarly, check how noisy a new car is before buying it. Create a well-insulated room in your home where you can be quiet or make a noise without bothering other people: thick carpet and curtains will help, and plenty of cushions to absorb the sound. The Noise Abatement Society is the national organisation concerned with limiting noise in our environment – write to them for information.

REDUCING NOISE LEVELS – WHO BENEFITS?

You

Lowering noise levels reduces stress-related symptoms like headache and backache, and will save your hearing too. Lower noise levels will enable you to hear pleasant, soothing sounds like birds singing and the wind in the trees.

Other people

Young people are particularly susceptible to hearing impairment from loud noise. Not exposing them to excessive loud noise will make them less stressed and protect their hearing.

The environment

Noise frightens and upsets wildlife. Noise pollution is often one of the effects of activities which are environmentally destructive, like road-building and quarrying.

TELEVISION

THE FACTS

Ninety-eight per cent of British homes now have a television, and 51 per cent have two or more. We watch an average of 3.7 hours of television every day, with children watching 2.7 hours a day and pensioners nearly twice as much. In all groups other than pensioners, television watching has declined slightly from a peak in 1986.

Though threatened by the same blind commercialism as American television, the public service tradition is still strong in Britain, ensuring a wide range of informative and entertaining programmes. Whatever the content, however, the succession of images on our screen is carefully controlled and formalised, since the aim of television is always to appear smooth and authoritative. This is nowhere truer than of television news programmes, regularly watched by nearly 20 million people each day, though compared with 1962, when 62 per cent of viewers thought the BBC news was always impartial and accurate, only 32 per cent have that faith today.

There is widespread concern about the way that television cuts people off from the world outside their living rooms, feeding them their attitudes and prejudices. For many people, television is like gas, electricity or water, to be switched on whenever it takes their fancy. Several researchers have shown that extended viewing tends to be associated with reduced attention span and poor imaginative abilities, though if watched with discretion, contemporary British television can be an excellent medium for important information and debate. Channel 4's environmental series *Battle for the Planet*, for instance, prompted more than 50,000 viewers to express their concern by phone or letter.

WHAT NEEDS TO CHANGE

The public service tradition needs to be upheld against those who argue for purely commercial broadcasting. Access to television programme-making should be widened to take in a broader cross-section of points of view and interests. Pressures to centralise the control of broadcasting should be resisted, and television employees and presenters should accurately reflect Britain's full range of social and cultural perspectives.

WHAT YOU CAN DO

- It often helps to be more aware of and discriminating in your viewing habits. Mark the newspaper or *Radio* and *TV Times* in advance so you can use it like a shopping list and avoid unwise spur-of-the-moment purchases.
- Remember you can switch off as well as on. You don't have to sit through something that's giving you no pleasure.
- Make a point of discussing programmes afterwards, especially with children.
- Don't expect children to limit their viewing if you can't control yours: 35-year-olds watch an average of eight hours more a week than 15-year-olds!
- Follow up programmes that interest you by writing for further details.

Learn more about television and who decides what should be put on: Stuart Hood's *On Television* (Pluto, 1987) is a good primer. Glasgow University Media Group's *Really Bad News* (Writers and Readers, 1982) exposes news bias on television, while Maire Messenger Davies's *Television is Good for Your Kids* (Hilary Shipman, 1989) opens a real can of worms.

UNDERSTANDING TELEVISION – WHO BENEFITS?

You

We spend a lot of time watching television, and get much of our information from it. Understanding what it does and how you can best use what you learn will help you to make the most of television without being engulfed by it.

Other people

Television can be a useful starting point for important discussions within households, groups and communities. Ideas which people hear about on television, including important green initiatives, can be quickly and widely disseminated.

The environment

A wide range of environmental issues is now being aired on television, though we should be wary of sensationalism and heed the ITN editor who said recently that one reason for current green interest was 'the hellishly good environmental stories we've been getting recently, like Chernobyl and the dead seals'.

APPROPRIATE PETS

THE FACTS

Half of all British homes own a dog or a cat or both. Our pets ate 651,000 tonnes of pet food in 1987 and pet food sales are currently running at £825 million per year, with £45 million a year being spent on advertising.

For many people, pets fulfil an important need for companionship, stimulation and protection. There is another side to keeping pets, however. Half a million stray dogs roam our streets, and nearly 1,000 a day are put down by the Royal Society for the Prevention of Cruelty to Animals (RSPCA). It has been estimated that Britain's dogs are allowed to deposit 100 tonnes of faeces and a million gallons of urine on our streets and public open spaces every day. As many as 400,000 dog bites are reported to the police every year, and one person in 50 is thought to be carrying roundworms (Toxicara canis) ingested from dog and cat excrement. Among schoolchildren it is between 8 and 14 per cent, and 100 children a year suffer serious eye damage (even blindness) as a result.

Although studies have shown that dogs only need a quarter of their diet to be meat and fish, and cats three-quarters, their owners almost invariably feed them larger proportions than this. One favourite ingredient, tuna, involves the indiscriminate killing of thousands of dolphins along with the tuna.

The suffering inflicted on other species kept as pets can be horrendous. The RSPCA reckons that over 80 per cent of tropical fish imported into Britain die within a year of arrival, and there is still a thriving black market in some rare and endangered species, especially tropical birds.

WHAT NEEDS TO CHANGE

There should be a national dog register, and all dogs should carry details of their owner, who would be legally responsible for that dog's conduct. Facilities for owners to deal with their pets' excrement ought to be widely available, especially in public open spaces. People should be able to have dogs and cats neutered easily and free of charge to prevent unwanted breeding. More ecological pet foods, using less meat and fewer imported ingredients, should be on sale in shops and supermarkets.

WHAT YOU CAN DO

- If you are thinking of getting a pet, weigh up the pros and cons very carefully. If in doubt, don't.
- Don't buy small tropical animals as pets; they will never be happy in our climate and only have a one in five chance of surviving the first year.
- If you do get a dog, get a small one rather than a large one.
- Feed your pet as little meat as it needs to keep healthy, using dry food rather than wet food from tins. You will save enormous waste and expense, and improve your pet's health: it has been shown that many pets are addicted to the additives in tinned foods.
- Never let your dog foul public open spaces. Write to the League for the Introduction of Canine Control for their pamphlet giving alternative suggestions.
- Worm your cat or dog regularly.

Make sure that your dog or cat is neutered as early in its life as possible – your local vet will be able to do this quickly and painlessly. The RSPCA produces a range of useful literature, and Pat Lazarus's *Keep Your Pet Healthy the Natural Way* (Macmillan, 1983) contains helpful dietary tips.

APPROPRIATE PETS – WHO BENEFITS?

You

The right pet, chosen carefully and treated respectfully, can give years of pleasure. It isn't worth the worry, guilt and frustration of keeping a pet that isn't really wanted.

Other people

Unaware pet keeping puts other people, especially children, at constant risk of infection and unprovoked attack. It puts the responsibility, which should be yours, on to the already over-stretched animal welfare organisations.

The environment

The chief beneficiaries of more aware pet keeping are the animals themselves, especially those who are left alone in their native habitats.

BEAUTIFUL AND REALLY USEFUL GIFTS

THE FACTS

In many shops which sell 'gift items', the amount of instant trash that you can buy at exorbitant prices is overwhelming. Not only is most of it ugly and non-functional; much of it is also ungreen in every aspect of its manufacture. Many cheaper gift items are made from over-packaged non-renewable materials – mostly plastic – in low-wage countries with poor factory conditions. The importers and retailers make the largest profits. Such a gift rarely benefits the recipient either. If they decide to keep it they will probably either resent dusting round it every week, or put it away until they can pass it on to another unsuspecting person – or until your next visit!

Many gifts which originate in Third World countries use rare plant and animal products. For example, 85 per cent of the world's rhinoceri have been killed in the last 20 years, for their horn. Scarce and beautiful geological specimens are also sought after, as are the cultural artefacts of tribal peoples – items which make sense in their own cultural setting but mean little on a Western mantelpiece.

With a little discrimination and imagination, however, the gifts you give can be both original and welcome, without involving environmental compromise. Many environmental and ethical organisations now produce comprehensive catalogues of useful and beautiful products, from organic seeds and recycled paper to cotton clothes from Third World co-operatives. 'Gift membership' of environmental groups is increasingly popular, and a number of attractive small 'green' shops, several of them in traditional tourist resorts, are catering for the growing interest in environment-friendly giving.

WHAT NEEDS TO CHANGE

The trend towards giving environment-friendly gifts should be encouraged. The gift trade should be supported in any moves it makes to interest its customers in the origins of its products, or in introducing imaginative green gift ideas such as bird-feeders, tree-growing kits, cotton T-shirts or greetings cards made from recycled paper. Local craft industries using local renewable resources should be encouraged.

WHAT YOU CAN DO

- Dispose of any ornaments and nicknacks which are cluttering up your life (see page 24). This will help to stop people who think you like them giving you yet more.
- When you choose presents, give yourself time and think carefully. Many wasteful and wasted gifts are impulse or last-minute purchases.
- Don't be tempted to buy over-packaged gifts just to impress, and try to select things which will give lasting pleasure.
- If you buy cosmetics, buy cruelty-free (see page 34).
- Don't buy anything made of ivory.
- Avoid precious metals, the production of which almost invariably causes severe pollution and social hardship.
- When in doubt, you could buy gift vouchers from a 'green' company, thus allowing the recipient to do the choosing.

Putting yourself on the catalogue mailing list of a variety of green-tinted organisations can solve a host of present problems, though it does mean thinking ahead. The possibilities include Greenpeace, The Woodland Trust, Friends of the Earth, CND, Co-operation, AA Enterprises, Traidcraft and OXFAM.

BEAUTIFUL AND REALLY USEFUL GIFTS – WHO BENEFITS?

You

You will have the satisfaction of knowing that what you give has not harmed the environment, and when your friends see that you are concerned about green issues you will almost certainly start to receive more useful gifts in return.

Other people

Buying beautiful and useful gifts will give real pleasure to their recipients, as well as supporting the many small businesses, both at home and abroad, which make environment-friendly products.

The environment

Endangered species are less threatened, and wasteful and polluting packaging is reduced. People who receive 'green' gifts often then become interested in doing something practical to help the environment.

YOUR PIECE OF LAND

THE FACTS

The ecologist Herbert Girardet once wrote: 'Land is life: land is constant while human life is transient upon it. It is the duty of every generation to leave the land as vigorous and fertile as they found it.' You may not be looking after very much land yourself, but about two-thirds of British dwellings have private gardens, which add up to more than 1,500,000 acres (600,000 hectares) in total. Nearly 50 per cent of men and almost 40 per cent of women do some gardening at least once a month. In 1985 we bought 40 million packets of seeds and 35 million rose bushes.

At the same time, however, we are in danger of losing the precious soil cover which is essential for plant growth, and ultimately for all life. Worldwide, about 4.5 million acres (1.8 million hectares) of productive land are lost each year due to destructive management which leads to erosion. If this remains unchecked, we could lose 18 per cent of the world's productive land area in the next 12 years. Soil erosion is *not* only a problem in other countries. At least 44 per cent of Britain's arable land (which includes the bare soil areas of many domestic gardens and allotments) is thought to be losing topsoil considerably faster than it can be replaced. Even on a very gentle slope (around 2°) heavy rainfall can quickly scar unvegetated areas to a depth of 6 to 9 inches (15 to 23 cm).

The other danger to our soil is pollution by pesticides, on which domestic gardeners spend £30 million every year. Soil can only be created by the organisms that live in it; if we spray indiscriminate poisons on to it, it will die. Land is indeed life, and we must let it live.

WHAT NEEDS TO CHANGE

Gardeners and farmers alike must wean themselves from an over-dependence on chemicals, recognising that the way to keep land in good heart is not to kill the organisms which create the soil, then replace nutrients with artificial fertilisers. We should understand our responsibility to pass land on, in at least as good a condition as we find it, to the next generation.

WHAT YOU CAN DO

- Always take care not to pollute the land you look after; or indeed any land.
- Don't dispose of any toxic chemicals (whether it be old paint or sump oil) by throwing them on the ground.
- Report any dumping of waste you see to your local authority Environmental Health Department; don't just ignore it.
- Don't use artificial chemicals on your garden; use natural alternatives instead (see page 62).
- Try to keep the surface of your garden covered, either with vegetation or mulch, to prevent soil erosion.
- Read about and use organic gardening techniques (see pages 56 and 60).

Reading matter concerning these issues tends to be rather depressing. Try Edward Goldsmith and Nicholas Hildyard's *Green Britain or Industrial Wasteland?* (Polity, 1986), or *Countryside Conflicts* (Gower, 1986). Friends of the Earth produce a very useful *A-Z of Local Pollution*, with practical hints on what to do about it. For inspiration, read John Stewart Collis's *The Worm Forgives the Plough* (Penguin, 1975). There is hope.

LOOKING AFTER YOUR PIECE OF LAND – WHO BENEFITS?

You

An unpolluted environment is a healthy environment. As people who live near waste infill sites so often discover, pollution has a habit of returning to haunt the polluters, sometimes years later.

Other people

Pollution is no respecter of property boundaries, but good land management can bring benefits to the whole of the surrounding area. Others will enjoy seeing and hearing the birds who come to your garden to feed on the worms in your fertile soil.

The environment

Land is the basis of the terrestrial ecological cycle, and is irreplaceable. Looking after the land and keeping it in good heart, year after year, benefits all the life that shares our land with us.

RECYCLING ORGANIC MATERIAL

THE FACTS

Life is constantly recycling itself. Indeed, within natural cycles there is no such thing as 'waste', just the constant decay of organic nutrients into the soil and the constant regrowth of new life. The process is very efficient: it has been estimated that although the Amazon rainforests grow on very poor soil, the lush growth is made possible because less than 1 per cent of the nutrients in the ecological cycle are lost from the system before they are re-used. By comparison, the most efficient agriculture we have devised only produces around a 15 per cent return on nutrient investment.

Most land in Britain has been farmed and gardened chemically for decades, but there is a growing realization that we will only achieve maximum sustainable yields from nature by working *with* natural processes rather than against them. Not only have we been gradually poisoning our land; we have also neglected to return to it the organic material that we consider to be 'waste'. Nearly 30 per cent of household waste is organic material: 9 million tonnes of potato peelings, vegetable trimmings, uneaten food and garden rubbish every year. Then there is the growing quantity of unwanted dung from intensive livestock units, not to mention the 300 million gallons (1,360 million litres) of sewage pumped into Britain's seas every day (more than half of it untreated or only partially filtered).

These examples all involve nutrients being taken from the soil and not returned: the result must eventually be poorer soil. There are now some experimental schemes for reclaiming organic material, but there is a great deal more to be done.

WHAT NEEDS TO CHANGE

It should be made easier to recycle domestic organic 'waste', with local composting schemes supported by government and the farming industry. Householders with gardens ought to make their own compost. Research should be done into ways of using the energy and nutrients in human and animal sewage, and pilot schemes established. The dumping of raw sewage must stop as soon as possible.

WHAT YOU CAN DO

- Waste as little food as possible: scrub root vegetables rather than peeling them, throw away less of the cabbage, try eating the whole apple including the core.
- Don't prepare more food than you can eat.
- Get into the habit of dividing organic household waste from the rest: keep a plastic bucket beside the sink.
- Give what you can to your pets or the birds that visit your garden.
- If you have a garden, either buy a small compost-maker or build a small compost heap – the books suggested below will tell you how.
- If you don't have a garden, offer your organic waste to a friend with a garden or allotment.
- See if your local council will take your garden waste separately; some have leaf dumps which will rot into useful leaf-mould.

The importance of recycling organic material is stressed in many gardening books. Two which give very good instructions on compost-making are Margaret Elphinstone and Julia Langley's *The Holistic Gardener* (Thorsons, 1987) and Geoff Hamilton's *Successful Organic Gardening* (Dorling Kindersley, 1987).

RECYCLING ORGANIC MATERIAL – WHO BENEFITS?

You

If you are returning organic material to your garden as chemical-free compost, you will certainly enjoy a healthier and happier garden. You will be building up the structure of your soil as well as recycling valuable nutrients.

Other people

Returning organic material to the soil means using fewer chemicals in the environment. Less dumped sewage sludge means cleaner rivers and excrement-free beaches, providing a healthier and cleaner outdoors to spend time in.

The environment

Policies to recycle organic material reduce pollution, and enhance biological productivity by rebuilding soil structure and giving back to nature the nutrients that we have borrowed.

WILDLIFE IN THE GARDEN

THE FACTS

Of all the habitats available to wildlife, one of the most valuable and yet most often overlooked is the garden. A mature suburban garden may provide a refuge for 30 different bird species, a dozen butterflies, half a dozen small mammals, 20 orders of insect, 200 different plants and literally thousands of different micro-organisms. A study of Buckingham Palace gardens revealed 21 nesting bird species, 57 species of spider, 90 different beetles, and 343 species of butterflies and moths – a tenth of all the species known in Britain.

Our gardens provide a wide variety of ecological niches. With the risks to wildlife posed by modern agriculture, gardens have become more important as wildlife habitats, providing vital sanctuaries for some species which are becoming quite rare in the wild. Fashions in garden design also have far-reaching implications for wildlife. After the post-Victorian penchant for formal flower beds and the post-war gravel-and-concrete garden, many people are again recognising the value of variety in their gardens. Following a practice advocated by William Robinson more than a century ago, more gardeners are now leaving wild and semi-wild areas, still carefully managed, but allowing birds, butterflies and mammals to share the land with the human beings.

It has been shown convincingly that a garden which has a wild or semi-wild area supports a far richer ecosystem than a conventional lawn, rose bed and shrubbery. As well as helping wildlife to flourish, it provides shelter, ground cover and a nutrient cycle. All of these would be time-consuming and expensive for the gardener to replace artificially.

WHAT NEEDS TO CHANGE

We need to recognise that our gardens are an important part of the landscape, ecologically as well as visually. We need to think in terms of sharing our gardens with wildlife, rather than seeing birds, animals and insects as a threat to our carefully laid plans. Landscaping around public works and buildings, and in public parks and gardens, should also give wildlife a high priority.

WHAT YOU CAN DO

- Plant native species in your garden (such as primroses, bluebells, campion and lady's smock). Buy them from a wildflower seed firm: don't dig them up yourself.
- Leave the grass and nettles to grow long at the far end of the lawn, and cut them only after the wildflowers have had a chance to set seed.
- Plant species which are attractive to wildlife (such as rowan, crab apple and honeysuckle for birds, buddleia and sedum for butterflies).
- Plant hedges rather than relying on fences and walls: hawthorn and blackthorn are particularly attractive to wildlife and offer good security.
- Put dog food out for any hedgehog that visits you (never give them milk); hedgehogs are welcome pest-eaters.
- Build a bird table, bird bath or nesting box – out of the reach of cats!

Write to the Royal Society for the Protection of Birds for their *Gardening for Birds* pack. John Stevens' *Wild Flower Gardening* (Dorling Kindersley, 1987) gives useful practical advice. Michael Chinery's *The Natural History of the Garden* (Collins, 1977) is *the* textbook for the enthusiast, who would also be advised to join the Urban Wildlife Group.

ENCOURAGING WILDLIFE IN THE GARDEN – WHO BENEFITS?

You

Your life will be enriched by the variety of wildlife you see in your garden. In addition, you will save time and money by leaving part of your garden wild or semi-wild.

Other people

Children love seeing birds and animals in their own gardens, and judging by the popularity of the 'open gardens' schemes run by the National Trust and other organisations, the joy of visiting a varied and well-maintained garden is one which is shared by thousands.

The environment

Diversity of habitat is known to help maintain long-term ecological stability, and it is largely through our gardens that we can all help in that process.

ORGANIC GARDENING

THE FACTS

The late 1980s have seen organic gardening come of age. No longer are composting and biological pest control seen as the province of weird back-to-nature fanatics. Ecological management and techniques which emulate nature are widely advocated today by gardening magazines and the gardening experts on radio and television.

Organic gardening is as much an approach to gardening as a set of techniques: working with nature rather than against it. It recognises that nature has sustained a rich mantle of life on the planet for millions of years, producing a yield and a range of crops that no gardener can hope to match. It sees gardening as the careful manipulation of natural cycles in such a way that they give us what we need in terms of food and beauty, but without unnecessary damage to soil, plants and wildlife.

The rapid post-war increase in chemical gardening, with a spray for every bug and a poison for every weed, may have given many gardeners instant solutions to specific problems. But we now know that the long-term consequences – the death of the soil and the indiscriminate destruction of wildlife – cannot justify the sustained use of a chemical arsenal. The garden suffers and in the long run we suffer too, from sterile soil and contaminated food.

The organic approach involves more than the questioning of unnecessary chemicals, however. A more holistic perspective recognises the dangers of losing traditional species, and of over-dependence on exotic hybrids controlled by an ever smaller number of large companies. It asks us to rethink what we mean by pests and weeds. It asks us to take responsibility for the future of the land we are fortunate enough to be looking after.

WHAT NEEDS TO CHANGE

Information and training in organic gardening techniques should be more widely available, as should organic garden supplies like non-chemical composts, manures and remedies. The patenting of rights in plants and plant material should be questioned, and the use of traditional species be more widely encouraged.

WHAT YOU CAN DO

- Get to know your garden thoroughly. Find out what sort of soil you have and what is already growing there. Then work out what your soil needs, if anything.
- Most gardens will benefit enormously from organic manure dug into the soil in the early spring at the rate of about 200 square yards (170 square metres) to the sackful.
- Whenever you see signs of disease or pest damage, think what you can do to help the plant, not just how you can kill the 'enemy'. Always use the mildest remedies first (such as picking caterpillars off your blackcurrant bushes and putting felt collars round your cabbage plants).
- If this doesn't work, write to the Henry Doubleday Research Association (HDRA) for their mail order list of stronger organic remedies.

Get a good practical guide like Lawrence Hill's *Month-by-Month Organic Gardening* (Thorsons, 1989), or Geoff Hamilton's *Successful Organic Gardening* (Dorling Kindersley, 1987). Consider joining the HDRA, Britain's foremost organic gardening organisation and the inspiration behind the television series *All Muck and Magic*: they offer a wide range of services, from seeds to gardening books.

ORGANIC GARDENING – WHO BENEFITS?

You

You will have the satisfaction of understanding your garden and how it works. If you grow any of your own food you will enjoy eating it more, knowing that it is entirely chemical-free.

Other people

You will be supporting the suppliers and nurseries catering for the increasing demand for their products, as well as the growing network of organic gardeners in Britain. Your friends and family will certainly benefit from eating your produce.

The environment

Gardeners who understand and work with the natural processes and cycles of their gardens are better able to comprehend the same processes on a larger scale, and ecological practices carried out on that larger scale will guarantee us all a future.

AVOIDING GARDEN POISONS

THE FACTS

Fifty years ago the most 'scientific' gardener used only a handful of chemicals: copper sulphate and lime against potato blight, derris for greenfly, and nicotine for caterpillars. Today, more than 100 chemical ingredients are available in nearly 500 formulations, each one often packaged under several different names. At least 10 of the 100 are implicated in cancer, and another 40 can cause damage to unborn foetuses. The widely used organophosphates reduce the liver's ability to detoxify the blood, and carbamates can harm the nervous system; 89 brands of pesticide are known allergens and irritants.

The dangers to health might be worth risking if these poisons made our gardens more productive, but they don't. They may kill the particular garden pest you are seeking to destroy, but they frequently do vast amounts of damage to the ecosystem of your garden. In the long run they do not even control specific problems. Insects like red spider mite and viruses like potato blight are causing more and more damage as they become resistant to biocides. The effects of horticultural poisons on wildlife can be disastrous, from the hedgehogs and garden birds killed by metaldehyde in slug pellets to the bees and other pollinating insects decimated by the indiscriminate use of spray guns.

Garden chemicals are costly too, especially given that nature has already evolved highly complex methods of keeping animal and plant populations in check. If you don't kill them, ladybirds and hoverflies will help to look after the aphids, and birds the sawfly larvae. The worms will aerate your soil far more efficiently than you can.

WHAT NEEDS TO CHANGE

Gardeners need to learn about the ecology of their gardens, and the role of each species – whether 'friend' or 'foe' – within that ecosystem. Careful research should be done into the risks of garden chemicals, and the results made public. Where there is a specific risk, it should be clearly stated on the product. The use of safer products ought to be encouraged, and highly suspect poisons banned.

WHAT YOU CAN DO

- Understand your 'enemies' and encourage garden friends (see page 58).
- Keep your plants healthy and, like nature, accept some losses.
- Find out about and use non-toxic organic solutions to garden problems. Always try milder techniques before bringing in the big guns, and even then use organic pesticides that break down quickly in the soil like the pyrethroids or derris.
- Avoid 'all-purpose' killers with names like Roseclear and Total Lawn Treatment, and don't be tempted into 'insurance spraying' for problems you don't have.
- If you must use pesticides, keep them in their original containers on a high shelf and wash yourself thoroughly after using them.

Find out about how your garden works and how you can help nature to do its work: Michael Chinery's *The Living Garden* (Dorling Kindersley, 1986) is excellent. Chapter 4 of Mike Birkin and Brian Price's *C For Chemicals* (Green Print, 1989) contains a valuable list of products and their dangers.

AVOIDING GARDEN POISONS – WHO BENEFITS?

You

Many garden chemicals are highly toxic, which is why farm-workers often wear gas masks and protective suits. Avoiding these chemicals reduces the risk of accidental exposure to them. If you grow your own food, you will be reducing your toxin intake even further.

Other people

One study showed that the children of non-chemical gardeners were six times less likely to contract leukaemia. Reducing our dependence on garden chemicals will mean that fewer people have to work in dangerous chemicals factories.

The environment

Ever since the publication of Rachel Carson's *Silent Spring* in 1962, the dangers of pesticides have been a major environmental concern. Abandoning toxic chemicals in your garden allows at least your piece of land to recover its health and vitality.

PRODUCING YOUR OWN FOOD

THE FACTS

Expecting somebody else to grow our food for us is a very recent development. Two hundred years ago most people grew at least some of their own food. Today convenience dictates that it will nearly always be easier to buy from the supermarket than to be involved in food production ourselves.

Nobody knows how much of our food is grown in private gardens and allotments because official statistics only cover produce which enters 'the market'. During the Dig For Victory campaign of the early 1940s, it was estimated that the proportion rose as high as 10 per cent of all food produced. Even today around one household in eight grows some food crop in their garden or greenhouse, and one in 40 maintains one of Britain's 480,000 allotments. Twelve million packets of vegetable seeds are bought each year, so the art of food production cannot be dead.

The main advantages of growing some of your own food are that you can control what goes on to and into it, and that you can enjoy it as fresh as possible. The few studies that have looked at costs suggest that if you spend money carefully, and treat gardening as a leisure activity rather than a money-earner, you can certainly grow many crops more cheaply than you can buy them. On the other hand, it does mean eating with the seasons, and dealing with both gluts and barren periods.

With the growing interest in organic gardening and the potential of small gardens, there has been a spate of innovations to help the small-scale ecologically minded food producer, from small compost-makers and strawberry barrels to organic peat-free gro-bags and miniature varieties of fruit bushes.

WHAT NEEDS TO CHANGE

We would do well to see our gardens as producers of crops as well as beautiful plants. One author has estimated that if an additional edible fruit tree were planted in one-tenth of Britain's gardens we could produce an extra 250 million lb (113 million kg) of fruit a year within five years.

WHAT YOU CAN DO

- Think about the potential of your garden to grow edible crops, which crops you could usefully use, and who would do the work.
- Unless you feel really committed to food-growing, start small-scale. You don't need to have a neat, single-purpose vegetable patch: many crops can be grown successfully in your flower beds.
- Don't grow more than you can use of one crop; many seed varieties will keep, so you don't have to use the whole packet.
- Start harvesting vegetables when they are young and small; you will often waste less in the long run.
- Feed your soil well: your crops will thrive, and thriving plants discourage pests and diseases.
- Whenever possible, pick produce just before you eat it.

Invest in a good organic gardening book, such as Rob Bullock and Gillie Gould's *The Allotment Book* (Optima, 1988) or Dick Kitto's *Planning the Organic Vegetable Garden* (Thorsons, 1986). Joining the Henry Doubleday Research Association will give you access to organic seeds, an information service and a national network of like-minded gardeners.

PRODUCING YOUR OWN FOOD – WHO BENEFITS?

You

You have the benefit of knowing that at least some of your food has only been fed and sprayed with the things you have chosen. Most gardeners give 'satisfaction' and 'doing something in the fresh air' as added advantages of their work. It also gives your body some exercise.

Other people

Your neighbours will appreciate any produce you have to spare, and fellow gardeners the exchange of seeds, plants and advice. Once they have been pried away from the television, many children love gardening, and the pride of eating their own crops instils a respect for natural processes.

The environment

Producing food from your own land reduces agricultural pressure on land both in this country and abroad, giving nature more breathing space.

WHERE FOOD COMES FROM

THE FACTS

Though the packets on the shelves of the supermarket may proclaim their 'naturalness', few of us stop to think what our food might have looked like in the fields. Unlike our predecessors, we are insulated from concerns about the land and what it can provide, often to the point where we have no idea where or how our food is being grown.

Until recently, people almost exclusively ate food that had been grown and processed near where they lived. Imported foods were a luxury: tangerines were a Christmas treat, and hot chocolate a drink worth celebrating in company. Yet today, when Britain is overproducing many agricultural products ranging from milk to grains, a third of our food is imported. Even with less intensive farming we could easily produce within Britain almost everything required for a varied and sufficient diet for all of us.

As a result of food industry pressure, Britain has recently fallen in line with a European Community (EC) policy of discouraging 'country-of-origin' labelling on both fresh and processed foods. However, many manufacturers and retailers continue to show place of origin. This is vital if we are to use our judgement in deciding where to buy our food from, thereby encouraging a food trade which supports ecological well-being and global justice.

WHAT NEEDS TO CHANGE

We could take more time to think where our food comes from, rather than taking it for granted and expecting exactly the same range to be on offer all the time. Education is the key to such a shift of understanding, especially in our children. Even more than adults they are lulled into the belief that food simply appears, quite magically and with no previous history. Foods must be labelled with their place of origin, since only then can we use our purchasing power to choose where we buy from.

WHAT YOU CAN DO

- Take an interest in where your food comes from.
- Look at the country-of-origin labels, and think about how that food has reached you and the effort involved in the process.
- Decide whether there are countries or firms that you won't buy from (see page 102), or whether there are any that you want to support actively.
- Support local growers and food producers (see page 68).
- If produce doesn't say where it was grown, ask the shop-keeper.

Find out about what grows where and who grows it – look at the labels and ask retailers. As far as home-grown food is concerned, a good book which sets food production in its green context is Charlie Pye-Smith and Richard North's *Working The Land* (Temple Smith, 1984), while the implications of food imports from the Third World (supplying about a fifth of our food) are clearly explained in Jon Bennett's *The Hunger Machine* (Polity, 1987).

KNOWING WHERE FOOD COMES FROM – WHO BENEFITS?

You

When you know where more of your food comes from you can start to make informed choices, and thus be more in control of who and what you support with the money you spend on food.

Other people

More informed and discerning consumers will mean an increased demand for good and wholesome food, thus giving its producers more say in the market. They will find it easier to make a reasonable living for themselves and keep their land in good heart.

The environment

When people who buy food take account of where and how it is grown, environmental policies concerning agriculture and food production will be better understood. The outcome must be a healthier environment.

BUYING LOCALLY

THE FACTS

In traditional non-industrial societies nearly all the food is grown locally, and very little is imported from other countries. It is usually grown and eaten in the same village or locality, and though to us it may seem a monotonous and spartan diet, the food supply is fresh, uses very little energy in its transport and processing, and its control is for the most part in the hands of local people.

In Britain we have a very complex system of food distribution, even of home-grown foods, though in recent years we have been growing an increasing proportion of our own food (now around 64 per cent, as compared with 46 per cent in 1974). This means that fresh foods are nearly always several days old before they reach the shops – the average for 'farm-fresh eggs' is eight days, for example – and it has been estimated that 20 per cent of some fragile crops becomes inedible in transit. The complexity of distribution also makes some foods very expensive. By far the largest cut goes to the distributors rather than the farmers: in the eight years to 1984 farming income rose by 42 per cent while retail prices rose by 166 per cent. The cost of transporting food around the country comes to about £8 billion a year, while total processing and distribution costs account for around 55 per cent of your grocery bill.

Membership of the European Community (EC) has undoubtedly made our food considerably more expensive. Though the EC's Common Agricultural Policy has helped some farmers and food traders to maintain a reasonable income, it has usually been the richer farmers who have benefited, leading to massive overproduction of a wide range of foodstuffs. Fraud is running at billions of pounds a year because of the complexity of price support and trade regulations.

WHAT NEEDS TO CHANGE

Wherever possible, shops should buy fresh produce from local suppliers, thus reducing transport costs and energy wastage. Farmers need to sell directly to consumers, and consumers – either as individuals or as groups – to buy regularly from local growers. More crops which are suited to our own agricultural conditions ought to be grown.

WHAT YOU CAN DO

- When possible, buy fresh produce grown in your own neighbourhood and avoid crops which have travelled long distances.
- If you live within easy distance of a farm or market garden, place a regular order with them for fruit and vegetables. See if your friends or neighbours are interested in sharing an order with you. You may find that the grower is happy to deliver a regular order.
- Look out for roadside signs advertising local produce, and buy from these suppliers.

Small greengrocers and market stalls often sell produce directly from the growers' boxes so you can see who you are buying from. Make a point of looking at the producer's name and address on egg boxes and milk cartons, and buy locally produced items when you can. If you live near a 'pick-your-own' farm, you can save money and get some exercise, while guaranteeing the freshness of your food. But remember to ask the grower what sprays are used, and when the last spraying was done.

BUYING LOCALLY – WHO BENEFITS?

You

Buying fresh produce from local growers (so long as it hasn't been bombarded with chemical sprays) benefits you in several ways. Fresh fruit and vegetables are richer in nutrients, and if you buy regularly from local suppliers you can almost always save money too. Potatoes by the sack from the farm gate, for example, are usually much cheaper than supermarket prices.

Other people

Buying locally grown and processed foods means that you are supporting local farmers, businesses and jobs. As a regular customer, you can often build up a good relationship with your neighbourhood grower.

The environment

Agriculture suited to local conditions and growing a variety of crops helps to keep land in good heart. Considerable energy and pollution are saved in not transporting so much food around the world.

WHOLEFOODS

THE FACTS

Wholefoods are simply undulterated, unrefined staple food-stuffs. They include wholegrains, pulses, nuts, fruits and veget-ables, fish, humanely reared meat and genuinely free-range eggs. Since wholefoods and wholefood shops began to reappear in the early 1970s, there has been considerable confusion – not helped by the food trade – between wholefoods and health foods. Health foods are often just as refined and heavily packaged as (and generally far more expensive than) their mainstream counter-parts.

There is no doubt whatsoever that wholefoods are healthier than processed foods. A varied wholefood diet is much more likely to provide you with nutritional balance than the processed alternatives. However, because of the topsy-turvy economics of the food trade, it is still the case that the more refined a product is, the cheaper it will be. Take bread, for instance, where white sliced (called 'a national disgrace' by the authors of *The Food Scandal*) is several pence a loaf cheaper than wholemeal. But the public is rapidly waking up to the health – and taste – that wholemeal bread offers, and we are now buying 132 per cent more of it (and 60 per cent less soggy white) than we were 10 years ago.

A recent survey showed that 27 per cent of us are aware of the importance of wholefoods, and there is a growing demand for them – even the House of Commons now has a wholefood menu.

WHAT NEEDS TO CHANGE

Grocery shops and supermarkets should increase their range of wholefoods, though prices need to be carefully monitored to ensure that advantage is not taken of people concerned about their health. Labelling ought to be clear, so we can see quickly which lines are wholefoods. And the misleading use of terms like 'natural' and 'wholesome' should be banned.

WHAT YOU CAN DO

- Buy wholefoods in preference to processed foods.
- Eat wholemeal (not just 'brown') bread and wholegrain pastas.
- Buy as much fresh fruit and vegetables as you can afford.
- Try varying your diet by introducing healthy wholefood staples like lentils, beans, rice and nuts – they offer protein and are just as nutritious as meat and dairy products. (Remember, however, that many of these items have been brought halfway round the world.)
- If you have a good wholefood shop nearby, buy as much as you can from it. If you can afford to buy in bulk you save money as well as your health.

Treat yourself to a meal at a good wholefood restaurant and see how tasty it can be. *Cook Yourself A Favour* (Thorsons, 1986) is a good introductory wholefood cookbook, while Sue Mellis and Maggi Sikking's *The Wholefood Express* (Food and Futures, 1986) shows that healthy meals needn't take ages to prepare. Janet Hunt's *The Holistic Cook* (Thorsons, 1986) includes a very good wholefood glossary, together with many basic recipes.

EATING WHOLEFOODS – WHO BENEFITS?

You

Your health will certainly benefit, as you will be eating a more balanced diet. If you are overweight you will probably find that you lose some weight. Cutting down on processed and packaged food as you eat more wholefoods may mean that you also save money.

Other people

The other people you cook for will experience the health and energy benefits of eating wholefoods, a particularly important consideration if you are preparing food for children.

The environment

Eating more wholefoods usually means eating fewer meat and animal products, which in turn means that less land is needed to grow the food you eat. Less processing uses less energy, and the minimal packaging of many wholefoods reduces waste and pollution.

ORGANIC PRODUCE

THE FACTS

Organically grown food is produced without the use of artificial fertilisers, chemical pesticides or growth hormones. Crops are grown on healthy soils built up using natural composts and manures. Livestock is kept in as natural a setting as possible, with plenty of space to move around in and an additive-free diet. Organic farming doesn't mean abandoning all chemicals – traditional non-toxic pesticides are permitted – and it certainly doesn't mean doing nothing to the soil. It is about building up a healthy and balanced ecosystem which can provide nutrient-rich food for many years to come.

There are now more than 1,000 organic farms in Britain – some quite large – though of course this is still a drop in the agricultural ocean. The problems of soil depletion, pesticide residues and nitrate pollution are showing ever more dramatically that intensive farming is unhealthy for us and for the land. And the number of people calling for change is growing rapidly. A recent study by a leading supermarket chain showed that 76 per cent of consumers thought all food should be grown without chemicals. Even farmers are moving against the excesses of 'agribusiness' – a survey showed that 81 per cent of farmers oppose the use of milk-promoting hormone in dairy cattle.

Although as yet it is difficult to get enough organic produce to fulfil demand, and 60 per cent of our organic produce is imported, at least four large supermarket chains are now selling organic fruit and vegetables, together with a limited but growing range of dried and processed organic foods.

WHAT NEEDS TO CHANGE

The government should encourage the shift towards organic agriculture, especially by providing financial support for farmers as they make the expensive and time-consuming switch from chemical to organic husbandry. Funds need to be made available for researching and monitoring organic systems, and widely accepted organic food standards are urgently needed. Retailers should make organic produce even more widely available, without charging unfair and exorbitant premium prices.

WHAT YOU CAN DO

- If you haven't yet tried organic fruit and vegetables, try them and see if you can taste the difference – you should be able to find a good range in your local Sainsbury's, Tesco, Waitrose or Safeway (though it's cheaper to buy from the grower).
- To be sure that produce is genuinely organic, look out for the distinctive symbols of the Soil Association, the Organic Growers Association, or Organic Farmers and Growers.

Alan Gear's *The New Organic Food Guide* (Dent, 1987) is an excellent introduction, listing 600 retail outlets throughout Britain. For the full horror of what pesticides are doing to our food, read Nigel Dudley's *This Poisoned Earth* (Piatkus, 1987) and Stephanie Lashford's *The Residue Report* (Thorsons, 1988). If you are really interested in organic farming, you could join the local branch of The Soil Association or spend a couple of days working on an organic farm in exchange for your bed and board, through a scheme run by Working Weekends On Organic Farms.

ORGANIC PRODUCE – WHO BENEFITS?

You

Eating organic produce ensures that you take in as few harmful chemicals and as many healthy nutrients as possible. Most people who regularly eat organic produce say they find it tastier and more satisfying than non-organic equivalents. Organic farming also makes countryside walks much safer.

Other people

The other people for whom you buy and prepare food will benefit too, a particularly important consideration where children, with their more delicate metabolism, are concerned.

The environment

Organic agriculture helps to maintain ecological balance in many ways. It supports a rich variety of wildlife and a diversity of habitats, reduces soil erosion and creates no toxic pollution.

RAW DEALS

THE FACTS

In our culture, the preparation of food almost invariably means cooking it in one way or another. The only foods that we regularly eat raw are fruit and salad vegetables. By contrast, native peoples like the Hunza of northern Pakistan and the Inuit of northern Canada eat a very high proportion of their food raw, and where they have not adopted Western eating patterns are renowned for their good health and longevity.

Some foods are digested better when cooked, and yield their nutrients more easily. For example, cooking expands the starch in plant fibres, causing the cell walls to rupture, and when meat is cooked the connective tissue is broken down, releasing nutrients for your digestive system to work on. Yet there is always some loss of nutrients during cooking, especially of the water-soluble vitamins like B and C, which are often discarded with the cooking water. If cooked food is not eaten immediately, exposure to the air causes further loss of nutrients through oxidation. Some studies of institutional food have shown alarmingly low nutrient levels, especially of vitamin C.

Most vegetables can be eaten raw, and attractive salads, made with a range of vegetables, nuts, cooked beans, pastas and dried fruit, are commonly available in restaurants and supermarkets. Lightly cooked vegetables, steamed or stir-fried in their own juices, are very popular. These cooking techniques can preserve up to 90 per cent of the nutrients available in the food. Eating more raw or lightly cooked food also fills you faster, providing fewer calories for the amount you eat and thus helping with weight problems.

WHAT NEEDS TO CHANGE

We need to realise the importance of food preparation techniques which conserve the nutrients in food. Fresh fruit and salads should be available on every restaurant and institutional menu, being subsidised where necessary to make them no more expensive than the alternatives. Up-to-date nutritional information ought to be available to caterers and teachers, and children should be encouraged to eat more raw and lightly cooked food.

WHAT YOU CAN DO

- Buy as much fresh fruit and vegetables as possible.
- Always buy fresh in preference to tinned or processed, though frozen foods (especially peas) do retain a high proportion of their nutrients.
- Wash produce thoroughly that you eat with its skin on, especially if it is not organic.
- Experiment with salads and salad dressings. Don't stop at lettuce, tomato and cucumber: add carrots, peppers, mushrooms, sultanas, celery and finely chopped cabbage.
- Cook your vegetables with just half a cup of water and a little oil at the bottom of the saucepan, or stir-fry them in the traditional Chinese way.
- Use a pressure cooker whenever you can to retain nutrients and save energy.
- Cook everything for as short a time as possible, though do – especially with meat – make sure that it's cooked right through.

Buy a good cookery book which takes these things into account, such as *Laurel's Kitchen* (Routledge, 1979) or Charles Gerras's *Feasting on Raw Foods* (Thorsons, 1987). Read Leon Chaitow's *Stone Age Diet* (Optima, 1987), which advocates a diet much closer to what our bodies were designed to work on, and gives some fascinating cross-cultural comparisons.

RAW DEALS – WHO BENEFITS?

You
Eating more fresh and lightly cooked foods provides you with important minerals and vitamins, helping to keep you healthy, fit and your natural weight.

Other people
Fresh produce tends to be more local produce, so you will be helping local growers, and your children will certainly benefit from more raw and lightly cooked foods – you may well be surprised at how quickly they take to them.

The environment
People who eat a lot of fresh food tend to ask for produce which has not been over-treated with chemicals, which helps the land in several ways (see page 72).

GROWING FOOD WITHOUT A GARDEN

THE FACTS

Even if you don't have a garden there is quite a lot you can do towards supplementing your diet with tasty and healthy fresh ingredients that you have grown or made yourself. One very easy way of growing food indoors is to sprout the seeds of a variety of grains and beans. When a seed sprouts its food value increases enormously, providing a very good source of vitamins – especially vitamin C – and minerals. They can be eaten absolutely fresh, and make an excellent addition to salads, sandwiches and stir-fries.

A wide variety of herbs can be grown indoors too, though both sprouts and herbs appreciate as much sun as possible. Kitchen herbs like thyme, sage, marjoram, chives, rosemary and parsley can all be grown in pots on the kitchen windowsill, and using fresh herbs means that you get their full flavour and nutritional value. Indoor herbs also provide fragrance – a natural alternative to chemical deodorants. If you have enough windowsill space, or a sunny balcony or conservatory, you could grow salad crops like tomatoes and peppers.

Making your own yoghurt is easy, and ensures that what you eat is additive-free and alive, unlike many shop-bought yoghurts. Similarly, you can use fresh yeast – another living organism – to make your own bread, wines and beers. Again, you have the satisfaction of knowing that the end result is wholesome and additive-free.

WHAT NEEDS TO CHANGE

In Britain today most people do not produce any of their own food. Doing the little you can to grow your own food helps you to appreciate what goes into producing it. Children, especially, gain a great deal of satisfaction from growing even a small proportion of their own food.

WHAT YOU CAN DO

- To sprout seeds all you need is two jam jars, a couple of muslin squares, two rubber bands, and a couple of ounces each of untreated seeds (e.g. mung beans and sunflower seeds).
- Wash the beans and put them in the jars.
- Cover them with tepid water, then put the muslins over the tops of the jars, securing them with the rubber bands.
- Change the water twice a day, and stand the jars with their necks tilted downwards, leaving the seeds damp but not submerged.
- The sprouts will be ready to eat in three to five days.
- Wash them thoroughly in a colander, and eat them fresh.

Try growing herbs on the kitchen windowsill: many garden shops sell indoor herb-growing kits. Ask at your local wholefood shop about yoghurt culture, wine-making kits and special sprouting trays which make the growing of sprouts even easier. Janet Hunt's *The Holistic Cook* (Thorsons, 1986) has an illustrated section on sprouting seeds together with instructions for making yoghurt, beers and wines; Lesley Bremness's *The Complete Book of Herbs* (Dorling Kindersley, 1988) will tell you all you need to know about growing herbs indoors.

GROWING FOOD WITHOUT A GARDEN – WHO BENEFITS?

You

Growing a little of your own food ensures a regular supply of essential nutrients, especially vitamin C, even during the winter months.

Other people

Children love watching things grow, and these simple methods bring the idea vividly home to them that all food must be grown. Their health will also benefit from eating home-grown food.

The environment

Only very small quantities of food can be grown indoors, but every little reduces the pressure on the land. Seed sprouting – widely used in traditional Eastern cookery – saves energy and is a very resource-efficient way of producing nutritious food. It is also cheap and easy.

CUTTING DOWN ON SUGAR

THE FACTS

Britons eat vast amounts of sugar – nearly 130 lb (60 kg) each year for every man, woman and child, or around 6 heaped tablespoonsful a day. Only half of that is added to food in the home; the rest gets into our bodies in sweets, snacks, drinks, and tinned and packaged food. Refined sugar has almost no nutritional value at all (just lots of calories) and though other sugars – including honey – do contain small quantities of nutrients, there is no such thing as a healthy sugar when eaten in large amounts.

Because it can be eaten in quantity without making us feel full, it is an important contributing factor in obesity, and therefore in heart disease. Sugar rots teeth, is suspected of contributing to allergies like headaches and dizziness, and is probably the commonest dependency in Britain today – a dependency which often starts within days of a baby's birth. Concern about these issues may explain why sugar consumption is currently dropping at a rate of about 20 per cent a decade. To counter this trend, the three major British confectionery manufacturers alone spend around £75 million a year on advertising (compared with the £4 million spent on advertising fresh fruit and vegetables).

Sugar is not only unhealthy for us; it has a long history of causing human misery and environmental damage. For many decades the sugar trade depended upon slave labour. Now, because the world market is largely in the hands of a few giant companies and demand for sugar is falling, farmers are still suffering. Land used for sugar in countries like Cuba, Brazil and Mauritius cannot be used to grow real food for local people, and becomes impoverished after years of growing a single crop.

WHAT NEEDS TO CHANGE

Official reports say that our health would benefit from halving our sugar consumption. Cutting direct sugar consumption only deals with part of the problem, however. A can of cola contains the equivalent of 7 teaspoons of sugar, while tomato ketchup often includes a fifth of its weight in sugar. We need to know exactly how much sugar of all kinds is included in foods; honest and accurate nutritional labelling is long overdue.

WHAT YOU CAN DO

- Put half the suggested amount of sugar in recipes and hot drinks.
- Try drinks and fruit puddings without sugar for a few days and taste the difference.
- Take the sugar bowl off the table and the tea tray.
- When you are tempted to buy a sugary snack, check whether something healthier – fruit, nuts or something savoury – wouldn't give you the same pleasure.
- When you do buy a sweet snack, eat one bit at a time and make it last much longer: it's the initial 'hit' of a large quantity of sugar that throws your body off balance.

Try cutting sugar out altogether for a few days and see if other things taste different. For the gory details about sugar and your health read Caroline Walker and Geoffrey Cannon's *The Food Scandal* (Century, 1985) or John Yudkin's *Pure, White and Deadly* (Penguin, 1988). Chapter 3 of Geoffrey Cannon's *The Politics of Food* (Century, 1987) gives a frightening but amusing account of how the sugar giants fight back. Richard North's *The Real Cost* (Chatto and Windus, 1986) shows how the sugar industry cripples parts of the Third World.

CUTTING DOWN ON SUGAR – WHO BENEFITS?

You
Your body will quickly start to benefit from eating less sugar; easing off on sugar is one of the simplest ways of losing weight. Your teeth will benefit enormously, and you will cut down on dental bills and misery. You will almost certainly feel more energetic and less sleepy, and reduce your chances of getting heart disease or cancer.

Other people
Your children will certainly benefit when you cut down on sugar: it is one of the biggest favours you can do for their health.

The environment
When it is not producing sugar, land can be used for nutritious crops instead, or returned to nature. Intensive farming of one crop (monoculture) is inevitably bad for the land because it takes out the same nutrients over and over again.

EASING BACK ON SALT

THE FACTS

Salt is a cause (though not so important a cause as excessive alcohol) of high blood pressure. And high blood pressure is in turn a major risk factor for heart disease and strokes. The World Health Organisation (WHO) recommends an upper limit of 0.17 oz (5 g) of salt a day, and points out that societies without high blood pressure problems generally consume less than 0.1 oz (3 g) a day. Nobody knows exactly how much salt Britons consume, but it is thought to average out at about 0.4 oz (12 g) a day, more than twice the WHO recommended limit. The number of people in Britain dying of circulatory disease is running at around 250,000 a year, of whom nearly a third die of strokes. This is the highest rate in the world.

Of all the salt we eat, as much as four-fifths of it is added to processed foods, which makes it harder than sugar to cut down on. Most tinned soups, bacon, pickles and sauces are particularly high in salt; they often contain large proportions of sugar, too. Around a third of our salt intake is added to foods we don't normally think of as being particularly savoury, like bread, biscuits and breakfast cereals. Another form of sodium – sodium citrate – is routinely added to fizzy drinks.

The way we traditionally cook things in Britain involves salt at almost every stage. Yet cooking vegetables in salt water makes them no better, greener or more tender, and there is no evidence that salt improves the baking quality of pastry. The extra salt we are supposed to need in hot weather to replace the body salts we sweat out is a pure fabrication, and except in very hot climates salt does not help to prevent cramps.

WHAT NEEDS TO CHANGE

Excessive salt must be acknowledged as a factor in high blood pressure and heart disease. Salt consumption should be reduced to no more than 0.17 oz (5 g) a day, and this guideline should be observed in meals served in restaurants and institutions. Labelling should clearly state the total salt content, and products with a very high salt content ought to carry a health warning.

WHAT YOU CAN DO

- Take the salt off the dining table, or at least keep it away from children.
- Try cooking vegetables, fish and eggs without adding salt; use herbs and spices instead – mint with potatoes and peas, caraway with cabbage, oregano in spaghetti sauce.
- Look at the labels of foods which might contain a lot of salt, especially breakfast cereals and processed meat products; avoid them.
- Never add salt to the food of babies and young children.

Add less salt when you cook, and aim to stop using it completely – you will get quite enough from the processed food you eat. Choose unsalted nuts and crisps rather than salted ones. The nutritional arguments for reduced salt intake are set out clearly in Chapter 7 of Caroline Walker and Geoffrey Cannon's *The Food Scandal* (Century, 1985), while *The Great British Diet* (Century, 1985) gives useful lists of lower-salt alternatives to many widely used ingredients.

EASING BACK ON SALT – WHO BENEFITS?

You

Your body only needs about 0.035 oz (1 g) of salt a day, roughly a tenth of what you are probably eating. Cutting back drastically on salt helps you avoid circulatory disease and strokes. Once you are used to a low-salt diet, you will probably find that you begin to appreciate the subtle flavours of foods which were previously smothered with too much salt.

Other people

The effects of salt on the circulation can start at a very early age. You owe it to your children to keep the salt content of their diet as low as possible.

The environment

Lower demand for salt reduces pollution in salt-producing areas like Cheshire. Salt is a major ingredient in many highly processed, high-value-added foods which waste large amounts of energy in production and packaging.

FOOD ADDITIVES

THE FACTS

The use of food additives has grown enormously in recent years, and has probably increased tenfold in the last three decades. About 200,000 tonnes, costing £300 million, are added to our food every year. Around 3,800 different additives are used for some 100 different functions, including bleaches, solvents, carriers, preservatives, antioxidants, emulsifiers, colourings and flavourings. Processed foods, which constitute 75 per cent of the average British diet, are rarely additive-free.

Some additives undoubtedly do improve the taste and nutritional value of our food. Most, however, do not. They are added to food to pass lower-quality food off as higher-quality, to turn simple ingredients into unnecessarily complex and expensive foods, to increase shelf life so that days-old food can be sold as fresh, and to make very similar products look quite different. They are used primarily to boost the profits of the manufacturers, with relatively little thought for your health: 93 per cent of additives have no nutritional value whatsoever and may, indeed, present specific health risks.

Britain allows more additives and has weaker controls than any other Western country. Fifty-seven different suspect additives (including the 'dirty dozen' azo dyes which have been implicated in hyperactivity and cancer) are still permitted in Britain, though public pressure has led many producers and retailers to stop endorsing their use. In order to capture the 'healthy eating' market, many manufacturers are now putting 'additive-free' flashes on their products, though these are often deliberately vague and misleading.

WHAT NEEDS TO CHANGE

The 25 or so additives for which there is clear evidence of toxicity, including all artificial colourings, should be banned. An additional 32 suspect additives ought to be severely restricted in their use, especially in foods designed primarily to appeal to children. The use of any unnecessary additives should be discouraged. Labelling needs to include all additives, with suspect additives highlighted; and misleading advertising in relation to food additives should be outlawed.

WHAT YOU CAN DO

- Eat as much fresh food as possible.
- Read the labels on packets and tins before you buy them.
- Avoid the processed foods containing the most additives (such as dessert mixes, cakes and fancy biscuits, tinned and packet soups, savoury mixes, processed meat products and anything highly coloured).
- If you have young children give them diluted fruit juice instead of squash; fruit, sandwiches and raw vegetables instead of sweets and biscuits.
- Learn about 'E numbers', and in particular steer clear of the E100 to 180 colourings, sulphur dioxide E220, the anti-oxidants E320 to 321 and monosodium glutamate E621.

Food Adulteration And How To Beat It (Unwin Hyman, 1988) is the best book on the subject, though Maurice Hanssen's *The New E for Additives* (Thorsons, 1987) and Erik Millstone's *Food Additives* (Penguin, 1986) are also illuminating. Chapter 4 of Geoffrey Cannon's *The Politics of Food* (Century, 1987) investigates the official cover-up of the risks of additives, while Tim Lobstein's *Children's Food* (Unwin Hyman, 1988) explains very clearly the risks to children of food additives.

UNDERSTANDING FOOD ADDITIVES – WHO BENEFITS?

You

Nobody really knows the long-term effects of a high-additive diet. However a recent survey found 'specific safety doubts and uncertainties' with 85 out of 299 permitted additives, so it is surely better to be safe than sorry.

Other people

Children are particularly at risk from additives, and should be protected as far as possible. The health of food workers would also benefit from a reduction in the use of suspect additives.

The environment

The production of many artificial additives, such as coal tar dyes and chemical bleaches, leads to pollution around the factories where they are manufactured. A move towards less processed food and more fresh food would also encourage more ecologically sound agricultural and food distribution systems.

WATCHING THE FAT

THE FACTS

In Britain we eat on average about 4.5 oz (135g) of fats every day, accounting for about 38 per cent of our calorie intake. Twenty-seven per cent of this comes from meat and 30 per cent from dairy products. Excessive consumption of fats, especially saturated fats, causes the furring up of the arteries, leading to circulation and heart problems. Heart disease is now the biggest killer in Britain, and a third of all heart disease deaths are of men under the age of 65. Scotland and Northern Ireland have the highest heart disease death rates in the world, followed closely by England and Wales. Eating too much fat can also cause certain cancers, and of course fats help make you fat.

Many dieticians suggest that we could usefully cut our fat intake by a third, that third consisting mainly of the saturated fats found in animal products, coconut and palm oil (much used in food processing), and hardened vegetable and fish oils. Small amounts of polyunsaturated fats, naturally present in vegetables, beans and fish, seem to protect us from circulation problems, but if consumed alongside a diet rich in saturated fats the advantage can be lost. Excessive fat intake is a particular problem for people with a high blood cholesterol level, but if fats are kept to a low level, cholesterol intake alone does not appear to be a cause for concern.

As with sugar and salt, there is a great deal you can do to cut down on 'obvious' fats like cream and fatty meat, but many fats, usually of the hardened saturated variety, are 'hidden' in biscuits, cakes, pies and pastries. Many of the oils we use in Britain are imported. Olive oil is probably the best choice for your health, but it is relatively expensive.

WHAT NEEDS TO CHANGE

People need to be alerted to the dangers of excessive fat intake. They should aim to cut their overall fat consumption by between a quarter and a third, and halve their saturated fat consumption. Clear labelling ought to show the fat content of all foods, distinguishing between the different types of fat; and low-fat foods should be widely available. Restaurants and institutional caterers need to reduce the fat content of their meals.

WHAT YOU CAN DO

- Spread less margarine or butter on your bread.
- Grill, bake or steam food rather than frying it.
- Steer clear of fatty meat, burgers, sausages and meat pies; buy lean meat instead – heart, for example, is cheap and tasty.
- Buy skimmed or semi-skimmed milk.
- Keep chips and crisps for treats rather than every day.
- Cut down on biscuits, cakes and pastries; go for healthy treats like fruit and nuts instead.
- Buy oils, margarines and spreads which are high in polyunsaturates and monounsaturates (corn, soya, sunflower or olive) but still use them sparingly.
- Don't re-use oil more than you have to, since it oxidises, and keep your oils in the fridge for the same reason.
- Try natural low-fat yoghurt, low-fat soft cheese and quark.

Try cutting as many fats as possible out of your diet for a week, and see if you feel any better. Read about the dangers of excessive fat consumption in Caroline Walker and Geoffrey Cannon's *The Food Scandal* (Century, 1985). For detailed suggestions about cutting down on fat, read *The Great British Diet* (Century, 1985).

WATCHING THE FAT – WHO BENEFITS?

You

Your general health will benefit if you cut down on fat and you will considerably reduce the risk of heart disease and cancer. Your complexion will also improve. In addition, you will probably find it easier to control your weight on a reduced fat diet, and may well feel more energetic.

Other people

Childhood obesity is at record levels in the Western world, as is the number of middle-aged men dying of heart disease. If you prepare food for other people in your family, a reduced fat diet will keep them healthier and help them live longer.

The environment

Reducing our saturated fat intake will mean using fewer animal fats. This in turn will mean less intensive livestock farming, thus benefiting both land and animals.

INCREASING FIBRE INTAKE

THE FACTS

Two out of five people in Britain say they are constipated, and one in five regularly take laxatives. This is largely because we eat so little fibre in our diet: currently about 0.7oz (20g) a day, compared with the 3.5oz (100g) a day or more eaten by Africans living away from Western influence. There, constipation, piles and Western disorders of the gut are almost unknown. In Britain, on the other hand, diverticular disease affects 40 per cent of the over sixties, and irritable bowel syndrome and cancer of the colon are both on the increase.

There are different sorts of fibre: the soluble fibre found in fruit, vegetables and pulses, and the insoluble fibre found mostly in cereals. The first helps to lower cholesterol levels; the second to bind food in the gut and move it rapidly through the intestinal tract, thus helping to remove the breakdown products of fats and proteins quickly.

Bread is an important source of fibre, though only wholemeal bread uses the entire grain (containing about 10 per cent fibre by weight compared with the 3 to 6 per cent in 'brown', granary or wheatgerm bread). Bran also features in many high-fibre diets, but it should be eaten cooked, since when raw it binds important minerals and prevents the body from absorbing them. In general, eating a balanced wholefood diet is better than adding bran and high-fibre supplements.

Fruit and vegetables are an important and balanced source of fibre, especially cabbage, root vegetables, peppers, mushrooms, courgettes and leeks. Other high-fibre foods include wholewheat pasta, flaked cereals (such as rolled oats), nuts, beans, peas and lentils. Many high-fibre foods make ideal snacks – a healthy alternative to chocolate and crisps.

WHAT NEEDS TO CHANGE

Our fibre consumption should be increased – ideally by between 50 and 100 per cent. Wholefood catering ought to be encouraged in schools, hospitals and restaurants; and wholefood ingredients need to be even more widely available. High-fibre foods should be clearly and accurately labelled, making it equally clear when such products also include high levels of fats, sugars and salt.

WHAT YOU CAN DO

- If you haven't already, change to wholewheat bread: it tastes better than other sorts, and is healthier. Don't be fooled by the 'healthy eating' flashes on granary and fortified white breads.
- Buy wholewheat low-sugar biscuits and cakes.
- Use wholewheat pastas and wholegrain rice.
- Buy as much fruit and vegetables as you can afford.
- Keep high-fibre snacks in your larder instead of sweets, crisps and sweet biscuits.
- Find out where your local wholefood shop is, and experiment with some of the ingredients they sell.

The Great British Diet (Century, 1985) includes a very useful section on high-fibre foods. Learn how to cook a variety of wholefood meals: *The Wholefood Cookery Course* (Thorsons, 1986) is a good place to start. Audrey Eyton's famous *F-Plan Diet* (Penguin, 1983) should be treated with caution. She does recommend a high-fibre diet, but she tends to over-emphasise fibre and many of her recipes are also high in fats and sugar.

INCREASING FIBRE INTAKE – WHO BENEFITS?

You

If you are among the 40 per cent of Britons who are regularly constipated, then increasing and balancing your fibre intake will almost certainly bring you enormous relief, as well as protecting you against a wide range of digestive illnesses.

Other people

The other people you cook for will also gain in health and vitality, though if you are moving from a very low-fibre diet to a high-fibre one, do it gradually so that your family's digestive systems have time to adjust!

The environment

High-fibre foods – grains, legumes, vegetables and fruit – are all found near the bottom of the food chain, meaning that more food can be produced per acre of land. This also makes it generally cheaper to live on a high-fibre diet.

UNDERSTANDING ALCOHOL

THE FACTS

Most doctors and nutritionists agree that one glass of wine or beer a day may help to reduce stress, and even help you to avoid heart disease. For good health, the recommended upper daily limit is 1½ pints (0.8 litres) of beer or its equivalent. Beyond this point both health and social problems may start.

Alcohol is a major cause of liver disease, particularly cirrhosis of the liver. It is also associated with a wide range of other disorders and diseases of the digestion, the gut, the heart and circulatory system, the lungs, the nervous system, the blood and the immune system. It is a major cause of high blood pressure and, because it contains many calories with no nourishment, it is even more fattening than sugar. In more than minimal doses alcohol is best thought of as an addictive poison: 500,000 people in Britain are thought to be alcohol addicts.

Alcohol is also a major cause of social damage and destruction. Of the 69,000 people killed or seriously injured on Britain's roads in 1987, a fifth were involved in accidents where at least one driver was over the legal limit. It has recently been shown conclusively that drinking during pregnancy can harm the baby. And alcohol abuse is estimated to be an important factor in one in nine divorces granted each year. The cost to the National Health Service (NHS) of alcohol-related diseases is £110 million a year, while the total cost to society of alcohol abuse is about £2 billion.

In 1987 Britons spent £17 billion on alcoholic drinks, more than half of what we spent on food. The government collects £5 billion a year in tax on alcoholic drinks, a quarter of the budget of the NHS. In real terms, beer costs 60 per cent of what it did in 1950 and whisky 25 per cent; as a result, the amount of alcohol we drink has almost doubled.

WHAT NEEDS TO CHANGE

There needs to be an intensive educational campaign about the risks of excessive drinking. Advertising and sponsorship by manufacturers should be carefully controlled, and the social drinking of non-alcoholic drinks more widely promoted. Alcohol addiction counselling ought to be easily available. The legal alcohol limit for drivers should be drastically reduced, and on-the-spot breath tests and penalties introduced.

WHAT YOU CAN DO

- Try to keep to 1½ pints (0.8 litres) of beer, a couple of glasses of wine or a single measure of spirits at a sitting.
- Try non-alcoholic drinks, or at least alternate alcoholic and non-alcoholic drinks.
- Dilute your drinks (for example, wine with sparkling mineral water, or beer with lemonade).
- If you are pregnant or thinking of becoming pregnant, cut out alcohol altogether.
- Never drive soon after drinking alcohol, and refuse to get in a car with a driver who has.

If you are regularly drinking more than the recommended amount each day, consider what alternatives would give you as much pleasure, and follow them up. If you think you need help to cut down, ask at your health centre or contact the local branch of Alcoholics Anonymous. *That's The Limit* is a helpful booklet published by the Health Education Authority, which should be available at your local health centre.

UNDERSTANDING ALCOHOL – WHO BENEFITS?

You

Keeping your alcohol intake below the recommended level will help to protect you against high blood pressure and kidney disease. It will also help with any weight problem you have.

Other people

It is very difficult to have a proper relationship with anyone whose primary relationship is with the bottle, so cutting down on alcohol will almost certainly improve your relationships (and, incidentally, your libido). Child battering is often alcohol-influenced, so children will be safer, as will anyone who happens to be on the road at the same time as you are.

The environment

Beer cans and drinks bottles are a ubiquitous form of litter, especially along roadsides. A great deal of gratuitous vandalism is associated with alcohol abuse, including the uprooting of trees and plants and cruelty to animals.

TEA AND COFFEE

THE FACTS

A recent survey suggested that the average British adult drinks four cups of tea and two of coffee very day: tea constitutes nearly half our total liquid intake. Both beverages contain high levels of caffeine, an addictive brain stimulant which also affects the digestive system. It is an allergen too, implicated in 10 per cent of arthritis cases, 24 per cent of allergic rashes and 77 per cent of recurrent migraines. A cup of coffee contains twice as much caffeine as a cup of tea (the same as in a can of cola or a cup of hot chocolate), because the caffeine in coffee is more thoroughly extracted. While coffee consumption in Britain has levelled off at three times the 1960 level, tea drinking is dropping at about 20 per cent every 10 years. It's worth noting that 10 per cent of the price of instant coffee goes on promotion.

The tea and coffee trades are among the most protected and centralised in the world: eight European and American firms control 90 per cent of the tea sold in the West, and growers find it impossible to negotiate reasonable terms. Coffee pickers in Kenya earn only about 45p a day, while Bangladeshi women tea pickers' wages can be low as 15p: 'slave labour', as one church aid agency has called it. Moreover, the terms of trade have caused the international price of tea and coffee to fall drastically in the last two decades, reducing the income of producing countries. The growing of these crops causes ecological damage on a massive scale, especially to the fragile soils of Central and South America. Coffee processing causes chronic water pollution, while the making of instant coffee (which now constitutes 90 per cent of our coffee consumption) is one of the most energy-intensive processes used by food manufacturers.

WHAT NEEDS TO CHANGE

The risks of excessive caffeine intake, especially by children, need to be understood and taken seriously. Healthy hot drinks should be easily available. Retailers ought to stock Third World brands of tea and coffee supplied by companies which support co-operative ventures in the countries of origin.

WHAT CAN YOU DO

- If you usually drink tea or coffee, try herb tea or fruit juice instead.
- Don't automatically offer your guests tea and coffee: see if they'd like to try something healthier.
- Don't encourage children to drink tea and coffee.
- Buy 'natural decaffeinated' rather than regular, but still try to cut down on the amount of coffee you drink.
- If you do buy tea and coffee, buy 'fair trade' coffee from your local wholefood shop, OXFAM, Traidcraft or Twin Trading.
- Buy loose tea rather than teabags; it's better quality and usually cheaper.

Try cutting out coffee altogether for a week and see if you feel any better or if any troublesome symptoms improve. If you think you may be allergic to caffeine, read Gwynne Davies' *Overcoming Food Allergies* (Ashgrove, 1985) for some practical suggestions about what you can do. Harold McGee gives some useful background and tips in *On Food and Cooking* (Allen and Unwin, 1986), while the chapters on tea and coffee in Richard North's *The Real Cost* (Chatto and Windus, 1986) explain the international background to the tea and coffee businesses.

KNOWING ABOUT TEA AND COFFEE – WHO BENEFITS?

You

Caffeine is the most widely used addictive substance in the world, and does you no good at all. Cutting down on it will almost certainly make you feel more energetic, improve your circulation and strengthen your immune system.

Other people

Your children will be healthier on water and fresh fruit juice than on endless tea and coffee, chocolate and cola. If you buy from 'fair trade' organisations, Third World plantation workers will also benefit directly from your choice.

The environment

These nutrient-draining crops take a great deal out of the land, as well as forcing peasants on to marginal land where slash and burn clearance for agriculture is an important factor in rainforest destruction.

EATING LESS MEAT

THE FACTS

Though more than four million Britons are now vegetarian and the number rises every year, there is nothing intrinsically unecological or unhealthy about eating meat. On the other hand, although the amount we eat has fallen steadily in the last 10 years, we still consume a great deal: 330 lb (75 kg) a year each. Some 85 per cent of it is home-grown. And it uses more than 80 per cent of our agricultural land: over half the grain we grow goes to feed livestock – a very inefficient way of using land to produce food.

Though there are societies like the Inuit in northern Canada who live on a high-meat diet, most native peoples eat meat only occasionally. Archaeological evidence shows that the diet of our ancient ancestors also included little meat. In any case, the meat and meat products on sale today bear little resemblance to wild meat. The meats you buy will almost certainly include residues of antibiotics, hormones and insecticides, nitrates and polyphosphates, and a large quantity of water (sometimes more than 15 per cent by weight). Fattening and processing techniques also create a high fat content, especially in 'meat products', where the mechanically recovered 'meat' can legally include fatty skin, rind, gristle and sinew.

To achieve high turnover and profits, most meat animals are more or less factory-farmed: chickens and pigs suffer the most. They are shut in and force-fed, and their manure pollutes water supplies instead of regenerating the land. As one writer has said, 'fat pigs make fat pigs', and being vegetarian is certainly healthier than eating agribusiness meat. One large-scale study showed that vegetarians can expect to live nine years longer than regular meat-eaters.

WHAT NEEDS TO CHANGE

Domestic science teachers should stop emphasising meat as an essential part of our diet; other sources of protein are at least as nutritious and more ecologically sound. Vegetarianism and 'demi-veg' need to be seen as entirely acceptable choices. Factory-farming techniques involving cruelty to animals should be outlawed. Strict guidelines for humane husbandry, easily understood by both farmers and consumers, should be legally enforced.

WHAT YOU CAN DO

- If you eat meat, buy smaller portions and serve smaller helpings, making up the quantity with other ingredients such as vegetables, beans and pulses.
- Use meat in stews, casseroles, curries and stir-fries rather than in 'lumps'.
- If you go to a restaurant which offers insufficient choice (or no choice at all) for vegetarians, it's worth asking them to change their policy.
- Try eating meat-free meals on one or two days each week.
- If you are interested in vegetarianism, you could buy a copy of *The Vegetarian* magazine, and write to The Vegetarian Society.

The arguments for eating less meat are well presented in *The Green Alternative* (Methuen, 1987) and *Blueprint for a Green Planet* (Dorling Kindersley, 1987). The status of meat in our diet is discussed in *The Food Scandal* (Century, 1985), while *Food Adulteration* (Unwin Hyman, 1987) contains the gory details of all the things that meat processors and retailers do to con us into paying top prices for third-rate products. Peter Cox's *Why You Don't Need Meat* (Thorsons, 1986) is a good introduction to the reasons for becoming vegetarian.

EATING LESS MEAT – WHO BENEFITS?

You
You don't need meat regularly to stay healthy, and you can save a considerable amount of money by eating less meat.

Other people
Your family's health will benefit from eating less meat, particularly of the processed varieties. The many Latin Americans who have been dispossessed of their land by cattle ranchers would be grateful if hamburger and corned beef consumption fell dramatically.

The environment
More of our food could be home-grown, easing the pressure on the land in food-exporting countries. The humane rearing of the fewer farm animals needed would alleviate untold suffering. Eating less meat also frees enormous areas of land for other uses, including wildlife and recreation.

FINDING HEALTHY MEAT

THE FACTS

Most of the meat and meat products on sale in Britain today are a great deal less healthy than they could be, and the main reason is that almost everybody involved in the growing, processing and selling of meat is much more interested in profits than in the well-being of farm animals and the health of the consumer. The government, backed by the meat industry, encourages the use of antibiotics, hormones and additives, and even lays down a minimum quantity of fat that a carcass can contain. The fat content of an intensively reared pig can be as high as 46 per cent.

Then there is the problem of the widespread infection of meat with bacteria. One author has said 'It would be hard to devise a better, more efficient system of recycling salmonella than modern livestock farming'. As early as 1979, a study of frozen chickens found 79 per cent infected with salmonella, and a 1986 report estimated the annual cost to society of poultry-borne salmonella to be as high as £10.7 million. Then there is the bacterium campylobacter (which is nearly as prevalent as salmonella); with listeria, noted for its severe symptoms, running third.

Only 10 per cent of British abattoirs come up to European Community standards; and 50 slaughterhouses received a harsh warning about hygiene standards in 1986. Though there are strict guidelines about storing cooked meats in supermarkets, a recent survey found that only 60 per cent of outlets were complying with them. Luckily, a small but increasing number of meat producers, processors and retailers are raising their stock humanely and selling clean additive-free meat, but there is still a very long way to go.

WHAT NEEDS TO CHANGE

The hygiene and handling standards of intensive stock-rearing need to be thoroughly overhauled, to ensure that animals are cared for humanely and that our health is not put at risk. Accurate information about the state of Britain's meat industry should be available to the public, and farmers and retailers who sell humanely reared, additive-free meat should receive government subsidies.

WHAT YOU CAN DO

- Cut obvious fat off meat before cooking it, and skim the fat from stews and gravies before serving them.
- Buy meat products from a reputable butcher who uses only lean meat.
- Prepare meat as quickly as possible, cook it immediately and thoroughly, and eat it as soon as possible.
- Only reheat cooked dishes that have been kept in the fridge, and then only once, making sure that they are thoroughly reheated.
- Always keep raw and cooked meats separately wrapped.
- Wash your hands, implements and work surfaces thoroughly after working with meat.
- If you suspect that you have food poisoning, report it to your doctor immediately.

Look out for 'real meat' shops and outlets. Several, like the Pure Meat Company and Red House Farm, operate a mail order service; while the Wiltshire-based Real Meat Company sells through over 40 shops in southern England. Write to Compassion in World Farming for a copy of their *Guidelines for Humane Animal Farming*.

FINDING HEALTHY MEAT – WHO BENEFITS?

You

Eating ecologically sound, humanely reared meat will help you to avoid the unpleasant experience of food poisoning. Eating less fatty meat will also help with any weight problem you may have, and reduce the risk of heart disease.

Other people

If you cook for other people, they too will benefit from eating healthier meat. Farmworkers and meat trade workers, who currently work in unhygienic conditions, will also benefit from a cleaner, healthier meat industry.

The environment

Happy livestock grazing in fields, manuring the land as nature intended, cause far less stress to both animals and land than intensive animal-rearing. Extensive grazing, where animals forage for most of their own food, saves on the production of animal feed and again reduces the pressure on the land.

HOW MUCH MILK IS GOOD FOR YOU?

THE FACTS

Advertising for milk and dairy products is almost invariably of the 'traditional countryside' variety, presenting a picture of olde-worlde wholesomeness. But in many respects dairy products are neither traditional nor healthy. We only started to consume them in such large quantities in the 1930s and '40s: milk consumption peaked in 1960 and cheese in 1986. Until the Middle Ages most people in Britain, like 90 per cent of the world's population today, drank almost no milk at all.

Milk is promoted as a high-protein, high-calcium food. In fact it is 87 per cent water. Only 3.3 per cent is protein (compared with 9 per cent in bread and 7 per cent in haricot beans). Milk is a fatty product: 3.8 per cent of full-cream milk is saturated fat. Dairy products supply 30 per cent of our total fat intake, and 40 per cent of the saturated fat. Milk is certainly a good source of calcium, but so are green leaf vegetables (like broccoli and chard), peas, potatoes and mushrooms, nuts and seeds, and dried fruits. Milk is increasingly likely to include traces of antibiotics and pesticides, while the threat of bovine growth hormone still lurks despite the protests of consumer groups and most farmers.

Many people find it hard to digest the lactose (milk sugar) in dairy products, and this gives rise to a wide range of allergic reactions. Clinical tests have shown that milk is implicated in 74 per cent of allergic skin reactions, and in 89 per cent of asthma and hay fever cases. Many nutritionists now support those who believe that cows' milk is generally unsuited to the human digestive system, and that consumption of dairy products is best kept below the equivalent of 1 pint (0.5 litres) of milk a day.

WHAT NEEDS TO CHANGE

We need to change our perception of dairy products, seeing them as useful and tasty additions to our diet rather than staples. The labelling of dairy products should be honest and accurate, especially concerning fat content. Low-fat dairy products and close equivalents to milk products should be even more widely available. Doctors ought to acknowledge the prevalence of intolerance to milk.

WHAT YOU CAN DO

- Buy skimmed or semi-skimmed milk to cut down on your saturated fat.
- Go for fresh milk rather than long-life or powdered milk.
- Gradually reduce the amount of milk you drink, and try organic soya milk in drinks and on cereals.
- Buy traditional, additive-free, mature cheeses, and choose low-fat cheeses in preference to high-fat ones.
- Use yoghurt instead of cream.
- Don't give cows' milk to babies; when they are weaning give them bottled water instead.

If your children have milk at school, ask if they can have skimmed or semi-skimmed milk, or fruit juice (not squash) instead. Ask for skimmed or semi-skimmed milk in cafés and canteens. If you suffer from asthma or hay fever, try cutting dairy products out of your diet for a week and see if it helps. For nutritional information about milk and dairy products, read Chapter 9 of Caroline Walker and Geoffrey Cannon's *The Food Scandal* (Century, 1985), and for a very readable argument against any milk at all, read 'The Great Milk Debate' in Leon Chaitow's *Stone Age Diet* (Optima, 1987).

KNOWING ABOUT MILK – WHO BENEFITS?

You

Cutting down on dairy products, and thereby your fat intake, will improve your circulation and help you lose weight. It may also alleviate allergic reactions for which there is no obvious cause.

Other people

Children drink more milk on average than adults, so providing them with low-fat and non-dairy alternatives will improve their health. Balance the milk decrease with an increase in bread, fruit and vegetables to ensure a good range of nutrients and sufficient calories.

The environment

Lower consumption of dairy produce, and therefore fewer dairy herds, will decrease pressure on the land, pollution from intensively reared cattle and the stress put on cattle by modern methods of agriculture.

EGGS FROM HAPPY HENS

THE FACTS

Although egg consumption has fallen by nearly 40 per cent in the last 20 years, largely as a result of worries about cholesterol, we still eat more than 200 eggs a year each, laid by the country's 50 million laying hens. Eaten in moderation, healthy eggs are a very good – though not essential – food. As well as a high proportion of usable protein, they contain a wide range of vitamins and minerals. They are also relatively cheap, and have binding and foaming qualities which are useful in cooking.

On the other hand, 90 per cent of the eggs we eat in Britain come from hens kept in battery cages, often five birds to an 18×20 inch (45×50cm) wire cage. The suffering of battery hens is unspeakable: they are unable to turn round, and lose feathers from rubbing and pecking; their beaks are trimmed and they become infected by bacteria. A very high proportion of battery hens – probably in excess of 90 per cent – carry salmonella bacteria, and a growing number of egg-related food poisoning cases are being reported.

Around 8 per cent of the eggs produced in Britain are now technically free range, and are becoming more widely available, though the relative costs of production do not justify the higher prices. Most 'free range' eggs still come from large flocks which many people consider to be kept at too high a density: free range flocks average 2,000 to 3,000 birds at 1,000 to the acre. The standard of the Free Range Egg Association is much more stringent: 3 square feet (0.9 sq m) of henhouse each, free access to open runs, and no debeaking or routine medication. For all the investment in equipment, food and drugs, a battery hen lays only 35 more eggs each year – 15 per cent more – than a free range hen.

WHAT NEEDS TO CHANGE

The battery farming of hens should be replaced by the widespread integration of small free range flocks into mixed farms as soon as possible, and small flocks ought to be encouraged with government financial incentives. The aim should be to do away with battery farming altogether. Egg retailers need to insist on strict guidelines for their free range eggs, and should not be allowed to charge unfair high prices for them.

WHAT YOU CAN DO

- Try not to eat more than two to three eggs a week. (This will keep your cholesterol intake to a safe level.)
- Although they are more expensive, buy free range eggs if you possibly can even if it means buying fewer eggs.
- Send an A5 stamped addressed envelope for a free copy of the Free Range Egg Association's list of approved farms and shops, and find out if you can get genuinely free range eggs from a local source. If you can, make sure the egg boxes are returned to them for re-use.
- Buy eggs in recycled cardboard boxes rather than plastic. If you have to buy eggs in foam plastic boxes, buy only those cartons labelled 'ozone friendly'.

Send £1 and an A5 stamped addressed envelope to Chickens' Lib for a copy of their booklet *Intensive Egg and Chicken Production*. Read Clare Druce's *Chicken and Egg* (Green Print, 1989) for more detailed information. Edwina Currie's book, due for publication by Sidgwick & Jackson in late 1989, should be illuminating!

EGGS FROM HAPPY HENS – WHO BENEFITS?

You

Eating genuinely free range eggs in moderation will certainly be better for your health, reducing your cholesterol level and ensuring that unwanted chemicals and bacteria are kept to a minimum. They taste better too.

Other people

The people you cook for will also benefit, as will the increasing number of small farmers trying to make a living from keeping poultry flocks in a more humane way.

The environment

If everyone insisted on free range eggs, 45 million battery hens would be rescued from degradation and disease and would experience fresh air and freedom of movement. The land would benefit from their manure, and poultry farming would again become part of the traditional pattern of mixed farming.

SWEET WATER

THE FACTS

Until mid-1985, when stringent European Community (EC) regulations came into force, the only official guideline on drinking water in Britain was that it should be 'wholesome'. With the exception of high lead levels in some city supplies, tap water 20 years ago was generally wholesome, but our public water supply is now threatened on several fronts. Until the EC commissioners recently ruled the practice illegal, the only way many British supplies could meet international standards was by averaging out the pollution figures and making pseudo-legal exceptions ('derogations') to the rules.

Nitrates from artificial fertilisers, domestic sewage effluent, and slurry from intensive livestock units are by far the worst problem. One million consumers in the Midlands and East Anglia are regularly supplied with tap water that exceeds the legal limit for nitrates. Excessive nitrates convert to nitrites in the human digestive system, thereby interfering with the uptake of oxygen by the blood. This is particularly dangerous for babies, sometimes causing what is known as 'blue baby syndrome'. Nitrates have also been linked with cancer. They create biologically dead streams and lakes by encouraging algae which use up all the oxygen in the water. Nitrate pollution has been called a 'time bomb', because it can take decades to seep through to the underground water supplies that we use.

Pesticide pollution of groundwater is also on the increase. At least 16 toxic pesticides are commonly found in drinking water and widespread testing is still woefully inadequate. Dangerous concentrations of metals like lead and aluminium, implicated in Alzheimer's disease, affect two million people's water supplies; while old pipes sometimes contain five times the EC limit of cancer-causing coal tars derived from pipe-sealing materials.

WHAT NEEDS TO CHANGE

The government must strictly enforce all the EC standards for drinking water. All water board test results should be publicly available. The use of nitrate fertilisers in agriculture must be discouraged by appropriate taxation and limitation, and strict control over a much-reduced arsenal of pesticides maintained.

WHAT YOU CAN DO

- If you are concerned about the quality of your tap water, ask your local Environmental Health Department to test it for you, and ask for a full breakdown of the results. This service should normally cost you nothing and Friends of the Earth may be able to assist you in interpreting the results.
- Do what you can to reduce the amount of water you use (see page 20).
- You could buy bottled water, though the non-returnable plastic bottles and the transporting of the water to your local shop are very wasteful of energy. Also, bottled water costs 1,000 times as much as tap water.

You can buy a water filter, but even if you pay in excess of £200 for a plumbed-in evaporation unit you will not eradicate all the pollutants from tap water. A cheap jug-type filter will improve the taste, however, by filtering out some pollutants and any organic impurities in the water. If you use one of these, change the filter unit regularly to prevent build-up of harmful bacteria. If you don't mind being too alarmed, read Brian Price's 'Pollution on Tap' in *Green Britain or Industrial Wasteland?* (Polity, 1986). Then write a strong letter to your local Member of Parliament and to your water authority.

INSISTING ON SWEET WATER – WHO BENEFITS?

You

Pollution in our tap water is one of the hardest forms of pollution to avoid. Improved water quality will benefit everybody, and help protect you from a range of ailments including cancer and Alzheimer's disease.

Other people

Babies and young children are particularly at risk from nitrate, pesticide and heavy metal pollution. Even if we act now, the problems will probably worsen for at least 20 years.

The environment

Nitrate and toxic waste pollution of inland and coastal waters is one of the most serious environmental problems we face. The casualties include birds, fish, small mammals and marine micro-organisms. All will benefit from cleaner water.

THE SOUTH AFRICAN CONNECTION

THE FACTS

The Commonwealth Eminent Persons' Group report on their 1986 visit to South Africa opens: 'None of us was prepared for the full reality of apartheid. As a contrivance of social engineering, it is awesome in its cruelty. It is achieved and sustained only through force, blighting the lives of millions.'

In an international survey of human rights, South Africa came last but five in a ranking of 120 countries, indicating a more repressive regime than Libya, Cuba or Mozambique. Twenty-two million blacks have no real vote, black infant mortality is 14 times that of whites and whites expect to live 13 years longer than blacks.

Britain is South Africa's fourth largest trading partner. After minerals, fresh and processed fruit are the largest imports, worth £74 million a year. Opinion polls among blacks in South Africa show that between two-thirds and three-quarters would like Britain to ban South African food imports (as the USA, Australia, Canada, New Zealand, Ireland, Sweden, Norway, Finland and Denmark already have). About a third of Britons believe that cutting trading links with South Africa would lead to positive political change within South Africa, and another quarter have no strong opinion. Around two million people in Britain have already stopped buying South African produce whenever possible. It is clear that concerted consumer action can be very influential, as in the Barclays Bank 1986 decision to withdraw its operations from South Africa.

Of course South Africa is not the only oppressive regime in the world. Other persistent offenders who regularly export large amounts of food to Britain include Chile, and Eastern European countries like Romania and Bulgaria.

WHAT NEEDS TO CHANGE

Shops and supermarkets should take account of consumer preference and ensure that alternatives to South African produce are always available. South African produce should always be clearly marked as such, and all foods ought to carry country-of-origin labels.

WHAT YOU CAN DO

- Make up your mind where you stand on this important issue, so that your purchasing decisions are in line with your beliefs.
- Read the Eminent Persons' Group's *Mission to South Africa* (Penguin, 1986) for a first-hand account. Then read Joseph Hanlon and Roger Ormond's *The Sanctions Handbook* (Penguin, 1987) for a fuller study of the possibilities for and effects of boycotts against South Africa.
- If you decide to buy only non-South African fruit, avoid Cape, Del Monte, John West, Outspan and Libby's. The Co-op is the only supermarket chain which almost never sells South African foods.

If you want to become actively involved in anti-apartheid activities in Britain, write to the Anti-Apartheid Movement; AA Enterprises is its fund-raising arm and produces an attractive mail order catalogue. *The World Human Rights Guide* (Pan, 1987) is a very accessible overview of worldwide repression, while membership of Amnesty International enables you to support political prisoners all over the world, including South Africa.

UNDERSTANDING THE SOUTH AFRICAN CONNECTION – WHO BENEFITS?

You

Understanding the implications and possibilities of international trade helps you to see where you fit into the pattern. It also helps you to recognise that combined consumer influence can affect decisions even at the highest levels.

Other people

The people who would stand to benefit most from sanctions against South Africa are the disenfranchised black population. Following political and economic reform in which the majority had a real say, they would gain both power and respect.

The environment

Vast ranches and squalid townships have replaced ecologically sound farming over much of South Africa. Social and economic reform would also bring more sustainable land use.

THE PROS AND CONS OF SUPERSTORES

THE FACTS

Supermarkets started springing up in American towns and cities in the early 1930s and reached Britain in the late 1950s, bringing a rapid increase in self-service. They considerably reduced retail overheads and, because products now had to 'sell themselves', there was a massive increase in advertising and promotion. The early 1980s saw a British boom in superstores, again following the American model – giant supermarkets, often carrying 50,000 lines or more, with in-store bakeries, cafés, hundreds of yards of shelving and acres of car park. Over half of all food purchases are now made in superstores and large supermarkets; for high-income households the proportion is 61 per cent.

Most of the large supermarket chains have responded rapidly to 'green consumer' demands, and additive-free products, organic produce and free range eggs are now widely available. Even healthier food is usually available, however, in your local wholefood shop. One-stop supermarket shopping is claimed to be efficient and economical, but how many people take into account car expenses and the 80 monotonous hours a year which the average shopper spends pushing trolleys along supermarket aisles and waiting in queues at the checkout? The average family buys more than 56 lb (25.5 kg) of packaged groceries every week, 18 lb (8 kg) of it packaging, which they have to pay for and then carry home. Thirty-six per cent of families do not have the use of a car.

One survey found that 70 per cent of people liked clothes shopping and 61 per cent enjoyed shopping for records and tapes, whereas 68 per cent often found supermarket grocery shopping tiring and 31 per cent said they frequently ended up with a headache.

WHAT NEEDS TO CHANGE

Supermarket chains must not only listen carefully to consumer concerns about health and environmental damage but also about unnecessary waste. The next green issues on the agenda include over-packaging and re-usable packaging, offering locally grown produce, honest and accurate nutritional labelling, and personal assistance for the disabled and those without access to a car.

WHAT YOU CAN DO

- Think about where you shop; don't just use the superstore because everyone else does.
- If you can, buy fresh food daily, using local suppliers and retailers (this helps to keep money and jobs within the local economy).
- Decide what you want to buy before you visit the supermarket.
- Try to avoid tins and packets: they are less healthy than fresh food and you pay for the packaging.
- Look out for nutritional and country-of-origin labelling.
- If you are shopping with young children, don't be swayed by advertising-induced demands for sweets; give them an apple or some dried fruit instead.
- Lobby your council for a bus service to 'out-of-town' shopping centres to reduce the use of cars.

Supermarket managers are increasingly aware that they must take their customers' green concerns into account, and most companies take customers' comments seriously. If something concerns you – if they don't stock organic vegetables or don't have recycling facilities outside, for example – use supermarket suggestion boxes or speak to the manager.

UNDERSTANDING THE PROS AND CONS OF SUPERSTORES – WHO BENEFITS?

You

To a large extent the psychology of supermarket selling relies on the trance-like state of the shopper. The less trance-like your state, the more likely you are to buy the healthy, environment-friendly food that you really need, rather than over-packaged junk.

Other people

The people you prepare food for will benefit from your wise buying decisions, as will the growers and manufacturers of healthy food and groceries.

The environment

When people buy healthier, more ecologically sound, minimally packaged and locally produced products they reduce waste and pollution, and save resources.

OVERCOMING THE THROWAWAY MENTALITY

THE FACTS

Nobody knows exactly what proportion of the things we buy are made specifically to be thrown away again almost immediately, but an informed guess would be about 15 per cent by weight and 25 per cent by value. We do know that nearly a quarter of the plastic and almost half of the paper used in Britain goes into packaging and very short-lived products like newspapers and plastic cutlery.

The 23 million tonnes of domestic rubbish we throw out every year might seem a lot, but add 100 million tonnes of industrial waste, 130 million of mineral spoil, 200 million of agricultural leftovers and 30 million of sewage, and you begin to see the scale of the problem. Government officials reckon that 55 to 60 per cent of domestic refuse could be reclaimed, and this is true of other sorts of waste too. The cash value of these materials is in excess of £2 billion a year, not to mention the £650 million it costs us to collect, transport and dispose of the discarded materials. The problem of waste is particularly intractable in our cities. Fourteen million tonnes a year of London waste are carried up to 40 miles (64 km) to landfill sites in seven counties.

We are running out of places to put our rubbish, and pollution problems at existing tips are growing ever more serious. In 1987 escaping methane from a tip in Derbyshire demolished a house and seriously injured the occupants. And leaking gas has been identified as a serious hazard at more than 600 tips nationwide, most of which have houses within 100 yards (83 m). Twenty per cent of household waste is officially classified as 'hazardous', releasing a cocktail of poisonous ingredients into land, air and water.

WHAT NEEDS TO CHANGE

It needs to be recognised at all levels – individual, community and nationally – that waste must be reduced. Packaging should protect and appeal, yet use minimal resources and be possible to recycle. We need to be aware that our 'waste' doesn't just disappear when we put it in the dustbin. Local authorities should promote anti-waste and recycling campaigns.

WHAT YOU CAN DO

- Before you buy anything, ask yourself whether you really need it. The less you buy the less you are likely to waste (and the less money you will spend filling your dustbin!).
- Buy things which come in the minimum of packaging (see page 108).
- Seek out products that come in packaging which can be recycled or, even better, used again – like milk in bottles.
- Mend things rather than throwing them away, and give potentially useful things to people who can use them instead of automatically throwing them in the bin (see page 24).

Start to separate your rubbish. Even though the collection of particular items like paper, glass and organic material is only just beginning in Britain, it is a good idea to get into the habit now (see page 110). The Friends of the Earth report *Once Is Not Enough* explains the issues involved, and the quarterly magazine *Resource* will keep you up to date.

OVERCOMING THE THROWAWAY MENTALITY – WHO BENEFITS?

You

A recent survey showed that 89 per cent of British housewives feel guilty about the amount they throw away. By recycling, re-using and reducing waste you can save on the guilt, together with the cost, the hassle, and the ever-present health risks of excessive piles of rotting rubbish.

Other people

Your 'waste' often deprives the poorer people of the world of vital resources. Reducing waste would help scarce food and other commodities to reach those suffering from poverty and hunger.

The environment

Nature has no concept of waste; you will look in vain for the rubbish tips of the virgin rainforest. The life-giving planetary ecosystem depends upon the constant recycling of materials and nutrients, and we can help by learning to work with these natural cycles.

BAGS OF WASTE

THE FACTS

More than a third of British domestic rubbish is packaging. The average household gets through nearly 22 lb (10 kg) of it every week – materials which they have paid for, and for which they then have to pay again to dispose of. The cost of producing and disposing of all this packaging has been estimated at about £12.60 per household per week. By using less packaging and more environment-friendly packaging, this could easily be halved, and the things we buy would still be safely and attractively wrapped.

Things obviously do need to be packaged – for security, for hygiene, and to a certain extent for convenience. This does not, however, explain why a less than ½ lb (0.2 kg) chocolate Easter egg is wrapped in nearly the same weight of card, plastic and foil, and costs three times as much as the equivalent amount of chocolate bought in bar form. Nor does it justify 10 individual portions of heat-treated cream in plastic and foil cups, set in a plastic dish and finished with a thick card lid.

Manufacturers are always looking for ways of adding 'perceived value' to make it seem as if you're getting more than you really are. And packaging is an ideal aid to this sort of persuasion, which often borders upon deception. Although industry has been slow to implement any change towards more environment-friendly packaging, there have already been some hopeful signs, like the replacement of CFC-blown plastic containers, a shift towards recycled cardboard egg boxes, and recycled brown paper bags at Safeway supermarket checkouts.

WHAT NEEDS TO CHANGE

We need to understand that it is we who pay – both in money and environmental damage – for excessive packaging. There needs to be a shift towards packaging which is attractive but not wasteful, and does its job well without harming the environment. Retailers should offer their customers minimally packaged goods, priced to reflect the true savings on materials.

WHAT YOU CAN DO

- Buy as little packaging as possible. Many items do not need packaging at all, and one layer of packaging is enough for most things.
- Take your own bags with you rather than getting new ones every time you shop. (Get into the habit of keeping a carrier bag in your pocket or a shopping bag on a hook just inside the front door.)
- Shop in places where you can use your own bags and containers: wholefood shops will usually be happy to provide this service.
- Buy things which come in packaging that can be recycled or re-used – recycled cardboard egg boxes, milk in bottles, and so on.
- Try to avoid plastic packaging, tins and aerosol sprays (see page 118).

Encourage your local shop or supermarket to provide more environment-friendly packaging. Safeway, Spar, Tesco and Sainsbury's have already taken steps in this direction, so encourage them to keep the ball rolling by asking for lightly packaged lines. Write to INCPEN, the Industry Council for Packaging and the Environment, for their information pack.

USING LESS PACKAGING – WHO BENEFITS?

You

The first noticeable effect of buying less packaging is that you will almost certainly save money. You will also spend less time battling with shrink-wrapped foil-coated wrappers, and there will be much less rubbish to put out each week.

Other people

Reduced packaging means cleaner streets and fewer smelly health hazards. It also means fewer disappointments for your children when the product inside the glossy wrapping looks nothing like the picture on the outside.

The environment

Less packaging requires fewer resources, and leads to less pollution around mines and factories. Reducing the paper used in packaging by 50 per cent would save 60 million trees every year. Less packaging also means that less land is needed for dumping our 'waste'.

SEPARATING RUBBISH

THE FACTS

More than three-quarters of the domestic rubbish we throw out could be recycled but less than 15 per cent actually is. During the 1939–45 war many people separated out metal, glass, paper and organic material in order to help the nation's economy. Today, householders in Germany, Denmark and Sweden are increasingly recognising that the separation and recycling of rubbish makes very good economic and ecological sense.

It is possible to separate out some sorts of rubbish – metals for example – at up-to-date waste treatment plants, and then use the rest to generate heat for local heating schemes or fuel pellets which can be burned like coal. Though this is much less wasteful than simply dumping rubbish in landfill sites, it is still a great deal less efficient than sorting rubbish in the home so that each element of it can be recycled in the best possible way. Here, Britain has a long way to go. Eighty per cent of local authorities now have bottle banks and 52 per cent have facilities for waste paper collection, but only 9 per cent have any facilities for collecting separated household rubbish. Less than 4 per cent recycle any plastic, and only 3.5 per cent encourage the refilling of glass bottles.

There are, however, a growing number of schemes in which it is successfully being demonstrated that separation and recycling of rubbish solves a wide range of pollution, energy and employment problems. In London boroughs like Richmond, full-time recycling staff are funded from the proceeds of recycled waste. In cities like Leeds and Sheffield, community projects benefit financially; while at one stage in Bristol 190 people were employed in a comprehensive 'wealth from waste' programme.

WHAT NEEDS TO CHANGE

It needs to be recognised that rubbish separation in the home is the key to successful recycling. Ninety-two per cent of the people questioned in one survey said they would be prepared to separate rubbish if their council gave them a lead, so local authorities – with government assistance – must be encouraged to set up experimental projects, using neighbourhood 'rubbish banks' and specially designed dustbins.

WHAT YOU CAN DO

- If you have a garden or gardening friends, separate out your organic waste (see page 56). This will stop your rubbish smelling too.
- Take your bottles to the bottle bank whenever you happen to be passing it.
- Find out where your nearest waste paper collection point is. If there isn't one, ask why not.
- This is an area where, unless you are lucky enough to live in a neighbourhood where recycling is taken seriously, you probably won't be able to do much more as an individual householder, so prod your local authority to take further action.

Find out whether any local charity, community or church groups have thought about raising money by collecting waste paper, glass or cans. With a buoyant market in these commodities, quite tidy sums can be amassed for good causes. The manufacturers' associations can be helpful in getting such schemes off the ground. The *Warmer* (World Action for Recycling Materials and Energy from Rubbish) *Bulletin* is a fascinating free quarterly publication.

SEPARATING RUBBISH – WHO BENEFITS?

You

Separating your rubbish may sound like rather an effort but it soon becomes second nature, like putting the plates and saucepans back in the right place. Your rubbish will stop smelling, and your dustbin space will be neater and cleaner.

Other people

It is well established that the recycling of separated rubbish provides useful employment for a large number of people. It also makes refuse collectors' jobs less unpleasant.

The environment

Separating rubbish means that far more of it can be re-used and recycled, saving the landscape from landfill dumps and enormously reducing our consumption of raw materials. This saves us cutting down trees for paper, opening new iron or aluminium mines in the Amazon forests, and using vast amounts of energy to make new products.

KEEPING CANS UNDER CONTROL

THE FACTS

Britons use more than 13.4 billion cans every year, about half of which are tin-plated steel and half aluminium. Though they could all be recycled, less than 2 per cent are. As many as 5.6 billion of those cans contains beers and soft drinks. (When you buy a canned drink, between 75 and 85 per cent of the price you pay represents the cost of making the can.) Another 3.9 billion are used for food, 2 billion for pet food, and 2 billion for paint and other non-foods.

Cans alone make up 9 per cent of the average household's rubbish. Every year nearly 2.5 million tonnes of valuable metal, potentially worth well over £1 billion, is thrown into holes in the ground. Aluminium is well worth recycling, since it is worth over £500 per tonne; tin-plated steel is harder to recycle, though there are waste recovery plants which can deal with it. Considerable energy and pollution could be saved by recycling cans rather than mining new ore deposits. For example, re-using aluminium uses only 4 per cent of the energy of extracting new metal from bauxite, and reduces air pollution by 95 per cent. The use of steel scrap instead of virgin ore reduces water use in steel-making by 40 per cent as well as reducing water pollution by 76 per cent.

So far there are less than 200 'can banks' operated by 60 local authorities in Britain. One big problem is that it isn't easy enough to distinguish steel from aluminium (in the USA aluminium cans are stamped with an 'A' to help identification). The can industry in Britain has established pilot recycling projects, but these are still very small-scale, and do not attempt to educate the public to use fewer cans.

WHAT NEEDS TO CHANGE

Customers need to know how much they are paying for the cans they buy and throw away, so they can make informed choices about which products to buy. Steel and aluminium cans should be labelled as such, and can collection points be widely available. For example, supermarkets should install them alongside bottle banks. The government ought to consider charging a small levy on cans to provide funds for recycling schemes.

WHAT YOU CAN DO

- Try to avoid buying things in cans whenever possible.
- Don't buy canned drinks. Go for draught, bottled and cartoned drinks instead, or water.
- Take re-usable bottles on picnics and hikes.
- Buy fresh food as often as possible, and frozen or packet food in preference to tinned.
- Never drop cans in the country or on the street: find a litter bin or take them home.
- Find out whether your local council or a local charity collects aluminium cans. Wash the cans out, open both ends thoroughly and stamp on them to squeeze the sides together. This will save space and smell, and they are then all ready for recycling.

Encourage your local authority and your supermarket to provide can recycling facilities. Write to The Can Makers Recycling Scheme, an industry-financed consortium, for information about their contribution to the recycling effort.

KEEPING CANS UNDER CONTROL – WHO BENEFITS?

You

Cutting down on cans, especially drinks cans, will save you a lot of money. They are also heavy to carry around, both before and after you throw them away.

Other people

Aluminium can recycling projects have provided funds for children's and pensioners' schemes, and employment – even on the current small scale – for several hundred workers.

The environment

Recycling cans saves vast amounts of energy (18,000 kilowatt hours of electricity are needed to produce a tonne of aluminium). It also reduces large-scale environmental degradation around bauxite and iron ore mines in countries like Australia and Jamaica.

PLASTIC AWARENESS

THE FACTS

The word 'plastics' covers a very wide range of materials, which have in common the ability to deform almost indefinitely under heat and pressure without breaking. Some plastics, like cellophane film and rayon, are based on plant cellulose, a renewable resource. The majority, however, including polythenes and PVC, are based on non-renewable oil and other hydrocarbons.

Over a quarter of all the plastics we use go into short-life packaging, and almost none of them are recycled, even though the technology exists to recycle most plastics. Plastic waste makes up between 5 and 7 per cent of domestic rubbish, 900,000 tonnes of it each year. One of the biggest environmental problems connected with the indiscriminate use of plastics is that most do not rot: a whale was recently found choked to death by more than 50 plastic bags, and seabirds and baby seals have frequently been found strangled by discarded plastic fishing nets.

More than 30 types of plastic are widely used in packaging, and since recycling works best when different materials are collected separately, this makes the recycling of waste plastic particularly difficult. In countries like the USA, plastic containers are stamped with a code to identify them. One of the most common plastics used in drinks bottles, polyethylene terephthlate (PET), is easily recycled if kept separate from other rubbish. The recycling of the 1.2 billion PET bottles we use each year would alone save 60,000 tonnes of plastic worth over £1,000 a tonne. Although only 3 per cent of these bottles are recovered at present, the plastics industry is belatedly planning to introduce experimental 'PET banks'.

WHAT NEEDS TO CHANGE

It needs to be acknowledged that, contrary to popular belief, most plastics can be recycled. To help recycling, each plastic container should be made of only one type of plastic, and should be clearly stamped to show what type of plastic it is. We need to think about the appropriate re-use of plastic containers, and the government should consider introducing a small levy on each container to fund recycling projects.

WHAT YOU CAN DO

- Take your own shopping bags or plastic carriers with you to the shops instead of using a new carrier bag every time.
- Avoid products that come with a lot of plastic packaging – fruit, vegetables and meat do not need plastic trays to protect them.
- Store food in the fridge in re-usable airtight containers, not clingfilm.
- Choose recycled cardboard egg boxes instead of plastic ones.
- Buy household and beauty products which come in simple refillable containers – and have them refilled rather than buying new every time (Body Shop and several other retailers provide this service).
- Remember that plastic containers can often be useful in the workshop or garden.

Since less than 4 per cent of local authorities provide any plastics recycling facilities, you will find it hard to recycle any of the plastics in your rubbish. Suggest to your local supermarket that they provide a PET bank, and write to manufacturers to encourage them to introduce returnable plastic containers.

PLASTIC AWARENESS – WHO BENEFITS?

You

Though the financial saving is not as great as with cans and paper, you will almost certainly find it cheaper to buy fewer things wrapped in plastic, and to recycle plastic packaging rather than buy new every time.

Other people

As with other recycling projects, recycling plastic creates more employment than it replaces, and less plastic waste means fewer rubbish tips in people's 'back yards'.

The environment

Plastic litters every beach in the world and will take centuries to decompose or be worn away. Plastic rubbish maims and kills thousands of birds and animals, as well as creating an unsightly mess in our streets and countryside.

BOTTLE BANKS

THE FACTS

Up till now, glass has been Britain's best attempt at recycling, and 14 per cent of the glass containers we use are recycled through the 3,400 bottle banks operated by 380 local authorities. This is partly because glass is relatively easy to recycle, and partly because the industry has been active in promoting recycling. There is far more that could be done, however. Holland recycles 62 per cent of its glass, and has one bottle bank for every 1,400 people. In Britain there are 16,000 people to each bottle bank, and 70 local authorities still have no bottle bank scheme. In Europe as a whole, 31 per cent of glass is recycled: only Ireland recycles less than we do.

We use six billion glass containers each year, amounting to 2 million tonnes of glass. Every tonne of glass that is recycled saves the energy equivalent of 30 gallons (136 litres) of oil, and replaces 1.2 tonnes of the raw materials – sand, limestone and soda ash – that go to make new glass. Even better than recycling is re-using, and we already have a strong tradition of this with milk and beer bottles. Over 8.5 billion pints (4.8 billion litres) of milk are delivered in milk bottles each year, and the average milk bottle is used 24 times. Here, too, we could improve the situation even further. In Denmark, for example, it has been illegal since 1981 to sell beer and soft drinks in non-returnable bottles.

As well as taking up space in landfill sites, glass containers which are not recycled pose environmental problems for human beings and wildlife alike. Each year more than 6,000 accidents involving hospitalisation are caused by broken glass; one broken bottle left on a beach can ruin a whole holiday.

WHAT NEEDS TO CHANGE

More bottles should be returnable. Britain needs to follow Denmark's lead in making re-usable bottles (on which a deposit is paid) the norm. There should be more bottle banks, eventually amounting to at least one for every 2,000 people. All supermarkets ought to have bottle banks and bottle recycling schemes. All glass containers should include information about re-use and recycling on the label.

WHAT YOU CAN DO

- Buy glass containers rather than plastic ones, since they are so much easier to re-use and recycle.
- Buy deposit bottles whenever you can (some soft drinks companies, like Corona, do still use them).
- Wash and return milk bottles promptly. Don't put them in the bottle bank.
- Take all your other bottles to the bottle bank (do it while you're passing rather than making a special trip). Take the tops off first, and make sure you put the bottles in the right holes – clear, green, or brown. Don't put in anything other than glass, and take boxes and carriers home with you again. Try to avoid using the bottle bank at night when people are sleeping.

Ask your local supermarket to provide a bottle bank and a re-usable bottle container: Sainsbury's, Tesco and Safeway are already pioneering such schemes. Write to British Glass for copies of *Save for the Future* and *Glass Recycling Facts and Figures*.

USING BOTTLE BANKS – WHO BENEFITS?

You

Every re-usable glass container you use saves about 4p. The financial rewards of using recycled glass are less obvious (apart from getting your deposit back on certain bottles), but recycling must make glass cheaper.

Other people

The less glass that is thrown away, the fewer landfill sites will have to be sited near people's homes. Children are often the innocent victims of broken glass which has been disposed of thoughtlessly, so recycling glass will save their pain and your anxiety.

The environment

Though the raw materials of glass are plentiful, their quarrying has a significant impact on the environment. Wild and domestic animals suffer many serious wounds from broken glass, and insects get trapped inside discarded bottles. Glass splinters on our streets and beaches are both dangerous and ugly.

AEROSOLS

THE FACTS

The recent change in attitudes towards aerosol sprays, and especially those which contain ozone-destroying chlorofluoro-carbons (CFCs), shows that the combined efforts of 'green consumers' can have a profound and rapid effect upon manufacturers. In 1987, over 80 per cent of the 800 million aerosol cans made in Britain used CFCs as a propellant. By the end of 1989 more than 85 per cent of aerosols, including all those made by the eight largest manufacturers, will be CFC-free.

Why the concern about CFCs? Because there are already hundreds of thousands of tonnes of CFCs in the atmosphere, and each chlorine molecule can destroy 100,000 molecules of ozone. The thin ozone layer, about 12 miles (20 km) above us, protects life on Earth from the sun's ultra-violet radiation which contributes towards skin cancer and eye disorders, crop diseases and smog pollution. Seasonal 'holes' in the ozone layer have now been reported over both the Arctic and Antarctic.

But CFCs are not the only problem associated with aerosol sprays. Because they are pressurised even when empty, aerosol spray cans are dangerous to dispose of. And because they contain so many different metals and plastics they cannot be recycled. This complex packaging also makes them expensive to produce: you can sometimes pay 30 to 40p for the can that you throw away when the product is finished. For most purposes there are simple alternatives to aerosols – hand pumps and trigger sprays – which helps to explain why sales of many aerosol products are now falling rapidly.

WHAT NEEDS TO CHANGE

A compulsory system for putting propellant information on aerosol cans should be introduced, and there ought to be an immediate ban on all non-essential uses of CFC aerosols. Other uses of CFCs (in fridges, solvents and foams) need to be phased out as quickly as possible. Manufacturers and retailers should sell spray products in non-aerosol containers that can be recycled.

WHAT YOU CAN DO

- Think very carefully before you buy any aerosols at all, even 'ozone-friendly' ones.
- Change to roll-on deodorants and hand-pump perfume sprays.
- Use wax polish and a paint brush instead of spray cans.
- A fly swat is much cheaper and more environment-friendly than an insecticide spray (which is also dangerous to you and your pets).
- Pipe cream with a piping bag rather than a spray can.

Check that your workplace or school has stopped using CFC aerosols. Write to Friends of the Earth for the latest edition of *The Aerosol Connection* (this includes information about all CFC-free aerosols and a lot of background facts too). John Gribbin's book *The Hole in the Sky* (Corgi, 1988) explains exactly what is causing the thinning of the ozone layer, and why it is so important for the health of human beings and other living things.

UNDERSTANDING AEROSOLS – WHO BENEFITS?

You

Buying alternatives to aerosol sprays will certainly save you money, especially if you change to refillable hand-pump and trigger sprays. Though it may seem like a very small contribution, you will be helping to save yourself and all of us from overdoses of ultra-violet radiation.

Other people

CFCs can last for more than 100 years in the atmosphere, so even an 85 per cent reduction now would only just stabilise the situation. Think of the effect of an increase of CFCs on our children's health and the environment.

The environment

All living things depend upon the fragile ozone layer for protection from the sun's ultra-violet radiation. Because such a depletion has never occurred before, nobody knows what the long-term consequences might be.

RECYCLING YOUR PAPER

THE FACTS

Every year we use the wood pulp from 131 million trees (more than two trees for everyone in the country) to make our paper and board. We use 8.7 million tonnes of paper a year, just under half of which is made in Britain, though only 10 per cent of the pulp used in British-made paper comes from home-grown trees. A large proportion of our paper could be recycled and used again, but only 29 per cent of it is, including less than 20 per cent of household paper waste: the average household throws away more than 6½ lb (3 kg) of paper every week.

The recycling of paper and board is important for many reasons, both economic and environmental. The recycling of paper could easily save nearly £1 billion in imports, and create up to 22,000 jobs. In environmental terms, recycled paper not only saves trees and reduces the need to plant vast areas of moorland with conifers. It also uses only 10 per cent of the water and 55 per cent of the energy that goes into making virgin paper, while producing less than quarter of the pollution (even taking the chemical de-inking of used paper into account).

Although Britain is a long way behind some other countries (50 per cent of paper in Japan and Holland is recycled), demand for used paper is now picking up. In the next four years the use of recycled newspapers and magazines is expected to double to 950,000 tonnes a year, which will make it economic for local authorities and charities to collect and recycle household paper in bulk. Two new recycled paper mills will come on stream in 1990, with several others planned.

WHAT NEEDS TO CHANGE

There needs to be a guaranteed market, with fixed minimum prices, for different kinds of waste paper. Waste paper collection schemes should be provided by the 49 per cent of local authorities which currently have no such scheme. And householders ought to separate paper waste. Large users of paper (like businesses and government departments) should introduce waste paper separation and recycling schemes.

WHAT YOU CAN DO

- Don't waste paper; re-use it as much as possible.
- Use both sides of each sheet whenever you can (playgroups and schools can usually use paper which is only clean on one side).
- Re-use envelopes.
- If your local authority or a local charity runs a paper collection scheme, use it.
- Certain kinds of 'white paper' (like writing paper, photocopier paper and computer paper) are more valuable than newsprint, so if you use a lot (in an office or business), collect it separately and tell the organisation that you can supply them regularly. Friends of the Earth support such a scheme in London.
- Buy recycled paper products (see page 122).

If your local authority doesn't provide any facilities for recycling paper, ask what they are planning to do about it. Ask your local supermarket to recycle all its cardboard packaging, as Sainsbury's are now doing at all their stores. If you are involved in charity work, write to the Charities Aid Foundation for a copy of *Waste Not*, which includes suggestions for raising money through waste paper collections.

RECYCLING YOUR PAPER – WHO BENEFITS?

You

Although it will take some time, recycling will eventually bring down the relative price of recycled products, thus saving you money. In the meantime, you will know that you are contributing to the reduction of unnecessary tree-felling and water pollution.

Other people

Paper recycling creates employment. As recycled and fairly chemical-free paper products become more widely available, you and your family will also be avoiding the health risks associated with highly processed paper products (see page 124).

The environment

The recycling of paper and board saves trees, and protects fragile moorland from harmful conifer planting. It also saves large amounts of energy and helps to avoid water pollution.

USING RECYCLED PAPER

THE FACTS

The main reason why paper is not recycled more in Britain is that virgin paper has been relatively cheap, so paper merchants have been able to claim that there is no call for recycled paper. This is a circular argument, since recycled paper remains expensive only because paper is not automatically recycled! In countries like Holland and Germany, recycled paper is almost always cheaper than virgin equivalents, and for uses like newsprint, recycled is cheaper in Britain too. These days almost all British newspapers use recycled paper; telephone directories are printed on recycled paper; and recycled paper waste is widely used to make cardboard boxes and cartons.

Recent concern about the chemicals used to bleach paper products (see page 00) means that customers are no longer exclusively asking for bright white, brand-new-paper toilet rolls, tissues, disposable nappies and filter papers. One manufacturer is already advertising 'natural off-white' products, an environment-friendly alternative to the bleached wood-pulp ranges.

Even 10 years ago it was hard to find a reasonable range of recycled papers, but now you can buy a very wide selection of colours and qualities. Several local authorities and government departments now use recycled paper for most purposes; the Department of the Environment, for example, is saving around £4,000 each year by using recycled paper. Virgin Records, The Body Shop and Sainsbury's all use recycled paper where possible, as do most environmental organisations.

WHAT NEEDS TO CHANGE

The biggest contribution that customers can make is to buy recycled paper products. To help in this, all recycled paper products should be clearly labelled and widely available. Stationery shops and office equipment suppliers ought to offer a wide range of recycled paper products, and individuals, businesses and organisations ought to use them.

WHAT YOU CAN DO

- Buy and use recycled paper products whenever you can.
- Start with tissues – kitchen roll, toilet paper and paper hankies. If all our toilet rolls were made from recycled paper (which doesn't have to mean grey, hard and scratchy) an extra half million tonnes of paper a year could be recycled and seven million trees saved.
- Buy recycled stationery. Many shops now stock it, but if you have problems finding it, write to Forestsaver, FoE Birmingham, Greenscene or Traidcraft for their recycled paper catalogues.
- Write to Friends of the Earth for a copy of their *Directory of Recycled Paper* which has examples of most available types.

If you are responsible for buying paper for a business or organisation, contact one of the main wholesalers like Paperback, Conservation Papers or Earthwrite to find out about buying recycled paper in bulk. You will almost certainly be pleasantly surprised by their prices. Friends of the Earth also have lists of mills, wholesalers and shops which sell recycled paper.

USING RECYCLED PAPER – WHO BENEFITS?

You

Using recycled paper products, especially unbleached and un-dyed ones, protects your health. In the near future they will almost certainly be cheaper too.

Other people

You will be helping the co-operative companies which supply a large proportion of Britain's recycled paper, and reducing the need for dangerous new rubbish tips close to people's houses.

The environment

We could easily reduce our need for pulp timber, and thus for tree-felling, by a third. This is very important at a time when we should be planting long-living trees to counteract the greenhouse effect. Using unbleached recycled paper would also reduce the huge discharges of chlorine compounds into the rivers below pulp mills – discharges which kill fish and other forms of aquatic life.

DISPOSABILITY

THE FACTS

We live in a convenience society, where everyday items from handkerchiefs to razors, kitchen towels to babies' nappies are increasingly of the disposable variety. This is particularly the case with those – mostly paper-based – products with which we clean up after ourselves, the 'disposable hygienics'. Every year we get through 3.5 billion disposable nappies and over 2 billion toilet rolls. Then we throw them all away and hope that we won't need to think about them again.

But everything has to come from somewhere, and everything must go somewhere. Disposable nappies alone use the wood from 30 million trees every year, and the chlorine-based chemicals used to bleach everything bright white cause serious pollution in the rivers and seas. The same chemicals, which contain toxic dioxins, are also thought to be a human health risk, especially to babies. Once used, the disposables create a formidable rubbish problem. They are not easy to recycle, they block drains and sewage systems, and can carry a wide range of viruses and bacteria.

Some countries, like Sweden, have recognised the environmental and health risks of these products, and have succeeded in shifting to safer formulations. Following an upsurge in public concern, unbleached paper disposables are now becoming more widely available in Britain. The next step is to re-introduce practices which are healthier for us and the environment, and less wasteful of valuable resources.

WHAT NEEDS TO CHANGE

Detailed information about the environmental and health implications of disposable products needs to be widely available, so that consumers can make informed choices. Non-bleached paper products should be widely available at reasonable prices. The producers of disposable products should contribute funds towards their collection and disposal, and research should be done into recyclable alternatives to disposable products.

WHAT YOU CAN DO

- Try to cut down on the quantity of 'disposable hygienics' you use.
- Don't use paper plates and plastic cutlery.
- Use towels and tea-towels in the kitchen instead of paper kitchen rolls.
- Use recycled paper products in preference to ones made of new paper, and buy unbleached off-white products rather than bright chemically bleached ones.
- If you have a baby, think very seriously about using terry nappies instead of disposables. You will save money, even though it might mean a bit more work.

If you use tampons, investigate the relative health risks of using them, as against sanitary towels. *The Sanitary Protection Scandal* (WEN, 1989) contains all the information you will need. This important book also looks at the real costs of using disposable nappies, and the alternatives, such as using cloth nappies together with washable absorbent 'biobottoms' (an American invention).

KNOWING ABOUT DISPOSABLES – WHO BENEFITS?

You

Disposable hygienics have been implicated in a range of health problems, including cancer and toxic shock syndrome. Using them with care will help to safeguard your health, and using them as sparingly as possible will also ease the pressure on your purse.

Other people

There is increasing concern about the effect of dioxins on the health of babies and young children. Using unbleached products or shifting away from disposables altogether will decrease the risks to your family's health.

The environment

Using fewer disposables saves trees, rivers and wildlife. Less dangerous household rubbish means less pollution, and less land needed for unhealthy and unsightly landfill sites.

LITTER CONSCIOUSNESS

THE FACTS

The 23 million tonnes of domestic rubbish we throw away in Britain every year creates serious problems when it comes to finding somewhere to put it all, but at least it is contained in bins, bags and boxes so the council can come and take it away. An even more intractable problem is the estimated 1 million tonnes a year of litter, thrown out of car windows and dropped thoughtlessly by passing pedestrians. Litter in the sea, thrown overboard without a second thought, affects every beach in the country. Recent developments like fast food outlets and 'free' magazines have made the problem worse: London's Westminster City Council collects 50 tonnes of litter, 7 per cent of all the borough's refuse, off the streets every day. Some obvious litter-encouraging businesses have shouldered the responsibility to provide adequate litter bins, but many have not.

Littering is illegal. While the litter problem gets worse, however, very little effort is made by the police and local authorities to take the problem seriously. In 1988 there were only 1,900 prosecutions for littering; 220 were in Cumbria and one was in London. The maximum fine for littering is currently £400; the average fine is £32. Of those prosecuted for littering, 6 per cent are women and 94 per cent men.

As the problem grows, the effort to combat litter has also grown. The Tidy Britain Group now has 10 active regional campaigns, attracting £3 million worth of government support and £5 million of industry sponsorship, much of it from the companies whose used packaging is most prominent among the litter being tackled.

WHAT NEEDS TO CHANGE

The litter problem wouldn't exist if people simply put their litter in a bin or took it home with them; what is needed is a widespread education effort. Well-designed litter bins need to be provided wherever litter is generated, and they should be emptied regularly. There should be stricter international controls on litter dumping at sea, and the laws against littering should be properly enforced.

WHAT YOU CAN DO

- Buy products with minimal packaging – individually wrapped sweets, for example, inevitably create more litter than ones sold loose in a paper bag.
- Avoid over-packaged fast food; you pay for the packaging you throw away.
- Avoid picking up 'free literature' you don't need; just say no.
- Don't drop litter: put waste in a bin or take it home with you.
- Don't let your children drop litter. It can be a tedious process, especially when they are under peer pressure to ignore you, but persevere: thoughtless children become selfish adults.
- Don't just watch someone littering without saying anything. If you can't bring yourself to challenge the litterer, pick it up yourself.

The Tidy Britain Group produces a range of literature, and the regional campaigns organise regular clean-up projects, which are always looking for volunteers. Various charities organise sponsored clean-ups – much more ecological than jelly-throwing or balloon races. Look out for details in your local paper or organise one yourself.

LITTER CONSCIOUSNESS – WHO BENEFITS?

You

Reducing litter gives you cleaner streets and junk-free country walks. As well as making your surroundings more attractive, less litter means fewer health risks.

Other people

Litter, especially glass, contributes to accidents – and children are often the victims. A cleaner neighbourhood will be safer and more pleasant for everyone.

The environment

As well as disfiguring our towns and countryside, litter can injure wildlife, block streams, kill marine life, and pollute land and water. Birds regularly choke on plastic waste, and small mammals often get trapped inside discarded containers.

RESPECTING THE COUNTRYSIDE

THE FACTS

Almost everybody likes a day in the country: 84 per cent of us do it at some time during the year. On a fine summer Sunday there will be 18 million people enjoying the countryside in one way or another. Yet rural areas are under severe pressure – from agribusiness, forestry, building, roads, power stations and cables, reservoirs and the pressures of unaware tourism. A 1985 survey showed that 68 per cent of us are very concerned about the future of Britain's countryside.

The way we relate to the countryside when we are in it can make a big difference. Although the greatest threats come from large-scale developments, visitors to the countryside are also often responsible for environmental damage. Examples are the severe bankside erosion of the Norfolk Broads, the scarring of Lakeland fells by hordes of hikers, and fires on the heaths of Dorset which have killed important populations of birds and reptiles. The people who live in rural areas must also play their part. For instance, the estimated 70,000 miles (110,000 km) of Britain's rights of way (nearly 60 per cent of the total) which are currently obstructed, ploughed up or overgrown need to be properly maintained so that we can all enjoy them.

The last 30 years have seen major and welcome changes to the provision of facilities for countryside recreation. In addition to 10 national parks, 40 areas of outstanding natural beauty and 850 miles (1,365 km) of heritage coastline, we now have 1,500 miles (2,400 km) of long-distance paths, 206 country parks and 239 landscaped picnic sites. Yet still only 26 per cent of us say that we know our local countryside well, while 72 per cent want to know more about what they can do and where they can go.

WHAT NEEDS TO CHANGE

Information about the countryside – where people can go, how they can get there, and what they can do – needs to be more widely available. The rights of way network must be properly maintained and adequately signposted. Land-use policies and strategies affecting the countryside should be integrated so that people working in it and visiting it can enjoy it together, without harming its ecological balance.

WHAT YOU CAN DO

- Find out about your local area: the nearest footpaths, woods, streams and parks.
- Buy a local large-scale map (they're called 'Pathfinder' and have green covers; most also show rights of way).
- Make sure you abide by the Country Code: guard against fire; fasten gates; keep dogs under control; keep to public paths across farmland; use gates and stiles to cross walls and fences; take your litter home; keep watercourses clean; don't over-pick or damage plants; and don't make unnecessary noise.
- More than a third of countryside visitors walk on roads or roadside footpaths, so be very careful on country lanes if you drive.

Write to the Countryside Commission for a free copy of *Out In The Country: Where You Can Go and What You Can Do*, a helpful booklet full of information about everthing from kite-flying to the legal aspects of using a metal detector. Find out about nearby countryside attractions from your local tourist information office or leisure and recreation department.

RESPECTING THE COUNTRYSIDE – WHO BENEFITS?

You

When those who visit and work in the countryside respect and look after it, you will be able to enjoy an unpolluted and unspoilt landscape whenever you go for a walk or a picnic.

Other people

The careful and integrated management of the countryside benefits farmers, other people who live in the country and all those who visit it.

The environment

Observing the Country Code will benefit the environment in many ways: keeping it clean, protecting plants and wildlife, and generally ensuring that your visit does it no harm.

COUNTRYSIDE CAMPAIGNING

THE FACTS

As Britain's population has grown and human activities have required the use of ever more land, machinery and chemicals, so the British countryside and the wildlife that inhabits it have suffered. Over the past 35 years the nation has lost 95 per cent of its lowland herb-rich grasslands, 80 per cent of its chalk and limestone grasslands, 60 per cent of its lowland heaths, 45 per cent of its limestone pavements, 50 per cent of its ancient woodlands, 50 per cent of its lowland fens and marshes, over 60 per cent of its lowland raised bogs, and a third of all upland grasslands, heaths and mires. Hedgerow loss has accelerated from 2,600 miles (4,200 km) a year between 1947 and 1979 to 4,000 miles (6,440 km) a year in the 1980s. Fifty-nine per cent of public footpaths in England and Wales are ploughed up or obstructed; and a recent survey of Buckinghamshire showed that the figure there was 82 per cent.

The Large Blue butterfly became extinct in 1979, but eight more butterfly species are endangered, and another 12 of our 55 breeding species are now officially classified as rare. Of 43 species of dragonfly, four have become extinct since 1953 and 10 have decreased to the point of being very rare. Thirty lowland and six upland species of bird have shown appreciable long-term decline in the last 35 years, including such favourites as the nightingale, heron and kingfisher. The otter has become extremely rare. Of Britain's 1,423 native vascular plants, 149 have declined by at least 20 per cent, and we risk the complete loss of species like the Early Star of Bethlehem and the Purple Coltsfoot.

There may now be growing concern in Britain about the importance of countryside conservation, but nobody should delude themselves about the scale of the problem.

WHAT NEEDS TO CHANGE

Central government and local authorities need to take seriously their commitment to countryside conservation policies. Planning procedures should be designed to give conservation a high priority, even when commercial or strategic considerations are important. The funding available for nature conservation ought to be increased dramatically: less than £10 million a year is spent by central government on our national parks.

WHAT YOU CAN DO

- Get to know your nearest countryside, and treat it with respect (see page 128).
- If you live in or near the countryside, keep an eye on what is going on in your neighbourhood. Watch out for notices of planning applications in your local paper: you are entitled to go and look at them at the District Planning Department.
- If you see changes that you don't like the look of, tell the Planning Department and your County Trust for Nature Conservation: the Royal Society for Nature Conservation (RSNC) will give you the address. You could also contact the local branch of the Council for the Protection of Rural England (CPRE) and ask what course of action they suggest.
- Talk to local farmers. They often feel isolated and misunderstood, and may well appreciate contact with local concerned residents.

The two best books to read are *Countryside Conflicts* (Temple Smith, 1986) and, for England, Derrick Mercer's *Rural England* (Macdonald, 1988). Angela King and Sue Clifford's *Holding your Ground* (Temple Smith, 1985) is also an excellent guide to local campaigning.

COUNTRYSIDE CAMPAIGNING – WHO BENEFITS?

You

Looking after the countryside and taking positive action when necessary ensures that Britain retains the variety and richness of its countryside, which will then be there to stimulate and refresh you whenever you want to enjoy it.

Other people

Countryside campaigning is an urgent and never-ending task. Those who do a great deal of this sort of work are delighted when new people want to become involved.

The environment

Thoughtless development of rural land is one of the biggest environmental threats we face. Protecting and conserving our countryside, especially the wilder and most unspoilt parts, benefits the rich variety of wildlife and habitat.

THE IMPORTANCE OF TREES

THE FACTS

Trees are a much-loved, dependable element of the British landscape, but they are far too often taken for granted, and have little chance of survival if they get in the way of a project like a motorway or a supermarket complex. Britain has retained less of its native woodland than any other European country; the last 35 years alone have seen the felling of nearly half of our old deciduous forest and almost 30 per cent of our hedgerow trees. And that was before the loss of 15 million to Dutch elm disease and a further 15 million to the storm of October 1987.

Though we import 90 per cent of our timber, 55 per cent of Britain's mixed and deciduous woodlands are unmanaged or deteriorating. Paradoxically, until recent tax law changes it was far more profitable to plant new conifer 'deserts' rather than manage existing woodlands. At one point in the mid-1980s there were plans to plant another 3 million acres (1.2 million hectares) of conifers (an area the size of Yorkshire) by the middle of the next century.

Trees are vital to the ecology of the planet, turning poisonous carbon dioxide into breathable oxygen, keeping the 'greenhouse gases' (especially carbon dioxide) in check, holding the soil cover in place, giving compost back to the soil, and providing the framework for rich and varied ecosystems. Trees cover 30 per cent of the world's surface, but they are being felled at an ever-increasing rate, especially in the tropics (see page 40). The trees of northern Europe are suffering from a wide range of pollutants, from acid rain to agricultural spraying. Fifty-two per cent of Germany's trees are already dead or dying; the percentage in Britain is thought to be between 25 and 30 per cent and increasing rapidly.

WHAT NEEDS TO CHANGE

We need to educate ourselves and our children about the importance of planting and looking after trees. More local authorities should establish tree nurseries, and encourage a wide range of tree-planting schemes, from single trees to whole new forests, using native species wherever possible. The owners of woodlands should be given financial help so that they can manage them on a sustainable basis.

WHAT YOU CAN DO

- Don't waste wood, though you should use it in preference to non-renewable resources like metals and oil-based plastics.
- Recycle paper (see page 120) and timber whenever possible. If you do joinery yourself, buy reclaimed building timber – it will be cheaper and better seasoned than new wood.
- Use hardwoods sparingly, and avoid tropical hardwoods completely (see page 40).
- Take care of trees and hedgerows.
- Learn about trees and their needs, and find out about local tree-planting groups that you and your children might join: Men of the Trees and The Woodland Trust should be able to help.

If you want to extend your knowledge further, the best tree identification guide is Alan Mitchell's *The Trees of Britain and Northern Europe* (Collins, 1985).

UNDERSTANDING THE IMPORTANCE OF TREES – WHO BENEFITS?

You

A treeless planet is an airless, dead planet. Ensuring a future for our trees literally ensures our own healthy existence, as well as providing endless beauty and inspiration.

Other people

The maintenance of healthy forest cover over large areas of our planet is one way of guaranteeing a worthwhile future for our children.

The environment

Healthy trees are a vital part of the environment, and do not deserve the fate we currently mete out to them. Trees and forests protect and feed the Earth's fragile mantle of soil, and keep the entire balance of the atmosphere agreeable to all life forms.

GREEN HOLIDAYS

THE FACTS

In a survey of activity holidays, one daily paper recently announced that 'the day of the green-tinted tourist has arrived'. With the tailing off of demand for overseas package holidays and the growing interest in all things environmental, there is certainly room for a wide range of leisure activities which help travellers to understand and work with their environment, rather than trampling it to death and throwing litter all over it.

The average Briton in the late 1980s takes between two and three holidays a year within Britain. In addition, nearly a third of us go abroad for a holiday. Those of us who stay in Britain are joined by 13 million overseas visitors, a quarter of them from the USA and nearly half from Europe. They spend almost £5 billion in Britain, while we spend rather less than that on our foreign holidays.

However, much tourism has disadvantages for us and the environment. Studies have shown that tourists are several times more likely to be ill than people who stay at home, and at the height of summer the roads and footpaths in popular tourist areas can be packed solid with cars and people, exhaust fumes and noise. Despite all this, the last two decades have seen a rapid rise in the number and variety of holiday opportunities for people who want to understand the places they visit more deeply than a half-day excursion allows. Walking, cycling and activity holidays are experiencing something of a boom, while conservation holidays (where you pay relatively little but work quite hard on environmental projects) are becoming increasingly popular.

WHAT NEEDS TO CHANGE

We need to question what tourism is really doing for us and for the environment. Projects which allow people to enjoy places without destroying them should be investigated and supported, especially in environmentally sensitive areas. Visitors ought to be encouraged to take an interest, and an active part, in conservation projects.

WHAT YOU CAN DO

- Think carefully about what you want from a holiday, then consider the easiest and most efficient way of getting it.
- A good range of options, including walking and cycling holidays, is given in the 'travel agents' section of *The Green Consumer Guide* (Gollancz, 1988).
- The British Trust for Conservation Volunteers organises a wide range of conservation working holidays at very reasonable rates, while the Field Studies Council's holidays cover themes from local history and wildlife to painting and rural crafts.
- When on holiday, respect the people and landscape of the places you visit, and take an intelligent interest in them without overwhelming them. As the American Sierra Club recommends: take only photographs; leave only footprints.

Green Print publishes a useful range of *Green Guides*, pointing travellers in the direction of interesting green-tinted sights and projects. So far the series covers France and England, with further volumes planned for Scotland, Wales, Europe and North America.

GREEN HOLIDAYS – WHO BENEFITS?

You

Knowing what you really want from your holiday and working out the best way to get it will result in more satisfying, enjoyable holidays. If you've chosen to do something creative or useful in the open air, you'll probably also feel healthier, as well as possibly saving money.

Other people

People who earn their living from tourism, and those who live and work in tourist areas, appreciate considerate and interested travellers.

The environment

Tourists who are considerate of the environment can help to protect threatened species and prevent erosion. Those who choose conservation holidays can also play an important part in helping the natural environment to look after itself.

PLANNED PARENTHOOD

THE FACTS

Though they may have been a few weeks out, the American Population Institute reckoned that the planet's five billionth human inhabitant was born on July 7th, 1986. The six billionth will probably be born in 2001 and the seventh billionth in 2012. Even the most optimistic demographers do not see the world's population levelling out until we reach 10 billion towards the end of the 21st century. It would be easy to think of population pressure only as a Third World problem, but it isn't. British trading and foreign aid programmes affect parenting decisions throughout the world. And many people believe that Great Britain is already overcrowded, not to mention the 4 per cent increase in population projected within the next decade.

The ecologist Garrett Hardin asks which of the freedoms we currently enjoy – how to travel, where to live, what to eat, and so on – will suffer if world population continues to increase at the present rate. His answer is 'all of them', and his conclusion is that we must therefore question our normally unquestioned freedom to procreate.

The reasons for people wanting and having children are many and complex, but it is clear that we need to think very carefully about our responsibility not to exceed the number of people that can be supported by the planet's resources. Being more aware of our sexual behaviour does not only mean being in control of our fertility. Since the advent of AIDS, we have had to learn to protect our health with safer sex, and people are increasingly recognising that sexual freedom must be balanced with sexual responsibility.

WHAT NEEDS TO CHANGE

Birth control advice and supplies should be widely and freely available, and all aspects of sexual responsibility should be part of every child's education. Research into effective, risk-free contraceptive techniques needs to be given high priority. Population policy must be taken seriously. Incentives that could be considered include tax benefits for small families and a small reward for people who choose to be sterilised.

WHAT YOU CAN DO

- Take your sexual responsibilities seriously, both in relation to contraception and to sexually transmitted diseases. Take joint responsibility for conception and contraception; don't assume (especially if you're a man) that the other person has taken the necessary precautions.
- If you are thinking about having a baby, try to sort out all the different reasons, and ask yourself whether having a baby will best fulfil your needs.
- If your children are old enough, discuss these issues with them.

Think very seriously if you are planning to have more than two children of your own. Any more will inevitably add to the overall increase in human population, which in the long run can only be at the expense of the rest of life on the planet. After 20 years of dormancy, population is again becoming an important environmental issue: write to the organisation Population Concern for their *Population Facts* leaflet.

PLANNED PARENTHOOD – WHO BENEFITS?

You

Having children when and how you want them means less anxiety and hardship, and more enjoyable parenting. Currently 18 per cent of conceptions end with an abortion and another 15 per cent are unplanned and unwanted, resulting in an annual population increase of 120,000.

Other people

While many 'unplanned' children have a full and happy childhood, a large number suffer from deprivation and lack of parental interest. Future generations will clearly benefit from population planning undertaken now.

The environment

The degradation of the environment resulting from excessive human pressure can be seen in almost every corner of the globe. Whatever other steps we take to look after the environment, population planning must be a prime concern.

THE GREEN BABY

THE FACTS

What could be more natural than a mother giving birth, and caring for her baby by ensuring that its simple needs are met? Yet the 780,000 British women who have babies each year know that birth is an occasion which is shared by an army of experts, from doctors and nurses to the makers of nappies, baby foods and soft toys. The 'baby industry' is worth more than £550 million a year, and much of it (including unnecessary medication, single-use disposable products, clothes which fit for only a few weeks and baby foods in excessive packaging) is about as un-green as you can imagine. It isn't just ecologically harmful; unnecessary drugs and chemicals can also be a health risk to both mother and baby. After reaching a low in 1985, infant mortality rates have recently started to rise slightly.

Ninety-nine per cent of all British babies are born in hospital, and 36 per cent of mothers bottle-feed their babies. By the time the baby is four months old, 74 per cent are bottle-feeding. Both practices use far more resources than home delivery and breast-feeding, and there is little medical evidence to show that either is safer or healthier. In Holland, where 29 per cent of births are home deliveries, the infant mortality rate is 8 per 1,000 compared with Britain's 9.4. Breast-feeding provides a baby with the correct balance of nutrients and costs almost nothing, whereas bottle-feeding costs nearly £350 a year.

The 68 per cent of British babies put in disposable nappies use nearly 3.5 billion nappies a year, or 3 million trees' worth (see page 124). The average baby eats £200 worth of tinned, bottled and packet food a year, produced by an industry which spends £4.5 million a year on advertising. The list goes on as the baby industry exhorts you to spend and spend on the one you love the most.

WHAT NEEDS TO CHANGE

We need to move away from seeing birth as a medical complaint and babies as an industry. Women should have as much information as they need, and be supported in their choices relating to childbirth. There should be more social acceptance of breast-feeding, and restrictions on advertising and 'free gift' systems. Employers ought to be flexible about parental leave from work.

WHAT YOU CAN DO

- For the birth itself, remember that the choice should be yours: if you want a home birth you are entitled to it by law. The Association for Improvements in the Maternity Services can provide information about the choices available.
- If you need help with breast-feeding, both the National Childbirth Trust and La Leche League have groups and counsellors nationwide. At least experiment with breast-feeding, and continue for as long as you can – both you and the baby will benefit.
- Do what you can to support mothers who breast-feed by accepting it as a natural part of everyday life.
- Only buy things that the baby really needs.
- Even if you still sometimes need disposables, use terry nappies and wool or cotton liners in preference.
- Use as few creams and powders as possible, and buy only natural cruelty-free baby care products.

Sally Inch's *Birthrights* (Hutchinson, 1982) is an excellent general book, while Penny and Andrew Stanway's *Breast is Best* (Pan, 1978) explains the benefits of breast-feeding. Karen Christensen's *Home Ecology* (Arlington, 1989) has a chapter covering every aspect of green babyhood.

GREEN BABIES – WHO BENEFITS?

You

Keeping babyhood simple and healthy saves a lot of stress and anxiety. It helps to give you a real connection with your baby, and the satisfaction of having done it yourself with minimal help from the 'experts'. You will also save a lot of money.

Other people

Your baby will benefit in many ways from having its early years relatively uncluttered by the baby industry. It will almost certainly be healthier and more self-reliant, and will have saved its country a large sum in medical costs.

The environment

A green baby makes minimal demands on resources and contributes minimally to environmental pollution.

PLAY AND PLAYTHINGS

THE FACTS

Every child needs stimulation: things to touch, taste, smell, look at, manipulate and explore. Toys can provide such stimulus, and have an important role in a child's world. Exciting and imaginative as toys may be, however, they can only be a small part of the real world. Though toy manufacturers might persuade us otherwise, a child cannot reach its full potential in a world consisting solely of scaled-down replicas of our materialist culture. Many of the things that fascinate a child simply can't be manufactured: snails and worms, sand and soil, flowers and grass – the world close to the ground that adults usually ignore.

Children's toys are a booming market, worth more than £3 billion a year. Toys are among the most advertised products you can buy – advertising which includes numerous plugs on primetime children's television – but do they deliver their promise of 'imaginative play'? Many do not, and every parent knows that it is a handful of toys – usually the most basic and adaptable ones – that receive the lion's share of a child's attention. The rest fill up toy boxes and shelves or get trodden underfoot. The environmental consequences of such waste are enormous. But worse than that, children learn from babyhood onwards that new consumer thrills will always replace yesterday's entertainment.

A small but growing number of parents and toymakers are bucking the trend, making imaginative and adaptable toys from safe, natural materials. There are over 1,000 toy libraries in Britain, lending a wide range of durable toys. And several cities have 'scrapstores' which pass useful industrial leftovers to schools and playgroups.

WHAT NEEDS TO CHANGE

We need to see play as an integration of the real world and the child's inventiveness and creativity. We should move away from the present emphasis on toys which 'do it all' and provide a constant escape from the world, and towards playthings which involve the child in the world. Manufacturers and retailers should experiment more with green-tinted playthings.

WHAT YOU CAN DO

- Pass on the toys your children no longer use: most children are overwhelmed by the number of things they own. If you can't bear to part with things, store them so they can be a pleasant surprise for the child in a few months' time.
- Throw out broken and unmendable toys; they're as frustrating to the child as they are to you.
- Give your children sand, water, paint and dressing-up clothes to play with.
- Buy durable, adaptable toys made from natural materials, and learn to say no when you can't see how your child will benefit from a particular toy.
- Tell relatives what sort of presents your children would like.
- See if there is a toy library near you (Play Matters will provide information).

Think about sharing bigger toys with friends or neighbours. Ask if they are interested in toy swaps for outgrown toys. Try to set a good example by not being obsessed with 'adult toys'. *Green Pages* (Optima, 1988) includes a range of 'green' toy suppliers, together with more about shared and recycled toys. Write to Letterbox Library for their catalogue of green-tinted childrens' books.

THINKING ABOUT PLAY AND PLAYTHINGS – WHO BENEFITS?

You

Both your patience and your purse will benefit from fewer, safer, more imaginative playthings. Your home will be less cluttered and your children less bored.

Other people

The main people to benefit are your children, who may sometimes lack discrimination but do recognise shoddy and unimaginative workmanship. They may even start to enjoy tidying up their simple, treasured possessions.

The environment

Fewer toys means using fewer – mostly non-renewable – resources, and creating less waste. With fewer material possessions, children may want to be outside more, appreciating and exploring their natural surroundings (see page 144).

CHILDREN AND FOOD

THE FACTS

Children are a huge market for the manufacturers of processed food. British pre-school-age children alone consume 50 million meals each week, worth more than £1 billion annually. Sweets, crisps, biscuits, soft drinks and ice-creams together account for £8 billion worth of business a year. Children may like these 'fun foods' (indeed, they are often addicted to them) but many of them contain dubious or second-rate ingredients, are overpackaged and overpriced, and do more harm than good.

The problem goes further than sweets and ice-cream. Children are eating six times as many chips as 20 years ago, three times as much branded breakfast cereal, twice as many frozen meat and fish products and three times as many sugary drinks. They are eating only a third of the amount of porridge and oat products, half the amount of fresh fish, and three-quarters of the amount of fresh meat. What effect does this have on their health?

Unhealthy fatty streaks have been found in the muscles of year-old babies. More than half of British children have tooth decay in their first set of teeth, at 12 the proportion is 91 per cent. Childhood allergy has increased 20-fold in three decades. Twelve per cent of teenagers are medically overweight. Untold numbers of children suffer from constipation and the early stages of haemorrhoids. Many of these complaints can be attributed to diet, particularly to an excess of sugar, fat and chemical additives. Numerous trials have shown that shifting to a healthier diet usually produces a marked improvement, especially in relation to hyperactivity and allergic reactions like rashes and asthma.

WHAT NEEDS TO CHANGE

All processed foods should be clearly labelled with ingredients and health risks. Misleading labelling and advertising ought to be banned, and ingredients suspected of being a health risk should not be allowed in food designed to appeal especially to children. We need to educate children, parents and caterers about healthy food, and make sure that attractive healthy alternatives are always available.

WHAT YOU CAN DO

- Unhealthy eating habits start young, so breast-feed as long as you can and then wean your baby on to mashed fruit and vegetables (like apple, carrot and banana) rather than commercial processed food.
- Do not introduce sugar and salt for as long as possible.
- When children start to eat solid food, give them small portions of adult food rather than convenience 'children's foods'. Good healthy foods that most children like include low-sugar baked beans, frozen peas, wholewheat pizza, wholemeal bread and fresh fruit.
- Talk to your children about healthy eating; tell them what is good for them as well as what to avoid and why. Involve them in meal planning and preparation.
- Without being dogmatic or inflexible, set a good example by eating a healthy diet yourself.

Talk to the catering staff at your child's playgroup or school to ensure that healthy choices are encouraged there. Ask the shops where your children buy snacks to stock healthy alternatives. If you think your child might be hyperactive, contact the Hyperactive Children's Support Group for advice. Tim Lobstein's *Children's Food* (Unwin Hyman, 1988) is essential reading.

UNDERSTANDING CHILDREN AND FOOD – WHO BENEFITS?

You
By ensuring a healthy diet for your children you will save yourself a great deal of anxiety and time waiting to see doctors and dentists. Both you and your children will almost certainly save a considerable amount of money too.

Other people
Though they may have the occasional problem with peer pressure, your children will thank you when they are healthy discriminating young adults.

The environment
Processed foods use vast amounts of resources in their manufacture and packaging. Reducing the demand for unhealthy children's food means less pollution, less unsightly litter and less waste.

SHARING NATURE WITH CHILDREN

THE FACTS

In a culture where we live mostly indoors, and where outside usually means tarmac, concrete and busy roads, it is essential to keep children in touch with the earth. It is important that they understand and experience natural cycles, changing seasons, the beauty and mystery of nature. It isn't enough just to be taught in a classroom. As Rachel Carson wrote: 'It is not half so important to know as to feel.'

There is no doubt that children are fascinated by nature. When Watch (the junior wing of the Royal Society for Nature Conservation) launched its 'Acid Drops' rain water testing project in 1987, over 20,000 children took part. A similar project for checking river water quality has already involved more than 3,000 school and youth groups. Both projects have produced far more detailed information than most official surveys.

A recent survey showed that 78 per cent of teachers believe that environmental education is central to a child's active participation in the world, while 67 per cent believe that even controversial issues should be examined in depth. Yet British children, unlike their Scandinavian counterparts, rarely leave their school premises and actually experience nature. Luckily the situation is now changing in many areas. More than 70 Leicester schools are involved in conservation projects, 15 Liverpool primary schools have nature gardens, and 25,000 schoolchildren visit the renowned Camley Street nature park behind London's Kings Cross station each year.

WHAT NEEDS TO CHANGE

Environmental, social and world development issues should be integrated into the school curriculum, and full use should be made of opportunities to experience nature at first hand. We ought to encourage children to explore 'real' nature, rather than limiting them to managed, 'safe' places, and we should get them actively involved in conservation projects.

WHAT YOU CAN DO

- Get out and experience the natural world more yourself, and take the children with you. Try to ignore initial complaints: once they get outside they will soon become absorbed and stop thinking of home comforts.
- Learn about the natural world together, sharing feelings and thoughts as well as the biological facts.
- Respond to the child's interests and concerns, and involve them in nature games, quizzes and treasure hunts.
- Find out whether your child's school is involved with any environmental projects, and see if you can help.

The nature organisation Watch has local groups throughout the country, involved in a wide range of activities. Another active youth organisation is the Young People's Trust for the Environment and Nature Conservation, which arranges environmental discovery courses for 9- to 13-year-olds. Joseph Cornell's *Sharing Nature With Children* (Exley, 1979) is a treasure trove of ideas for nature games and exercises.

SHARING NATURE WITH CHILDREN – WHO BENEFITS?

You

Taking an interested child can make your country walks even more enjoyable, and may well get you out into the fresh air more often.

Other people

Children are quite naturally fascinated by and concerned about the natural world. As one six-year-old girl said, watching a film about the rainforests, 'I don't want the trees to be felled because I get a feeling here in my heart.'

The environment

What happens to the environment ultimately depends upon our children. Teaching them about nature and helping them to appreciate its complexities and mysteries will help to safeguard the natural environment for many years to come.

LEARNING –
A LIFELONG PROCESS

THE FACTS

Education in Britain today is undergoing major change. Many, with a variety of political convictions, would use the word 'crisis'. At present the aim seems to be to produce workers for a technologically sophisticated, internationally competitive, highly skilled economy. Yet this approach to education as a form of job-training is, for a growing number of pupils, simply not working. Both unemployment and truancy are at record levels, while classroom unrest reflects the boredom felt by many young people. Only 57 per cent of school-leavers will find a proper job, while 21 per cent of 15- and 16-year-olds are missing from school on any given day, a third of them for no obvious reason.

Green-thinkers suggest that we must widen the concept of learning, concentrating on quality rather than quantity, since the problems arising within schools are simply a reflection of problems within society. Learning is a lifelong process, they say, and should provide each of us with the tools and skills we need to fulfil our individual potential.

Many teachers agree that the concept of learning should be widened and, despite lack of funding, several exciting new educational projects have been developed. Resource centres have been set up all over the country, and teachers have a wider range of materials to draw on than ever before. At the same time, and also despite financial constraints, educational opportunities have widened for adults too. Whatever happens to our education system, the attention it is currently receiving can only be a good thing.

WHAT NEEDS TO CHANGE

Education needs to take account of individual needs, covering a wide range of intellectual, creative and manual skills. It should use the skills and experience of the community. In this way the boundaries between school and non-school can be transcended, offering school facilities to anyone who can use them, and using the non-school world as an additional classroom for children.

WHAT YOU CAN DO

- Take an interest in your children's education and talk to them about important issues, both local and global.
- Point them in the direction of interesting books, television programmes and local events.
- Establish a relationship with their teachers so that you are all working together.
- If you have an interest or skill that you would like to share, let the local school know; many schools appreciate being able to ask local people to give talks or organise projects.
- Think about what *you* would like to learn. Your Local Education Authority (LEA) runs evening classes, as do universities and the Workers' Educational Association. Many LEAs now run evening classes on environmental issues.

Books of interest to 'green educationalists' include Richard North's *Schools of Tomorrow* (Green Books, 1987) and the excellent sourcebooks *Earthrights* (Kogan Page, 1987) and *Greenprints* (Kogan Page, 1989). The bi-monthly magazines *Green Teacher* and *Libertarian Education* will keep you up to date with many new ideas and issues.

LEARNING FOR LIFE – WHO BENEFITS?

You

The traditional idea of education ending at 16 is very limiting, especially to those who find school uninspiring. A broader vision of education will help you to look for and learn from the teachers you need throughout your life, and encourage you to pass on your skills to others.

Other people

Children, particularly the less academic ones, will certainly benefit from a more flexible approach to education. Most teachers will appreciate your involvement in your children's education, and those to whom you pass on your skills or knowledge will benefit too.

The environment

Having a wider range of creative and practical skills will help us all to look after the environment, while a clearer picture of what learning is all about will prevent much senseless environmental destruction.

HOLISTIC HEALTH

THE FACTS

Despite a health budget which doubles every 10 years and ever more sophisticated technology, Britons have not become noticeably healthier in recent years. Indeed, indicators like infant mortality rates are now beginning to rise after many years of decline. More and more people are suffering from 'mystery illnesses', and one in three of us feels 'run down', 'headachey' or 'blocked up'. Nobody believes that this is the way things should be. So why aren't we well? Many people believe it is because we only think of health in terms of 'getting bodies to work properly', ignoring the mental, emotional and environmental aspects. There is a tendency to look for specific causes for ill-health – a clear-cut virus or bug that can be blamed and eradicated with a pill or a potion.

A green perspective is vital, both for new and helpful diagnoses of human illness and in finding appropriate remedies. Most of us live in an environment so polluted and stressful that it is hardly surprising that our systems can't cope. Many of the things we are given to 'make us better' are polluting our bodies even more. Many health experts now believe that 'doctor-induced' illness accounts for a very high proportion of ill-health, a phenomenon not helped by patients' routine demands for medication. Some modern remedies are extremely questionable ecologically. There is increasing concern about treatments such as radiation and chemical tranquillisers. And 3.5 million medical experiments are carried out on live animals each year, tests which produce very little useful information.

WHAT NEEDS TO CHANGE

We need to see good health in terms of a relaxed mind, a creative spirit and a healthy environment, not just as a body which does what we want. We also need health care professionals who acknowledge these connections. And we need an environment which is not filled with health-threatening pollutants. Drugs and surgery should be used only when less intrusive methods will not work.

WHAT YOU CAN DO

- Tell yourself that you have a right to be healthy, that feeling good is *not* just an occasional fluke.
- When you feel under the weather, don't just think about your symptoms. Allow yourself to feel what is really going on, and see if you can hear what your body is trying to tell you.
- When you visit your doctor, ask all the questions you need to, and always ask whether the remedy being prescribed is the mildest one that might work effectively.
- Read the rest of this 'health' section, which will give you more specific suggestions.

Read Patrick Pietroni's *Holistic Living* (Dent, 1986), which includes a very readable introduction to the idea of seeing things as a whole. For a well-reasoned account of how the medical profession can make you ill, read Ivan Illich's classic *Limits to Medicine* (Penguin, 1977). Write to the British Union for the Abolition of Vivisection for details of their 'Health with Humanity' campaign.

HOLISTIC HEALTH – WHO BENEFITS?

You

Health is far more than a mere absence of illness. You cannot understand what true well-being is until body, mind, spirit and environment are all taken into account.

Other people

Few things assist healing more than being among other fulfilled and vibrant people. Well-being breeds well-being. More specifically, you will have more energy for family, friends, work and leisure.

The environment

The life-supporting systems of the planet we inhabit are connected at every level. When we understand that good health depends to a large extent on living in an unpolluted environment, we will all start moving towards a clean and cruelty-free planet.

NATURAL HEALING

THE FACTS

Natural healing is a philosophy and an approach rather than simply a particular set of techniques. It is a belief that the human body is superbly equipped to resist disease and heal injuries, an approach which counsels against drastic action until simpler, cheaper and safer alternatives have been tried. Natural techniques include rest or massage for a headache rather than aspirin, trying a warm pad on a backache instead of relying on valium, going to an osteopath or chiropractor with your back pain rather than expecting surgery.

At least one in 10 of us (and some surveys suggest as many as one-third) have consulted an alternative medical practitioner in the last year. This does not include the millions who are treating themselves with remedies they have read about or been told about by friends. With few exceptions, natural healing techniques are not available on the National Health Service (NHS), which means that you have to be highly motivated to find out about them. Yet it has been estimated that it costs as much to treat an average 'natural healing' patient for a year as to keep someone in an NHS hospital for three days.

For the most part the mainstream medical establishment has attempted to denigrate natural healing techniques (perhaps most notably in a 1986 British Medical Association report). This is hardly surprising, given the vested interests involved; the latest threat is to ban the sale of many natural medicines. Yet the tide is turning very quickly, and a recent survey of 200 GPs showed that 59 per cent of them referred patients to alternative practitioners, and 42 per cent wanted further training in alternative medicine.

WHAT NEEDS TO CHANGE

Some 'natural therapies' may deserve to be wholly or partly discredited, but they must be judged on their results, and not according to the necessarily blinkered criteria of the medical establishment. There needs to be far more exchange of training and experience within both 'mainstream' and 'alternative' medicine, and greater recognition of the skills of alternative practitioners. Where appropriate, natural healing techniques should be available within the NHS, and the full range of natural remedies ought to be freely available to experienced practitioners.

WHAT YOU CAN DO

- When you don't feel well, think of the simplest and safest thing you could do to help you feel better; for instance, a hot bath, a massage from a friend, some herbal tea (e.g. peppermint for stimulation and chamomile for relaxation), a short rest on your bed or a 20-minute walk in the fresh air.
- Allow yourself to cry if you need to.
- Find out whether there are any alternative practitioners in your area. You might be interested in homoeopathy, herbalism, massage or osteopathy, for example. Talk to other people who have been to these practitioners.
- If you don't feel better soon, consult a doctor you trust.

Natural healing can seem a very complex subject, and you may well become engrossed in studying herbalism, massage, or one of the many other branches of alternative medicine. Two excellent books to start you on your exploration are Mark Bricklin's *The Practical Encyclopedia of Natural Healing* (Rodale, 1983) and Stephen Fulder's *The Handbook of Complementary Medicine* (Oxford, 1988).

NATURAL HEALING – WHO BENEFITS?

You

Safe and simple remedies – when appropriate – will always be kinder to your body than the relative battering rams of drugs and surgery. Though not generally available on the NHS, they are usually cheaper than mainstream medicines.

Other people

When your friends see that safe and simple treatments are benefiting you, it will not be long before they are trying them too. Techniques like massage and co-counselling build links between people and help them to see that we can all be healers.

The environment

Natural remedies generally use renewable resources, and safer remedies cause less pollution, both to us and to the environment around the factories where they are produced. They do not involve cruel and unnecessary animal testing.

HELPING YOUR BODY TO HELP ITSELF

THE FACTS

The human body is built to be resilient, to bounce back quickly when it is thrown off balance. Yet stress and pollution have reached the point where we are constantly being bombarded with quantities and combinations of things which our bodies cannot cope with, from lead in the air and aluminium in drinking water to noise and overcrowding. The Western diseases of cancer and coronary thrombosis have reached epidemic proportions. Yet, to a large extent, they are preventable.

An increasing number of doctors are beginning to acknowledge the links between problems with our immune systems and a wide range of diseases, from arthritis and asthma to cancer and AIDS. Though our bodies are continually dealing very effectively with small indiscretions, we are increasingly tipping the balance into areas where our natural defences can no longer cope. The resulting symptoms – headaches, sneezing, sweating and so on – can be suppressed with drugs, but the more these symptoms are ignored, the louder our bodies shout for help. If we continue to ignore the pleas, they will eventually give up the unequal battle.

A small but rapidly growing number of people have started to do what they can to help their immune systems to keep them healthy. This means not putting excessive stress on the system, while building up the body's natural defences.

WHAT NEEDS TO CHANGE

We need to remind ourselves that nature is the best – if not ultimately the only – healer. For effective healing we must deal with the causes of ill-health, and not just the symptoms. Given a healthy lifestyle and a healthy environment, our bodies know what is necessary for healing to take place. We have to take responsibility for looking after our own bodies, instead of expecting the experts to do it all for us.

WHAT YOU CAN DO

- Avoid environmental pollutants as far as possible, especially the most obvious ones like exhaust fumes. For instance, if you have a choice, walk through a park rather than along a main road.
- Avoid toxic chemicals whenever possible (see pages 28 and 72).
- Eat as healthily as you can: more fresh food and fewer additives (see pages 70 to 87).
- Stop or cut down on smoking (see page 162).
- Watch your alcohol and caffeine consumption (see pages 88 and 90).
- Rest when you need to.
- Take some regular exercise (see page 166).

Read up about the immune system and how it looks after your body: Michael Weiner's *Maximum Immunity* (Gateway, 1986) is a good introduction, and includes many practical suggestions. If you are concerned about the rising incidence of cancer (one in three of us will suffer from cancer at some time in our life), two excellent and very positive books are Shirley Harrison's *New Approaches to Cancer* (Century, 1987) and Ian Gawler's *You Can Conquer Cancer* (Thorsons, 1987).

HELPING YOUR BODY TO HELP ITSELF – WHO BENEFITS?

You

Who, given the choice, wouldn't want to be healthy and in charge of their own health? Accurate information and practical suggestions about self-help health care are the keys.

Other people

Helping yourself to good health encourages those around you to do the same. Much of this exploration can usefully be done in self-help groups.

The environment

When people realise that pollution and stress are directly responsible for their ill-health, it is much easier to gain support for pollution control campaigns in every area of environmental concern.

DRUGS AND MEDICINES

THE FACTS

Last year in Britain we consumed more than £1,500 million worth of drugs. The level of prescriptions, at 300 million a year, is running at nearly twice that of the early 1960s. Though many drugs cost less than the prescription charge to produce, their price to us and the National Health Service is currently rising at between two and three times the rate of inflation, with the profits of pharmaceutical companies at record levels.

Over 17,000 different drug products are licensed for use in Britain, even though the World Health Organisation has shown that no more than 200 are needed for all but very obscure applications. The amount spent on drug-related research is thought to be about £400 million a year; advertising and promotion, often in the guise of 'independent' (though sponsored) research, another £180 million. It has been estimated that because of over-prescription, wrong diagnosis, the excessive prescribing of brand names rather than cheaper 'generic' drugs, and drugs which are simply not used, around half of the money currently spent on drugs is wasted.

A leading doctor has suggested that two-fifths of all patients suffer unwanted side-effects from the use of drugs, and that one in 10 hospital cases is the result of medicinal drug misuse. Despite increasing awareness of the dangers of over-dependence on tranquillisers, doctors continue to write more than 25 million prescriptions for them every year. Because medicine containers only need to describe the active ingredients of their contents, many suspect colourings, sweeteners and preservatives go unmentioned, often undoing the benefits of the medicine itself.

WHAT NEEDS TO CHANGE

The most important thing that needs to change is the belief in 'a pill for every ill'. Drugs work by changing the way our bodies function, and they usually deal only with symptoms, not with underlying causes. We need much better information about what different drugs do, what the side-effects are, and what alternatives exist. Drug companies have to be far more accountable and provide accurate information about their products. Doctors must recognise the right of the patient to ask questions, and to receive a full and honest reply.

WHAT YOU CAN DO

- Sort out your medicine cabinet and take all the drugs you no longer need back to your chemist for disposal.
- The next time you are offered a prescription by the doctor, ask what the drug is designed to do, what its side-effects are, and whether he or she can suggest a non-drug alternative.
- If your doctor seems too busy, ask your local pharmacist instead; if your medicine is not prescription-only, they will also be able to tell you if it would be cheaper to buy it without the prescription.

There is plenty of gripping reading matter on the subject. For a general overview, start with Jenny Bryan's *Drugs for All* (Penguin, 1986). Then for the full gory details go on to Vernon Coleman's *The Health Scandal* (Sidgwick & Jackson, 1988) and Joe Collier's *The Health Conspiracy* (Century, 1989). Going to the doctor's will never be the same again.

UNDERSTANDING DRUGS AND MEDICINES – WHO BENEFITS?

You

More informed choice about what you put in your body means that remedies will be more appropriate to the causes of your illness. As a result you are likely to be healthier and more in control of your life. You may also save money.

Other people

The people close to you will understand your treatments better, and you theirs. Knowledge will replace worry and helplessness. And understanding drugs and their effects will help you safeguard your children's health.

The environment

Using fewer drugs frees resources for other uses and reduces the pollution created by pharmaceutical factories. It also reduces the cruel and senseless suffering of animals used to test every new drug that comes on to the market.

ALLERGIC REACTIONS

THE FACTS

The word 'allergy', which means literally 'a different response', was coined only in 1906. It means an out-of-the-ordinary reaction by the body's tissues to certain physical substances. Mainstream medicine tends to play down the incidence of allergic reaction, though some doctors working in the field now think that it could be affecting the lives of as many as 80 per cent of us.

Nowadays we are surrounded by substances (from industrial chemicals to food additives) in such abundance and variety that it is hardly surprising that our bodies react against them, exhibiting a range of symptoms such as rashes, shivering, migraines and sneezing. Reactions to different substances vary enormously from one sufferer to another, though allergens known to affect a relatively large number of people include excessive milk or sugar, agricultural sprays, additives and preservatives, industrial effluents, chemicals used in the home and at work, medicines, exhaust fumes, chlorine in tap water, and cigarette smoke. Coping with all these additional allergens often makes it more difficult for sufferers to handle plant pollen during the summer months; hence the growing problem of hay fever. Though it is often possible to isolate a particular allergen, it is the cocktail of allergens which brings many people's natural defences to the point where they can no longer cope.

The situation is gradually changing, but the conventional medical solution is still too often to treat the symptoms without exploring the causes. Some environmental health experts – 'clinical ecologists' – can now be consulted through the National Health Service, but this more holistic approach is not easily available.

WHAT NEEDS TO CHANGE

We need to acknowledge that allergic reactions to our poisoned environment are widespread and all-pervasive. Only then can we see clearly that it is the environment that we need to change, rather than simply suppressing the symptoms. Allergy sufferers certainly need to be helped to identify the particular substances to which they are allergic, so that they can be avoided, but above all we need to ensure that our food, air and water are as free as possible from harmful chemicals.

WHAT YOU CAN DO

- If you suffer from obscure symptoms which seem to surface without any warning (headaches, rashes and fatigue are the commonest), see if there is any common factor behind them. For instance, is it something you ate or something about the room you were in?
- Fairly common allergens include the lactose in milk, the gluten in some grains, caffeine, and nicotine. You could try a few days without each and see how you feel.

Where possible allergy is concerned – and it's always worth checking persistent symptoms to see if they are allergic reactions – there is a great deal you can do to help yourself. For illuminating case histories, read Barbara Paterson's *The Allergy Connection* (Thorsons, 1985) and, for practical advice and information, Ellen Rothera's *Perhaps It's An Allergy* (Foulsham, 1988). Two important self-help and campaigning groups in this field are Action Against Allergy and the National Society for Research into Allergy.

UNDERSTANDING ALLERGIC REACTIONS – WHO BENEFITS?

You

There is nothing more frustrating than persistent symptoms which do not respond to conventional treatment. Identifying an allergen, and being able to keep well simply by avoiding it, will give immense relief. Recognising the scale of environmentally induced illness also helps you to keep your domestic environment as pollution-free as possible.

Other people

Children are especially prone to allergic reactions, and the relief of identifying what they are allergic to saves parental worry and the child's suffering.

The environment

Other living things are also allergic to environmental pollutants, and are often much more sensitive than human beings: a good example is the poisoning of trees by acid rain. A less polluted environment would reduce strain on all organisms, bringing health and well-being to more than just ourselves.

DIETS AND SUPPLEMENTS

THE FACTS

The aim of good nutrition is to provide your body with just the right amount of each of the things it needs to keep everything in balance, and a healthy diet includes each of these essential nutrients in the correct quantity and proportion. What 'dieting' means to most people, however, is losing weight. About 50 per cent of women and 10 per cent of men have at some time in their lives tried to lose weight by undergoing one of the many hundreds of diets now available. Most diets of this kind simply don't work, because they are treating the symptoms rather than the causes of excess weight. They can often leave you both demoralised and even plumper than you were before. Obesity is usually the result of mild (or worse) addiction to food. This addiction is in turn the outcome of years of unhealthy eating habits and unbalanced attitudes towards food, and is more usefully seen in this light (see page 160).

Many slimming diets include one or more courses of dietary supplements, the sort of vitamin and mineral tablets which appear in the advertisements in health magazines. More than £60 million worth of dietary supplements are now consumed in Britain every year. This abundance of dietary supplements is a very recent phenomenon, making it hard to choose those that will genuinely help you and your family to be healthier. Nearly all nutritionists agree that if your everyday diet is healthy and balanced, you should have little need for supplements. As one author puts it, 'the supplement addict who ignores the importance of a wholefood diet is like the jogger who spends more time selecting a pair of running shoes than actually running'.

WHAT NEEDS TO CHANGE

We need to shift away from diets which look only at the symptoms of unhealthy eating. Instead, we need a more integrated approach which includes accurate information and genuine support for those who want to change ingrained eating habits. To be successful, any weight control diet must look at attitudes towards food as well as the benefits of healthy nutrition. Dietary supplements should be subject to the same controls as any other medicines (see page 154).

WHAT YOU CAN DO

- Fresh food is the key to good nutrition: buy as wide a range of fresh fruit and vegetables as possible.
- Try to avoid processed foods.
- Try to get some outdoor exercise every day.
- Only take dietary supplements if you really feel you need them for a specific reason. In such a case take the advice of a qualified naturopath rather than believing the claims in advertisements.

Geoffrey Cannon and Hetty Einzig's *Dieting Makes You Fat* (Century, 1983) takes the lid off the theory and practice of dieting, while Leonard Mervyn's *Complete Guide to Vitamins and Minerals* (Thorsons, 1986) will tell you all you need to know about supplements. Never take dietary supplements for a long period of time just as a matter of course: two to three weeks should be sufficient for most ailments. Buy supplements made from natural ingredients rather than chemical imitations, and always follow the dosage on the bottle. The Institute for Optimum Nutrition and the Green Farm Nutrition Centre both offer dietary counselling and advice.

UNDERSTANDING DIETS AND SUPPLEMENTS – WHO BENEFITS?

You

Your health will certainly benefit from a balanced diet, and healthy food is nearly always cheaper than expensive courses of dietary supplements.

Other people

If you are preparing food for others, they too will benefit from a shift to a more balanced diet. This is especially important for children, since food habits are learnt at a very early age.

The environment

Eating a healthier diet, especially of fresh fruits and vegetables, uses a fraction of the energy and resources that go into processed food. As with drugs and medicines, dietary supplements usually involve extensive packaging and advertising, leading to the waste of yet more valuable resources.

CHECKING ADDICTIONS

THE FACTS

Addiction means being so dependent on a particular stimulant that you feel that you can't live without it. Some substances (like morphine and heroin, amphetamines and barbiturates, nicotine and alcohol) change the chemical balance of your body, causing painful withdrawal symptoms if regular doses are not available. Many doctors make the distinction between true addiction of this sort, and habituation, where a strictly physical dependence is replaced by a psychological – though often no less powerful – dependence.

Misleadingly, the word 'addiction' is frequently used only in relation to illegal drugs (including cannabis which, unlike nicotine and alcohol, is not physically addictive). There are thought to be about 50,000 people in Britain addicted to such drugs, compared with around three million regular users of tranquillisers, two million heavy smokers and three million people who find it difficult to control their alcohol intake. Many health experts would define excessive and uncontrolled intake of refined sugar and salt as drug-like dependencies, which would take in most of the 32 per cent of the population who are overweight.

Though those who study addiction vary in their analysis of its causes, it is generally agreed to be largely the result of unmet emotional needs. These emotional needs are then drowned in addictive activities which bring temporary escape and relief. Until 10 years ago it was thought that certain medicinal drugs could in many cases 'cure' addiction. Recently, however, it has become increasingly obvious that the only real solution lies in providing addicts with mental and emotional support, for ultimately they themselves must want things to change.

WHAT NEEDS TO CHANGE

Addiction needs to be recognised for the widespread phenomenon it is, without artificial distinctions being made between 'acceptable' and 'non-acceptable' addictions. Addicts do not need judgement and blame; they need help to channel their energy and creativity in a positive way. Official and commercial endorsement of all known addictive substances ought to be monitored and discouraged: health must come before profits.

WHAT YOU CAN DO

- Consider the things you think you can't live without: see how many are genuinely life-enhancing needs and how many might be addictions.
- The next time you feel you are not in control of your eating, smoking, drinking, television watching or whatever, sit down and make yourself comfortable. Then ask yourself what it is that you really want. Awareness of your actions and exploring the alternatives open to you are the keys to working with addiction.
- If you are offered the more highly addictive drugs, whether illegal or legal, simply say no.

Janet Pleshette's *Overcoming Addictions* (Thorsons, 1989) is a good introduction to the subject, with a wide-ranging resource list covering specific addictions from caffeine and sugar to heroin and tranquillisers. Susie Orbach's *Fat is a Feminist Issue I* and *II* (Hamlyn, 1978 and 1984) are still the best books on the subject of compulsive eating. (See page 162 for more about smoking and page 88 for more about alcohol.)

CHECKING ADDICTIONS – WHO BENEFITS?

You

Most ex-addicts would agree that it is vitally important to be in control of your own life, and not to be ruled by your addictions. Not only do you gain self-respect: you will almost certainly feel healthier and more attractive, and you will save money.

Other people

A great deal of anti-social behaviour is addiction-related, from domestic violence to drunken driving. Your enhanced self-esteem will be reflected by the confidence placed in you by friends and family.

The environment

Vast resources go into supplying addictive behaviour. Large areas of Central and South America are devoted to coca planta-tions, and even greater acreages to producing cane sugar. The land, and local people, would benefit enormously if consumption of these dangerous crops were cut back, thus freeing the land for food crops.

AVOIDING THE BIG SMOKE

THE FACTS

Fourteen million smokers in Britain get through nearly a quarter of a billion cigarettes every day. The tax revenue from tobacco products – about two-thirds of what the smoker pays – yields around £7 billion annually to the government. In 1987, £1.2 million was spent on anti-smoking campaigns.

There is irrefutable evidence that smoking kills, which explains why the proportion of smokers in the population has fallen from 47 per cent in 1972 to 33 per cent now. Smoking – even light smoking or living with a smoker – can cause lung cancer, duodenal ulcers, bronchitis and emphysema. More than 100,000 deaths each year are caused directly by smoking, and the annual cost to the National Health Service of smoking-related illnesses is about £500 million.

While the overall percentage of smokers is falling, many parents and teachers are worried about increasing smoking among teenagers, especially girls, who are 50 per cent more likely than boys to smoke regularly. By the time they are in their late teens, about a third are regular smokers. With home markets declining, cigarette companies are increasingly targeting their products at the Third World, 'finding new people to give cancer to' as one author puts it.

As a crop, tobacco is very demanding of nutrients, and rapidly degrades the land on which it is grown. In countries like Bangladesh it also takes land away from vital food crops such as rice. About half of the tobacco smoked in the Common Market is grown in Europe – mostly in Greece, Spain and Portugal – and about 60 per cent of the income of European Community tobacco farmers comes from agricultural subsidies which are currently running at about £1 billion each year.

WHAT NEEDS TO CHANGE

The government must change its double standards in relation to this addictive drug and ban tobacco advertising and sponsorship. They should also insist on a blunt 'Smoking Kills People' warning on cigarette packets. All public buildings ought to be made non-smoking, both for health and safety's sake. Addiction counselling should be easily available through the National Health Service, with adequate resources for publicity and back-up services.

WHAT YOU CAN DO

- If you have never smoked, don't start, and make it clear that your friends should not smoke in your home, car or office: get a 'no smoking' sign from your health centre and put it somewhere prominent.
- If you smoke only occasionally, stop altogether.
- If you are a regular smoker, ask at your local health centre for information about 'smokestop' classes, or write to ASH for details about the steps you can take to cut down.
- For those who have tried and failed to give up, you could at least change to a low-tar brand.

The chapter on cigarettes in Richard North's *The Real Cost* (Chatto and Windus, 1986) puts the international industry in perspective. A Health Education Authority leaflet called *A Smoker's Guide to Giving Up* should be available at your local health centre, while Judy Perlmutter's *Kick It!* (Thorsons, 1987) is one of the better self-help books currently available.

AVOIDING THE BIG SMOKE – WHO BENEFITS?

You

Steering clear of the pollution of tobacco smoking is one of the single most important ways in which you can protect your health. It has been estimated that a non-smoker will live an average of seven years longer than a smoker.

Other people

Research has increasingly found that non-smokers who inhale a smoker's 'sidestream' smoke are at risk as well as the smoker. Partners and children of smokers have a dramatically increased risk of cancer and chest infection.

The environment

Growing less tobacco would free land for food crops or allow it to return to wilderness. It would keep nutrients in the soil, reducing the need for dangerous pesticides and unnecessary fertilisers, and would save the 2.5 million acres (1 million hectares) of Third World forest timber currently used each year for curing tobacco.

WATCHING STRESS LEVELS

THE FACTS

Stress is inherent in life. We cannot stand up or walk without tensing muscles which oppose and balance each other. Eating puts a stress on our digestive system and exercise stretches our heart muscles and blood vessels. Yet there is a difference between healthy energy-enhancing stress, and chronic debilitating stress. In our world of noise, pollution, glare, competition, fear and rapid movement, unhealthy stress has become one of the most common reasons for ill-health. It has long been acknowledged that ailments like indigestion, gastric ulcers, migraines, high blood pressure and obesity are stress-related – they are some-times called 'the stress diseases'. But in recent years stress has also been implicated in a wide range of serious conditions, including cancer, hardening of the arteries, rheumatism and chronic infections. Fifty-two per cent of Britons now die of circulatory disease compared with 6 per cent of Japanese; 26 per cent from cancer compared with 0.5 per cent in Burma. Thirty years ago the British figures for these diseases were 34 per cent and 16 per cent.

Traumatic events (like the loss of a partner or being made redundant) have been shown to have a direct effect on health, though over-emphasising such events can mask the constant worries and frustrations which take a daily toll on our health. Many techniques for stress management have been developed in the last 20 years. Most of them involve letting go of the symptoms of stress – holding the breath, rigidity in the body, the suppres-sion of feelings – as quickly as possible, so that everyday 'healthy' stress does not become chronic stress. Training in stress manage-ment usually involves a critical re-examination of lifestyle, together with the learning of relaxation techniques such as meditation, breathing and yoga.

WHAT NEEDS TO CHANGE

A great deal of emphasis is placed on stress management, but much more needs to be done about removing the sources of stress: noise, air pollution, glare and constant rapid movement. Restful environments ought to be created in urban settings: quiet, open, pollution-free places where people can relax. Stress management techniques should be readily available to anybody who needs them.

WHAT YOU CAN DO

- Awareness of your breathing pattern and learning how to relax are the keys to stress management. Try the following exercise for a few days.
- Lie down on your back, put one hand on your tummy and the other hand on your chest.
- Let your breath go, then breathe in very gently, feeling your tummy rise slightly.
- Now breathe out, taking a little longer than you took to breathe in, thus helping your metabolism to slow down.
- Pause for a couple of seconds, then start the cycle again with an in-breath.
- Do this breathing cycle for two or three minutes several times each day, getting gradually slower each time, and see if it makes any difference to how tense you feel.

A very good introduction to stress and its management is John Mason's *Guide to Stress Management* (Celestial Arts, 1985), while Beric Wright's *Executive Ease and Dis-Ease* (Gower, 1987) covers this increasingly common problem. Several organisations offer training in relaxation, with classes, tapes and books.

WATCHING STRESS LEVELS – WHO BENEFITS?

You

Watching stress levels helps you to deal with potential problems quickly and appropriately, and to become more aware of the harmful stresses you need to avoid. Learning to relax gives your body a chance to heal itself thoroughly.

Other people

Other people will find it much easier to spend time with you if you are relaxed and able to cope with the inevitable strains and stresses of today's world.

The environment

It is not only the human beings on this planet who are suffering from excessive stress: the indirect victims include wildlife killed on our roads and the trees killed by exhaust fumes. Taking life more calmly makes us much more aware of our surroundings. And setting aside peaceful oases in our towns and cities provides vital refuges both for us and for all living things.

EXERCISE

THE FACTS

Britons today are in general a pretty unfit lot, preferring to watch athletics and skiing on television than to get out for a brisk walk. In a 1986 official survey of leisure activities, only 23 per cent of the respondents said they had been for a walk of two miles or more in the previous four weeks. Just over eight million of us take part in a physically active sport once a month or more, but that still leaves 48 million who don't. Lack of exercise starts very early: a survey of 500 Glasgow secondary school children showed that two-thirds never took any vigorous exercise, and obesity and lung problems are increasingly being seen in children.

The benefits of regular exercise are well known. It helps to prevent coronary heart disease, heart failure, rheumatism, arthritis, backache and asthma. It tones muscles, improves your figure, makes you more alert, helps you to relax and sleep better, improves the digestion, and increases suppleness, strength and stamina. Yet we still don't do it.

This is largely because exercise has become divorced from life in general, rather than being an integral part of it. Ours is the age of the exercise machine, the gymnasium and the sports centre, while fewer and fewer of us do jobs which involve a healthy amount of strength and stamina. Another problem is that exercise tends to be associated with sport, which is fine for those for whom the idea of sport holds no terrors, but it can easily put off the many people with unhappy memories of strict gym teachers, forced effort and unattainable perfection. Exercise for pleasure has nevertheless increased in recent years, with attendance at keep-fit classes rising fourfold and leisure swimming doubling in the last decade.

WHAT NEEDS TO CHANGE

We need to understand the importance of regular exercise in keeping healthy and move away from our over-dependence on labour-saving technologies. People need access to a range of exercise resources, from footpaths and safe places to swim, to fully equipped sports centres. Community-based health classes and projects which include exercise as an important element should be encouraged.

WHAT YOU CAN DO

- If you get out of breath quickly, your legs ache after climbing a couple of flights of stairs, you find it hard to bend down and tie your laces or get out of an armchair, you need some exercise badly.
- As long as you choose the right sort of exercise and build it up gradually, you can't hurt yourself. If you have any doubts, ask your doctor.
- To begin with, try walking more and faster. Walking briskly for 20 minutes every day will soon build up your stamina.
- Use the stairs instead of the lift, and walk up escalators.
- Remember to get some exercise regularly; you can't store up fitness for your old age.

If you want to visit a sports centre or join a local class or group, ask your local leisure and recreation centre what is available; your local health education unit will be able to help, too. The Health Education Authority (HEA) and the Sports Council produce an excellent free booklet called *Exercise: Why Bother?* The HEA also produces a comprehensive exercise resource list.

EXERCISE – WHO BENEFITS?

You

Regular exercise helps to control high blood pressure, stops your arteries furring up, and reduces the chances of a heart attack. It needn't be hard work, and as you do it more you'll almost certainly enjoy it more.

Other people

Many forms of exercise, from team sports to hill-walking, are enjoyable group activities, helping to develop mutual understanding and communication.

The environment

Some outdoor sports, particularly the ones which involve machinery, do considerable environmental damage, but increased levels of physical exercise will tend to get people out into the open more and increase their awareness of the natural world.

VIOLENCE AND NON-VIOLENCE

THE FACTS

One recent survey showed that two-thirds of television news items involve violence of one sort or another, from international wars to car accidents and domestic assaults. Another showed that by the age of 15, the average British child, watching 19 hours of television a week, had witnessed 6,500 killings and 10,400 shootings. Crimes involving violence towards other people in Britain are currently running at about 160,000 a year, or one every three minutes; three times as many as 20 years ago.

The people who suffer from the violence in our society tend to be those conventionally thought of as weaker. Ninety-four per cent of the victims of domestic violence are women. One in five girls and one in 10 boys has been sexually abused. Of the 21 million people killed worldwide in the 120 major wars since 1945 (thought of by most Britons as the start of 'peacetime'), 61 per cent have been civilians – compared with 5 per cent civilian casualties in the Second World War.

It is still widely assumed that violence is an innate part of human behaviour, and that men especially will inevitably resort to violence when they feel attacked. In recent years, however, many techniques of non-violent conflict resolution have been developed. These techniques include counselling programmes for men who assault their partners, conciliation techniques for industrial disputes and, on a much broader level, negotiation skills for diplomats attempting to avoid involving their countries in violent confrontations. At a time when previously icy super-power relations are thawing, more and more people are acknowledging that only genuine communication and co-operation will give us any hope of a stable future.

WHAT NEEDS TO CHANGE

We need to stop thinking of violence as inevitable, and we should refuse to support violence at every level from playground bullying to state militarism. We need to protect children from gratuitous violence, and allow them to express strong feelings in non-violent ways. A nationwide network of counselling and support groups is needed for the survivors of violence, and for those who want to understand their violent behaviour.

WHAT CAN YOU DO

- When you next feel violent, find a way of expressing the feeling without hurting anything: beat a pillow if you are in the house or shout if you can find a private place to do it.
- Find somebody to talk to about your feelings.
- If you feel angry towards a child, try to be firm and gentle rather than aggressive.
- If you are suffering from someone else's violence, go to your local Citizens Advice Bureau, or ring Childline or your nearest Rape Crisis Centre.

Violence on a global scale is graphically illustrated in *The Gaia Peace Atlas* (Pan, 1988). The best practical guide for women suffering from violent behaviour is *Sexual Violence* (Women's Press, 1984), while Sarah Nelson's *Incest* (Stramullion, 1987) fulfils the same function for incest survivors. For positive suggestions about working with children on these issues, read *A Manual on Nonviolence and Children* (New Society, 1984). Daniel Sonkin and Michael Durphy's *Learning to Live Without Violence* (Volcano, 1982) is a helpful workbook for men who want to understand their own violence.

LEARNING ABOUT VIOLENCE AND NON-VIOLENCE – WHO BENEFITS?

You

Constant fear of violence prevents you from enjoying your surroundings and relationships, and has been implicated in a wide variety of health problems.

Other people

Co-operation and understanding are always better keys to relationships than confrontation and judgement.

The environment

The 15 million bomb craters and vast areas of defoliated forest in Vietnam, the desertification of Ethiopia, and radiation from bomb tests in the Pacific, are all the direct results of a single-minded faith in violent means. On a more domestic scale, many environmentalists believe that the violence we do to our surroundings, from shooting rare birds to the careless dumping of toxic waste, mirrors the violence endemic in our society. Living in harmony with each other will help us to live in harmony with nature.

PEACE WITHIN YOURSELF

THE FACTS

Regular meditation and contemplation are an integral part of many cultures' spiritual practice. Deep breathing and profound relaxation have been practised in eastern Asia for thousands of years. The 1960s saw a resurgence of interest in such methods in the West, mostly in the form of yoga and meditation, and a recent survey suggested that more than one million people in Britain regularly practise one of these techniques.

Most people find it hard to concentrate on one thing for any length of time – ours has been called a 'blip culture' – though it has been shown by many researchers that living more peacefully brings clear benefits in terms of health and personal fulfilment. Techniques such as yoga and meditation are demonstrably effective in the treatment of asthma, cancer, AIDS, chronic pain, high blood pressure and anxiety. One study of 2,000 people who meditate regularly showed that they needed medical treatment only half as often as a non-meditating control group. Another group using biofeedback as a calming technique showed a 20 per cent decrease in cardiac risk over a four-year period, while immune response has been observed to increase during periods of relaxation as short as 20 minutes.

Living peacefully goes far beyond specific techniques, however, and many people who regularly stop and take time to turn inwards find that it is possible to be both calm and active (or even calm and busy). 'The peace that the world cannot give' is how many Christians put it, though it is possible to give the peace that we find within ourselves back to the world.

WHAT NEEDS TO CHANGE

We need to take more time to 'find' and understand ourselves, rather than constantly resorting to outside stimulation. We have to rediscover our deep connections with each other and with the forces that shape the world we inhabit, allowing ourselves to dream and imagine, to experience the joy of knowing that we belong and have a purpose in being here. The spiritual dimension must be acknowledged alongside the material.

WHAT YOU CAN DO

- If you already relax or meditate on a regular basis, make sure that it continues to take priority over other activities.
- If you have never tried any form of meditation, try taking 20 minutes for yourself each day, and sit comfortably on a chair with your eyes closed.
- Breathe easily and slowly, and each time your attention begins to wander, bring it gently back to your breathing – some people use a mantra (a calming syllable or word) repeated over and over again to help focus their attention. See if this helps you to remain calmer for the rest of the day.
- Find out about yoga classes in your area.

Think about joining or forming a local meditation group, or even going to a weekend 'retreat'. Open Centres is a network of meditation centres and retreat houses, and produces a helpful directory. Two useful introductions to meditation are Erica Smith and Nicholas Wilks' *Meditation* (Optima, 1988) and Ian Gawler's *Peace of Mind* (Prism, 1989). Peaceful living in its global context is the subject of Jonathan Schell's *The Fate of the Earth* (Picador, 1982) and Fran Peavey's *Heart Politics* (New Society, 1986).

FINDING PEACE WITHIN YOURSELF – WHO BENEFITS?

You

People who regularly take time for contemplation, meditation, yoga, or silent prayer find that it helps them to remain centred and calm, even at times of great upheaval. Many find that it also helps them to make sense of and see the vital connections between different aspects of their lives.

Other people

Once you are relatively calm and centred, you will almost certainly find that your relationships with other people become easier, more fulfilling, and deeper.

The environment

Calm, relaxed people tend to inflict less damage on their surroundings. They don't usually drive fast cars, shoot birds or go in for other environmentally destructive activities. Taking time to sense the importance of things that money can't buy helps to put everything back in perspective.

NATURAL FIBRES

THE FACTS

More and more people who buy clothes are asking for pure natural fibres – wool, cotton and silk – rather than synthetics. Ninety-eight per cent of women in one recent survey mentioned natural fibres when asked what they looked for when buying clothes, and 72 per cent (80 per cent of the under-25s) bought only pure cotton underwear. Until recently it looked as though artificial fibres were set to take over, having risen from a 13 per cent market share in 1951 to 40 per cent in 1971. But cotton is still the most popular fibre; it has held a 52 per cent share for several years, with wool maintaining around 7 per cent.

Though some artificial fibres, like rayon, are made from wood cellulose, most are oil byproducts. Natural fibres, on the other hand, are renewable resources. They are also generally kinder to our skin, non-allergenic, more adaptable and longer-wearing than artificial fibres. Yet even the growing of natural fibres has some impact on the environment. Most of Britain's 25 million sheep graze moorland areas which cannot sustain other forms of agriculture, but they also prevent rich natural ecosystems from developing. All the cotton we use is grown chemically, often causing widespread soil degradation; and what is considered to be the best-quality silk involves the asphyxiation of the silkworm moth in its cocoon. Most natural fibres are also routinely treated with moth-repelling insecticides before being made into clothes.

Although demand is now declining following intensive campaigning, the cruel trade in animal furs still continues at the rate of around 20 million furs a year, including over half a million wild animals caught in vicious steel-jawed leg traps.

WHAT NEEDS TO CHANGE

Manufacturers and retailers should provide all-natural-fibre alternatives wherever possible. Support should be given to projects which produce natural fibres in a more ecological way, and to small-scale clothes manufacturers using natural fibres. All animal fur products ought to indicate where the fur has come from and how the animal was killed.

WHAT YOU CAN DO

- Buy natural fibre clothes whenever possible, especially clothes which go next to your skin.
- Write for a catalogue to some of the small mail order companies specialising in natural fibre clothes, like Natural Fibres, Cotton On, Denny Andrews and Nightingales.
- Never buy clothes and accessories which incorporate animal furs, even 'farmed' ones. As well as the suffering endured by farmed fur-bearing animals, they can cause severe damage to wildlife if they escape.

If you find it difficult to obtain all-natural-fibre clothes in the shops you normally buy from, ask why they do not have what you want. Read the chapter on cotton jeans in Richard North's book *The Real Cost* (Chatto and Windus, 1986) to see how even an apparently natural and innocuous product can have such far-reaching social and environmental implications. Write to Lynx, Britain's active anti-fur-trade campaigning organisation, for information about their activities, or visit their shop in London's Covent Garden.

NATURAL FIBRES – WHO BENEFITS?

You

If you are one of the estimated 10 per cent of people who react to some synthetic fibres, your health will benefit from wearing natural fibres. They are generally more comfortable and let your skin breathe more easily.

Other people

Children quite often find that certain fabrics – usually synthetics – irritate their skin, a good reason for dressing yours in pure cotton and wool whenever possible.

The environment

Despite their impact on the environment, the growing of natural fibres is far more energy-efficient and creates less pollution than making chemical-based ones. Unlike petroleum, which is the basis of most synthetic fabrics, all natural fibres are renewable resources.

NEW, NEARLY-NEW AND SECONDHAND

THE FACTS

In Britain we spend about 6 per cent of our incomes on clothes, about £15 billion every year, which is nearly as much as we spend on alcohol and half as much as we spend on food. People enjoy shopping for clothes; one recent survey found that 70 per cent of us actively enjoy it (more than any other sort of shopping). Yet, for whatever reason, most of our clothes are ones we don't wear, or wear less than once a year. There are around £30 billion worth of clothes sitting in British drawers and wardrobes simply gathering dust and being nibbled by moths. It seems rather a waste.

At the other end of their lives, we throw out nearly a million tonnes of clothing a year, together with another million tonnes of carpets, rugs, bedding and other household textiles. An increasing proportion finds its way to charity shops and jumble sales. But a lot more old clothing could be recycled, especially if we were to shift some of the things we keep but never wear, as happened during the appeal for warm clothing after the Armenian earthquake in December 1988. There is still a thriving trade in second-hand clothing, where charities like OXFAM have considerable expertise in the sorting and recycling of clothes. Clean sorted rags are in demand too, with cotton for filling and insulation fetching between £100 and £150 a tonne.

If we were all to pass on the clothes we don't wear, mend and darn more, and buy more of our clothes second-hand, we would have more to spend on the new clothes that we really need and use far less energy and fewer resources in the process.

WHAT NEEDS TO CHANGE

After a period in the 1970s when 'conspicuous thrift' dressing was in vogue, we have gone back to demanding that everything we wear must be both stylish and brand-new. There needs to be a shift back towards the social acceptance of recycled and durable clothing, and not only for the poor and the elderly. Experimental projects for recycling and exchanging second-hand clothing should be encouraged and made attractive. Basic sewing skills should be part of every child's education.

WHAT YOU CAN DO

- Check your wardrobe (and your children's) regularly, and give away anything you no longer need. Pass clothes on to friends who might like them, check the local paper for jumble sales they could go to (the organisers will often collect), or take them to the charity shop.
- If you don't already have them, learn some basic mending skills like sewing and darning: mend torn and worn clothes rather than letting them rot at the back of dark cupboards.
- Find out where your local second-hand clothes shops are and look in from time to time. Watch out for jumble and car boot sales.

A useful book full of ideas for recycled clothes is Carolyn Chapman's *Style on a Shoestring* (Hutchinson, 1984), while Debbi Thompson's *Glad Rags* (Wildwood House, 1984) is an entertaining guide to London's second-hand clothes shops.

RECYCLING CLOTHES – WHO BENEFITS?

You

Your purse will certainly feel the difference if you choose to buy a judicious combination of new and second-hand clothes. The chances are that you will feel more comfortable too, as well as enjoying looking for interesting and unusual clothes.

Other people

If you have children, especially young ones, you can save pounds by getting involved in clothes exchanges with other parents. Recycling clothes creates employment, as well as raising funds for a wide range of good causes. Reducing competition in world clothing markets is also likely to improve the bargaining position of Third World workers.

The environment

As with other sorts of recycling, buying or swapping second-hand clothes reduces the demand for the raw materials and energy used to make new ones.

BUYING CLOTHES DIRECT

THE FACTS

The fashion industry has some of the biggest retail mark-ups you'll find in any business. Often, less than a quarter of the shop price goes to the makers of the clothes and the producers of the fabrics that go into them. In this country clothing workers (90 per cent of whom are women) receive some of the lowest wages. In a recent survey of the Yorkshire rag trade, a third of the women earned less than £2 an hour, while piecework rates for Asian women clothing workers in the West Midlands can leave them with as little as 60p an hour.

Forty per cent of imported clothes – about 18 per cent of all the clothes we buy – come from the Third World, where low wages and bad working conditions are common. One Korean woman, working in a large garment factory, writes of the constant plague of tuberculosis, athlete's foot and stomach diseases, yellow faces from inadequate lighting, and constant harassment from supervisors. Another 40 per cent of imports come from southern Europe, especially Italy and Portugal, where 13-and 14-year-old children regularly work long days in clothing factories.

One way of ensuring that clothing workers are properly compensated for their work is to buy directly from them whenever possible. Several organisations and companies now buy clothes directly from workers' co-operatives in the Third World, and the number of specialist mail order clothes manufacturers in Britain is growing too. They still only account for less than 1 per cent of all the clothes we buy, but between them they offer an exciting range, while properly rewarding the manufacturers.

WHAT NEEDS TO CHANGE

The pay and conditions of workers in the clothing industry need to be properly monitored, and minimum wage and safety levels enforced. Small co-operative clothing businesses and experimental projects in direct trading should be supported, and clothing retailers ought to bring pressure to bear on suppliers to ensure proper working conditions for their employees.

WHAT YOU CAN DO

- If you don't already, you could consider making some of your own clothes.
- Look at the labels in the clothes you buy and see where they were made.
- For special occasion clothing, look out for adverts for clothes mail order companies in newspapers and magazines, especially those who are making clothes rather than just marketing other people's, and send for their catalogues.
- Write to OXFAM and Traidcraft for their catalogues of clothes from the Third World; these often include descriptions of the co-operative projects you are supporting by buying their products.

A good way of finding out which small clothing firms are making the sort of clothes you want is to ask the regional craft agencies for their literature.

BUYING CLOTHES DIRECT – WHO BENEFITS?

You

By buying clothes directly from the manufacturers you will almost certainly be able to buy more interesting and individual clothes, as well as saving money in some cases. Buying directly often means that you can specify exactly what you want.

Other people

Those you will be helping include the workers in small businesses in this country (often in inner-city and economically depressed rural areas), and those in poorer countries who will receive a proper reward for a change.

The environment

Buying directly saves much of the energy and resources that go into transporting clothes around the country; some small businesses also tend to be more environmentally aware than large factories.

CLOTHES CARE

THE FACTS

The average Briton at the end of the 1980s owns nearly three times as many clothes as a typical 1950s consumer. Not only do we have many more garments to look after; we also wash and clean them more often. Only 33 per cent of homes had a washing machine in 1957. Today the figure is 82 per cent, and 36 per cent of British households also have a tumble dryer. The evidence suggests that many of today's clothes suffer more damage during washing, cleaning and drying than they do while being worn. In addition, automatic washing machines and tumble dryers use a prodigious amount of water and energy.

When it comes to detergents, the manufacturers' competing claims that their products can wash clothes cleaner than anyone else's have led them to add a variety of extra ingredients. Many of these do very little to get your clothes cleaner and some of them do considerable environmental damage. The phosphates in most detergents can cause ecological imbalance in freshwater lakes, while the enzymes in 'biological' detergents cause dermatitis and other allergic reactions in sensitive people. The bleaches, artificial perfumes and optical brighteners used in many detergents are largely unnecessary, do not degrade easily in the environment, and can be harmful to wildlife. Because they remove oil from the skin, all detergents are potential skin irritants, and detergent residues can upset the digestive systems of babies and young children.

Most natural fibres are routinely treated with long-lasting pesticides, usually one of the organochlorides, before being made up into clothing. Though this helps to keep moths at bay, such pesticides are implicated in a range of health problems.

WHAT NEEDS TO CHANGE

Washing machines and tumble dryers should state clearly on their labels how much energy and water they require in normal use, so that buyers have sufficient infomation to help them choose. 'Environment-friendly' washing powders and liquids which do not contain phosphates, bleaches, enzymes and brighteners should be widely available at reasonable prices (see also page 28).

WHAT YOU CAN DO

- Pass on any clothes you don't need (see page 174).
- Keep drawers, wardrobes and airing cupboards clean to discourage clothes moths; keep your pets' bedding clean too.
- Think carefully about how often you need to wash your clothes; it's too easy to use the washing machine just because it's there.
- Don't wash clothes in water which is hotter than necessary.
- Use 'environment friendly' detergents like Ecover and Clear Spring (see page 28).
- Use the least amount of detergent to gain the required result, but remember that clothes don't always need to be sparkling bright in order to be properly clean.
- Don't automatically put clothes in the tumble dryer if the weather is fine; fresh air is healthier and infinitely cheaper.

If you are thinking of buying a washing machine, look for one which is energy and water efficient. A 'cold fill' machine can use twice as much energy as a 'hot fill' one, but a twin tub uses only about half the water and energy of an automatic. One author has called tumble dryers 'an extremely efficient device for devouring money'. A washing line for dry days and a ceiling-mounted drying rack or clothes horse indoors is usually sufficient.

UNDERSTANDING CLOTHES CARE – WHO BENEFITS?

You

Looking after your clothes without cleaning them to destruction means that you can look your best without risking your health or damaging your favourite garments; it will also save you a considerable amount of money.

Other people

Many young children are thought to be allergic to the chemicals in detergents; using gentle and natural products will help prevent skin rashes and irritation.

The environment

Our rivers and seas will certainly benefit from a reduction in phosphates and other detergent ingredients, as will the wildlife which depends on unpolluted water.

IS YOUR JOURNEY REALLY NECESSARY?

THE FACTS

The frequency and speed with which we travel around is one of the biggest changes in Western life over the last century. The methods of transport we use have changed drastically too. In 1890, 80 per cent of the distance travelled was covered by foot or bicycle; now it is less than 3 per cent. The other 97 per cent, of which more than four-fifths is accounted for by private cars, uses large amounts of fuel, time and land, and creates serious land and air pollution as well as a great deal of noise and danger. Petrol-driven vehicles, of which Britain has nearly 23 million, are a highly inefficient and polluting way of converting non-renewable resources into useful work.

Most of us see easily and widely available transport as an essential part of everyday life. Indeed, with the closing of many local shops and services, it has become so. Yet, holidays excepted, few people actively enjoy travelling. The road industry's own calculations put the cost of urban congestion at £8 billion a year, while public transport delays account for 2.8 billion wasted and uncomfortable passenger hours each year.

For most of us, simply wanting to travel is sufficient justification for doing it; we do not ask ourselves why we travel. Yet less privileged people do not make the same assumptions about accessibility. Out-of-town superstores with massive car parks are out of bounds to the 37 per cent of households without cars, while children and old people have their freedom curtailed, not expanded, by motorways and the centralisation of schools and community centres.

WHAT NEEDS TO CHANGE

We need to be aware that travelling, particularly the 97 per cent which involves vehicles and engines, has important and far-reaching environmental consequences. It should be easy for everyone to get to the places they really need to, but we ought to investigate and clarify the costs as well as the advantages. Official transport policies should reflect all these costs.

WHAT YOU CAN DO

- Think about the implications of each journey you make, and in particular – unless you are walking or cycling for enjoyment and exercise – ask yourself whether your journey is really necessary. Every journey is a compromise between speed, comfort and cost, though costs like stress and environmental damage are often overlooked.
- Walk or cycle whenever you can.
- However you travel, leave enough time to get where you are going in as unstressful a way as possible.
- Don't automatically use the car, especially for short journeys – 41 per cent of all car journeys in urban areas are less than 3 miles (5 km).
- For longer distances, public transport is far more 'environment-friendly' than cars, so make sure that you know what services are available and use them (see page 192).

Experiment with different ways of making regular journeys, and vary the way you travel according to the weather and the season. Join the transport campaigning group, Transport 2000, in working for a sensible transport system.

CHECKING WHETHER YOUR JOURNEY IS NECESSARY – WHO BENEFITS?

You

The average British adult spends nearly 300 hours a year – 37 working days – travelling. Think of the stress and boredom you could avoid by organising your life so that you needed to travel less than at present. Then think of the money you could save.

Other people

Our present transport system makes much of our environment unsafe for living things both human and non-human. Children and old people are particularly at risk on our roads.

The environment

Decreasing travel means using fewer non-renewable resources and creating less pollution. It also means using less land for transport, thus saving landscape and wildlife: 110 sites of scientific interest will have been destroyed by road developments alone during the 1980s.

USING YOUR LEGS

THE FACTS

In 1914 the average Westerner travelled 1,640 miles (2,640 km) a year, 1,300 (2,090 km) of them on foot. Today the figure is something like 8,000 miles (13,000 km) a year, of which no more than 400 are travelled on foot. It is becoming increasingly common to find people who get up early to jog or work out on their exercise bike, then get in the car to drive the couple of miles to work. On the other hand, a full third of all travel time is spent walking, and more than 30 per cent of journeys are on foot. Walking accounts for 80 per cent of journeys of less than a mile, yet official transport statistics ignore these short journeys as being unimportant when formulating an overall transport policy.

Because priority has consistently been given to wheeled vehicles on our public highways, they have become extremely dangerous places for pedestrians. A walker is four times more likely to be killed per mile travelled than a car traveller, and more than 60,000 walkers are killed or seriously injured on British roads every year. Children are the main victims.

Two hundred people a year die from falls on badly designed and poorly maintained paving. A recent survey showed a long list of problems besetting pedestrians: 46 per cent were concerned about pavement maintenance, 42 per cent with the growing issue of dog dirt, and 37 per cent with the bad behaviour of motorists where pedestrians are concerned.

An increasing number of schemes for pedestrian precincts and the 'calming' of local traffic are already in place. York and Wolverhampton city centres and the Covent Garden area of London show what can be done, given imagination and a willingness to experiment.

WHAT NEEDS TO CHANGE

Local plans and the vetting of planning applications should always take into account the needs of pedestrians. Local shops and public buildings such as libraries, schools and health centres need to be easily accessible on foot, with special provision for disabled people. Pedestrian facilities should be integrated with public transport to reduce the need for car travel. Walking has to be made safe, convenient and enjoyable for everyone.

WHAT YOU CAN DO

- Always think before you set out on a local journey, and walk if you can.
- Leave enough time to walk to the shops or the health centre, and keep boots and an umbrella by the front door so you're not put off by a spot of rain.
- Try to get out in the open air at least once a day, and include some good walking in your holiday plans (see page 134).
- When you drive, remember that walkers have as much right to cross the road as you do to drive on it.
- Keep to speed limits in built-up areas, and always watch out for children: don't just assume that they will keep out of your way.
- Never park on the pavement: it's neither fair nor legal, and can be dangerous.
- If you come across a dangerous piece of paving on your walks, notify the transport department of your local council.

If you feel strongly about the rights of walkers, send a stamped addressed envelope to the Pedestrians Association, which has produced some excellent and helpful literature. Transport 2000 is running an important Feet First campaign, aimed at local councils, and Friends of the Earth have a very good leaflet called *Traffic Calming in Residential Areas*.

USING YOUR LEGS – WHO BENEFITS?

You

Regular walking is a very important open-air form of exercise, toning up your muscles and improving posture and circulation. It can also create a sense of balance and general well-being.

Other people

Given safe footpaths, your children will benefit from walking to and from school; while reduced car use – especially in residential areas and town centres – improves air quality, cuts noise and congestion, and dramatically lowers accident rates.

The environment

Walking allows people to enjoy and appreciate the beauty of nature, and thus to value it more.

HOW ABOUT THE BIKE?

THE FACTS

In 1953 Britons cycled nearly 13 million miles (21 million km), and 12 per cent of the total distance travelled (using all forms of transport) was covered by bike. By 1973 the figure had fallen to 2.2 million miles (3.5 million km), less than 1 per cent of total distance travelled. But in recent years cycling has started to make something of a comeback. Between 1974 and 1984, cycle mileage rose by 56 per cent (compared with an overall traffic growth of 31 per cent). In London, cycle use tripled in the same period. In 1983 and 1984 more new bicycles were sold in Britain than new cars.

Bicycles remain largely functional machines: 29 per cent of bike trips are to and from work, 26 per cent for shopping, and 11 per cent for getting to and from school. A quarter of cycle trips are recreational. As car ownership has grown, however, our roads have become increasingly dangerous for cyclists. Cyclists are now four times more likely to be hurt per mile travelled than they were 30 years ago, and 17 times more vulnerable on the road than car drivers. The reasons for this are mostly to do with lack of care by drivers and lack of special provision for cyclists, though 23 local authorities have recently completed cycleway projects. Oxford City Council now provides 'official bicycles' for its staff.

Cycling is indisputably a green activity. A cyclist can travel 1,600 miles (2,575 km) on the amount of energy contained in 1 gallon (4.5 litres) of petrol, using up very little space and causing no pollution. Purpose-built urban cycleway costs around £100,000 a mile, compared with £23 million to £30 million a mile for urban motorway. Cycling also offers healthy exercise, takes up a fraction of the parking space needed by cars, and currently provides employment for 11,000 people in Britain.

WHAT NEEDS TO CHANGE

Central and local government should research and fund systems of cycleways, and facilities for cyclists should be included in plans for all new residential and commercial developments. Cycle parking facilities should be provided at schools, shops and offices. Car drivers should be specifically trained in cycle-friendly driving.

WHAT YOU CAN DO

- If you have a bike, keep it in good condition, and use it.
- Make sure that you can get it out easily when you need it.
- Learn how to ride safely: *The Highway Code* gives basic information, while the Royal Society for the Prevention of Accidents can provide more detailed information.
- If you don't have a bike, think seriously about getting one and learning to ride it: a good second-hand bike costs less than £100.
- If you drive a car, treat cyclists with respect: they have just as much right to the road as you do but do not have the same physical protection. Look out particularly for young cyclists who may not have as much experience and road sense as adults.

All cyclists should have a copy of the cyclists' bible, *Richard's Bicycle Book* (Pan, 1986). Look out too for *New Cyclist* magazine, full of useful ideas and information. The Cyclists' Touring Club puts recreational cyclists in touch with each other, while Friends of the Earth's Cities for People Campaign covers cycling and the environment.

GETTING ON YOUR BIKE – WHO BENEFITS?

You

In a recent London survey, 66 per cent of regular cyclists said they cycled because it was cheap, 53 per cent said it provided much-needed exercise, and 43 per cent said it got them where they wanted to go faster than any other form of transport.

Other people

Cycling is a very sociable occupation, allowing parents, children and groups of friends to relax together even if they are of different ages and levels of fitness.

The environment

The bicycle is one of the most environment-friendly machines ever invented. Cycling pollutes neither land nor the atmosphere, is kind to wildlife, and reduces the amount of land that needs to be covered in concrete and asphalt.

DRIVING ECOLOGICALLY

THE FACTS

The problems on our roads may already seem bad enough, but planners believe that we shall soon be a nation of two-car families, the country's vehicle population rising to 40 million (nearly twice the present number). Yet motorways like the M25 are already carrying twice their design capacity, the average speed of traffic in London has dropped to 11 miles (18 km) an hour, one person is killed or seriously hurt every seven minutes on our roads, and cars are known to be a major cause of atmospheric pollution.

At the end of the 1980s, car manufacturers are still enjoying booming sales, but while cars give enormous personal freedom to those with access to them, the public is rapidly becoming disenchanted with their side-effects. One recent survey showed that 69 per cent of those questioned were very concerned about pedestrian safety, 54 per cent were bothered by traffic noise and 33 per cent thought that cars should be banned from town centres. Yet, despite the environmental costs of the car, £2.4 billion a year is paid out to industry as tax relief on company cars. Though the government raises over £13 billion a year in car-related taxes, this figure pales beside the estimated £8 billion a year lost to industry through traffic congestion, the £8 billion that goes on road building and maintenance, and the £3 billion lost each year through road accidents and their consequences. In the absence of more adventurous and environmentally sound transport systems, the car may be a convenient way of getting from A to B, but a less efficient and more dangerous way would be hard to devise. The relatively non-polluting 100 miles per gallon (35 km per litre) car already exists – why can we not yet buy it?

WHAT NEEDS TO CHANGE

The car must be seen as the environmental menace it is, and be integrated into a comprehensive transport system rather than being seen as the best way of getting around. Encouragement should be given to small, fuel-efficient, non-polluting cars, with price differentials to persuade people to buy them. Manufacturers should take account of current environmental concern, and produce a truly 'green' car which uses the latest technology to boost fuel economy and reduce pollution.

WHAT YOU CAN DO

- If you have a car, resist the temptation to use it just because it's there. Walk, cycle or use public transport instead.
- Share car space whenever possible: full cars are four times as efficient as driver-only cars.
- Think about getting rid of the car and hiring one when you really need it.
- Drive carefully: being behind the wheel doesn't give you the right to be thoughtless and selfish. Leave enough time to drive with minimum stress and rush.
- Keep to speed limits in built-up areas, and on the open road keep between 55 and 60 miles (88.5 and 96.5 km) per hour; this gives 20 to 25 per cent better fuel efficiency than driving at 70 to 80 miles (110 to 128 km) per hour. Slower driving is safer driving: the chances of being killed or seriously hurt rise dramatically with increased speed.

When buying a new car, choose as small a car as possible, with good lead-free fuel economy and the latest anti-pollution technology – Audi Volkswagen are currently the frontrunners in the field. Read Stephen Plowden's *Taming Traffic* (Deutsch, 1980) for some radical ideas on what to do about the car.

DRIVING ECOLOGICALLY – WHO BENEFITS?

You
Driving less often and more safely reduces your chances of being killed or hurt on the roads, and lessens the risk of cancer from air pollution. It reduces the stress in your life, and will almost certainly save money too.

Other people
Less traffic on the roads means safer streets for everyone, and makes our towns and countryside quieter and less polluted. Driving carefully particularly benefits pedestrians and cyclists.

The environment
Driving considerately reduces the carnage of wildlife on the roads, decreases the pollution which is killing trees and warming the atmosphere, and keeps the amount of land needed for new road building to a minimum.

LEAD-FREE PETROL

THE FACTS

Lead was first added to petrol in the early 1920s as a lubricant, to extend the life of a car's exhaust valves. It was known then that lead was poisonous, but it has become increasingly clear that it is an extremely *dangerous* poison, affecting people's brains and central nervous systems. Babies and young children are particularly at risk. Though lead emissions have been falling for nearly 15 years, motor vehicles are still spewing out over 2,500 tonnes of lead a year, concentrated near main roads and in town centres.

In 1985, in Sweden, every petrol station with more than one pump was obliged to supply unleaded fuel and a 4 per cent price differential was introduced: within a year 67 per cent of those drivers whose cars would take unleaded petrol were doing so. Britain has been slower to make the change, but three years after its introduction and with the introduction of a 10p price difference, 50 per cent of petrol stations now supply unleaded fuel and 25 per cent of drivers are using it. There is still a great deal of ignorance and misinformation about the practicalities of making the change. Contrary to many people's fears, 'unleaded cars' will also run on leaded (though leaded will 'poison' a catalytic converter), and unleaded petrol will not damage an engine designed to take it, nor adversely affect performance and fuel consumption.

Despite a slow start, the move to unleaded petrol in Britain is now gathering momentum. Forty per cent of British cars will now take unleaded, and about 60 petrol stations a week are converting pumps to take unleaded fuel. Both the Minister of Transport and the Queen have converted to unleaded, along with the entire Hertz hire fleet.

WHAT NEEDS TO CHANGE

By the end of 1990, all new cars sold in Britain will use unleaded petrol; what is now needed is education and widespread availability. The price differential between leaded and unleaded petrol should be enough for drivers to perceive a real cash incentive for using unleaded, and government departments and local authorities should set an example by converting to unleaded at the earliest opportunity.

WHAT YOU CAN DO

- First find out whether your car will take unleaded petrol: both CLEAR and the Society of Motor Manufacturers and Traders have detailed lists, and your local dealer should be able to tell you.
- If it will, start using unleaded immediately.
- If it needs converting – and several manufacturers will do the conversion free – then have it converted as soon as possible.
- If you are thinking of buying a new car, make sure that it will run on unleaded petrol, and try to make sure that any company or hire cars you use will take unleaded.
- Wherever possible, don't let children play near busy roads.

If you have any influence over company decisions about car purchase, make it known that you favour cars which take unleaded petrol; three-quarters of Britain's cars are company cars, and such policies can make a big difference. Write to CLEAR, the Campaign for Lead-Free Air, and find out about the dangers of lead in the atmosphere from vehicle exhausts and other sources.

LEAD-FREE PETROL – WHO BENEFITS?

You

A wholesale shift to unleaded fuel would cut your risk of brain damage, senility and cancer. Blood lead levels in one US survey showed a 37 per cent drop after a 50 per cent reduction of lead in petrol. It is also cheaper to use unleaded petrol.

Other people

Young children, especially those who play on city streets and transfer lead-containing dust into their mouths on sticky fingers, are particularly at risk. They will certainly benefit from reductions in atmospheric lead.

The environment

Atmospheric lead is also poisonous to wildlife, especially to birds and fish. Nearly 40 per cent of the world's lead production is used as fuel additives, creating further pollution problems as well as being extremely wasteful.

CATALYTIC CONVERTERS

THE FACTS

Cars may be useful for getting us where we want to go, but it would be hard to devise a more efficient way of polluting the atmosphere. As well as 2,500 tonnes of tetraethyl lead a year, British cars give out vast amounts of carbon dioxide (one of the major 'greenhouse gases'); nitrogen oxides which combine with hydrocarbons to produce poisonous smog; 100,000 tonnes of unburned cancer-forming hydrocarbons; 4.5 million tonnes of poisonous carbon monoxide; and a quantity of black smoke which now exceeds that given off by coal fires.

All this is well known, and the technology exists – in the form of catalytic converters which filter out most pollutants – to reduce the pollution dramatically. In the USA the compulsory fitting of catalytic converters has cut carbon monoxide emission by 90 per cent, and hydrocarbons and nitrogen oxides by 75 per cent. Half the world's catalytic converters, 15 million a year, are made in Britain by Johnson Matthey. They are nearly all exported. Apart from the luxury Toyota Celica and three Volkswagen models, you can't yet buy a car in Britain fitted with one. Under current government guidelines it will be the end of 1992 before the fitting of catalytic converters to new cars becomes commonplace, by which time pollution from vehicle exhausts will have risen by another 5 per cent.

As with the conversion to unleaded petrol, there are misconceptions about the effects of catalytic converters. The facts are that the cost range is roughly £100 to £300 depending on the size of the car; they last the lifetime of the car; the performance difference is less than 2 miles (3.2 km) per hour at top speed; and there is no effect on fuel economy. They cannot be used with leaded petrol, so both pollution-reducing measures must be introduced together.

WHAT NEEDS TO CHANGE

Since the technology exists (British cars for export already incorporate catalytic converters), the date for their compulsory fitting should be brought forward. Individual manufacturers should be encouraged to offer catalytic converters to customers asking for them. Tax concessions for purchasers of 'clean cars' should be introduced, as in Germany and Sweden.

WHAT YOU CAN DO

- The only long-term solution to exhaust pollution is to burn less fuel and to burn it more efficiently, so always check that your journey is necessary before you set out.
- Write to Johnson Matthey for a free copy of *Cutting Car Pollution: The Role of Catalytic Converters*, so that you are clear about their benefits.
- If you plan to buy a new car, check which models can be bought with catalytic converters: you can point out to your dealer that in Europe companies like Volkswagen, Fiat, Volvo, Nissan, and even Rover fit them at no cost.

Make sure you understand the pollution created by cars: Michael Allaby's *Conservation at Home* (Unwin Hyman, 1988) has a well-illustrated section on the subject. At work, especially at a time when companies and organisations are trying to improve their 'environment-friendly' image, press for a change to cars fitted with catalytic converters.

CATALYTIC CONVERTERS – WHO BENEFITS?

You

Using catalytic converters will dramatically reduce the levels of health-threatening atmospheric pollutants, and is the only short-term way of making our roads safe to walk beside. Motorists are particularly at risk, breathing in these poisons through their vehicles' ventilation systems.

Other people

Whenever you drive, you are adding to the already dangerously high levels of pollutants in the air: a recent survey in the London Borough of Southwark showed carbon monoxide at an all-time high, more than twice the recommended safety level. Cyclists and pedestrians, in particular, will thank you for making the change.

The environment

Nitrogen oxides, which in dry conditions combine with hydrocarbons to form a poisonous smog, are probably the most important factor in the death of millions of trees. Carbon monoxide and lead are also harmful to many animals and plants.

HELPING PUBLIC TRANSPORT TO SERVE YOU

THE FACTS

Although the number of journeys travelled by car has more than tripled in the last 30 years, most forms of public transport still carry as many passengers as they did in 1960. Rural areas have suffered from public expenditure cutbacks, with 5,000 miles (8,000 km) of railway and 2,300 stations being closed in the mid-1960s, and local bus services being cut by 29 per cent in three decades. In urban Britain, on the other hand, public transport is gaining in popularity as the roads become more crowded. In the last two years, bus use in London has increased by 13 per cent and use of the Underground by 44 per cent, while car commuting has fallen by 21 per cent.

After a dip during the 1970s, rail travel is back up to its 1961 level, and an average of six stations a year are being opened or reopened. Bus travel has stabilised at about two-thirds of its 1961 level. In 1961 a quarter of all travel was by bus: today it is less than a tenth. Sixteen per cent of us regularly use public transport to get to work or school each day, and women and children use it nearly twice as frequently as men.

Public transport is considerably more energy-efficient than using your own car. While a car with one occupant can carry that person between 4 and 6 miles (6.5 to 9.5 km) on 0.2 gallons (1 litre) of fuel, a bus carrying 40 passengers uses 0.2 gallons (1 litre) for 32 miles (50 km) of individual travel. And a train carrying 300 passengers achieves 35 miles (56 km) for 0.2 gallons (1 litre) per person. Public transport is generally quieter, cleaner, faster and uses much less land area. It is also much safer: your chances of being killed or seriously hurt while travelling by public transport are 13 times less than when going by car or motorbike.

WHAT NEEDS TO CHANGE

We need to stop thinking of public transport as the poor cousin of the private car, and see it instead as vital to this country's mobility, especially for the 37 per cent of households that have no car. Investment should be made in integrated transport systems which use land, resources and capital to the best advantage, and provide a comfortable and efficient service at a fair price.

WHAT YOU CAN DO

- If a journey is too far or too difficult to walk or cycle, always think about using public transport.
- Make sure you have local timetables handy (perhaps pinned by the front door). Keep the numbers of your local bus and railway stations by the phone for easy reference.
- Find out whether you are eligible for any railcard or bus pass schemes.
- Watch out for public transport bargains, like cheap fares for pensioners or a special coach trip to do your Christmas shopping.

If you travel quite a lot, national timetables are a good investment: you can buy the British Rail one at main stations and the National Express coach one directly from them. The most important transport pressure group is Transport 2000, which produces a range of useful literature. The Railway Development Society campaigns for better rail services, and the Community Transport Association is a national network of community-based public transport operators – write to them for more information.

HELPING PUBLIC TRANSPORT TO SERVE YOU – WHO BENEFITS?

You

As the inhabitants of countries like Holland and Switzerland know, an efficient integrated public transport system is comfortable, fast, convenient, and relatively cheap and stress-free.

Other people

A renewed emphasis on public transport helps the many people – such as the elderly, children, mothers, and those with disabilities – who have become increasingly isolated as our society has become more and more car-based.

The environment

A shift to public transport provision helps the environment in a host of ways. It uses less land, fewer raw materials and less energy, destroys less wildlife and fewer natural habitats, and creates less noise and pollution. It also helps to save our towns and countryside from ever larger road schemes and ever more traffic.

STOPPING TO THINK ABOUT WORK AND MONEY

THE FACTS

Money and work seem so central to the way we see the world that we hardly ever stop to think about what they really are, or to remember that the concepts were invented no more than a few thousand years ago. Until then we lived quite happily without either. In our culture, work is the time we spend doing things for other people, and money is the reward; but there are cultures where there is no distinction between living and working, or between the fulfilment of basic needs and the gaining of material reward.

The 1980s in Britain have frequently been characterised as the 'me decade', when corporate and personal gain have triumphed over community responsibility and ecological concern. In many areas this is undoubtedly true; yet opinion polls consistently suggest that Britons have not mislaid their morality. A 1979 Gallup poll found that 34 per cent wanted tax cuts and 34 per cent wanted better services; by 1987 the figures were 11 per cent for tax cuts and 66 per cent for better services. Sixty-seven per cent oppose water privatisation and 56 per cent the selling of the electricity industry, largely on health and environmental grounds. President Bush's inaugural speech included an exhortation to espouse values other than the material, and many church leaders and politicians are making similar noises.

We live at a time when the future of conventional work and conventional money are increasingly being questioned. A recent survey of work satisfaction showed that freedom, respect and challenge headed the list; money was way down the field. Twenty-seven per cent of us now think that the money markets will suffer an irreversible crash within the next five years. It would seem prudent to be making contingency plans.

WHAT NEEDS TO CHANGE

We need to do some fundamental thinking about the nature of work and money, based on the concepts of quality of life, people's real needs and ecological sustainability. Research into different ways of organising work and resources should receive high priority, and practical projects be encouraged.

WHAT YOU CAN DO

- Take some time to think what work and money mean to you. Which of the things you do give you real satisfaction? Are they the things you are paid to do? And what do you consider to be the truly valuable things in life? Can money buy them?

- To set you thinking about a wide range of possibilities, try reading James Robertson's *The Sane Alternative* (Robertson, 1983): one of his tenets is that our current money system is fundamentally corrupt. See what you think.

As far as work is concerned, two important and very positive books are Charles Handy's *The Future of Work* (Blackwell, 1985) and John Osmond's *Work in the Future* (Thorsons, 1986). If you are unemployed and thinking about these issues, Guy Dauncey and Jane Mountain's *The New Unemployment Handbook* (NEC, 1987) is a mine of stimulating ideas. For those who would like some sound economic theory with their visionary ideas, there is Paul Ekins' *The Living Economy* (RKP, 1986).

STOPPING TO THINK ABOUT WORK AND MONEY – WHO BENEFITS?

You

If work and money rule your life, it can help a great deal to get some perspective on what they are and what they represent. It may well help you to see ways of changing your circumstances in order to gain more control.

Other people

It sometimes seems that all relationships between people have a price tag. Thinking about what gives you real satisfaction and what has true value can help you to appreciate certain aspects of relationships which can never be given a cash price.

The environment

The same is true of nature. Is the value of a walk in the forest really the amount you are willing to pay at the turnstile? And how much is the last giant panda worth?

CREDIT AND DEBT – WHO PAYS?

THE FACTS

In May 1988 the total amount of money owed by ordinary people to shops, companies and financial institutions was over £37.9 billion – £670 for every woman, man and child in Britain. This figure excludes mortgages. Between 1982 and 1986 the amount spent on advertising by credit card companies rose from £9.3 million to £16.7 million. In 1986 the total Third World debt topped $1 trillion for the first time, though even this is nothing compared with the public debt of the USA, currently running at $2.3 trillion.

What do these figures mean? They certainly mean that there are a lot of very rich lenders making their money 'work for them'. They also mean that nearly all large organisations, whether states or corporations, operate in a permanent state of debt. As one major aerospace company put it in a full-page advertising campaign: '$695 million worth of credit: the banks of the whole world trust us!' Many observers suggest that the domestic 'credit boom' is largely due to the deregulation of financial institutions, though the beginning of the boom predated deregulation by several years. Automation of credit has also played an important part, with many transactions now taking place with a computer rather than a human being.

What is certain is that there is now a debt crisis, both nationally and internationally. It is estimated that about 40 per cent of Third World debt will never be repaid. A recent survey showed that 34 per cent of 16- to 21-year-olds had debts they couldn't easily service, and 22,930 houses were repossessed in Britain in 1987 because their owners defaulted on mortgage repayments.

WHAT NEEDS TO CHANGE

We must stop blaming people – and nations – that get into debt. Lenders need to take more responsibility for ensuring that borrowers can afford the credit they seek. Creative ways should be found to provide credit for people who have little or no conventional 'security', and repayment terms should be carefully controlled and monitored.

WHAT YOU CAN DO

- Don't purchase things on credit without thinking very carefully about your overall finances.
- Always check repayment terms, and if in doubt, don't, or at least get professional advice.
- Take cheaper, shorter-term credit in preference to longer-term.
- Use credit cards and store cards as cautiously as possible.
- Think about insuring your credit against illness or redundancy, and look into the possibility of joining a credit union, which can offer its members low-cost loans.

A common reaction to debt problems is to do nothing in the hope that they will simply go away. They won't. If you think you have problems, get some good advice straight away. Your local Citizens Advice Bureau will almost certainly be able to help, and Michael Schluter and David Lee's *Credit and Debt: Sorting It Out* (Marshall Pickering, 1989) is a very practical and helpful guide. For an international perspective on the debt crisis, read Susan George's *A Fate Worse Than Debt* (Penguin, 1988).

UNDERSTANDING CREDIT AND DEBT – WHO BENEFITS?

You

There are few things as futile and time-consuming as worrying about money. It can easily make people ill – sometimes even suicidal. Being in control of your finances will save your time and your health.

Other people

Financial worries ruin relationships and make family life very difficult too. In Third World countries, debt too often creates a cycle of poverty, famine and misery.

The environment

Many people believe that the environmental crises we currently face are the result of overdrawing our 'resource account' with the global 'bank'. Personal and corporate bankruptcy are quite painful enough; the possibility of planetary bankruptcy needs to be faced if we are to succeed in averting it.

CHECKING WHO YOU'RE WORKING FOR

THE FACTS

Of the 25 million Britons in employment, nearly three-quarters work for companies in the private sector. Though most work in small businesses, six million work for companies with more than 100 employees. This isn't the whole story, however, since many small and medium-sized businesses are owned by large 'parent companies'. Thus, although the company you work for, and those you buy goods and services from, may have the same name and even some of the same directors as the family firm that has owned it for decades, the chances are that it is now owned by one of Britain's 600-odd regularly quoted public companies. Many of these are multinationals with worldwide activities: the world's largest 500 companies have aggregate sales equivalent to 23.6 per cent of the world's total annual income.

To give just one example, Booker is a UK-based food and agriculture giant, founded in 1899 and now turning over £1.26 billion a year. It has nearly 200 subsidiary companies, including 55 per cent of the cash-and-carry food outlets in Britain, Loseley Farm ice-cream, the 230 Holland and Barrett health food shops, and the company which markets Harold Pinter's screenplays. While it has a big stake in the 'healthy eating' market, it also puts large resources into genetic engineering and the centralisation of the world's seed business.

The larger the company, the more difficult it is to ensure that its activities are compatible with your own standards and beliefs. Around 28 per cent of the top 600 quoted companies are involved in military sales, 16 per cent have an active involvement in South Africa, and there isn't a large pharmaceutical or detergent company that doesn't test its products on animals.

WHAT NEEDS TO CHANGE

Companies should encourage their employees to take an interest in company policies and the structure and policies of the parent company. Companies ought to publicise their social, ethical and environmental policies alongside the financial ones, and take account of shareholders' and employees' concerns in these areas.

WHAT YOU CAN DO

- If you would like to know more about the company you work for, or plan to work for, ask for a copy of the parent company's latest annual report, which will give you a good idea of its activities and policies. If your employer doesn't have a copy, ring the head office and ask for one.
- If you don't know who owns the company you work for, or want to see the range of activities undertaken by the parent company, ask in your local library to see a recent copy of the annual *Who Owns Whom?*
- If there is anything that you want to follow up, such as a particular environmental or employment policy, try ringing the parent company's public relations department – you might be surprised at how helpful they are. You don't have to say who you are!

New Consumer runs a 'good business advice service', with researchers who can advise you on specific questions. Michael Kidron and Ronald Segal's *Book of Business, Money and Power* (Pan, 1987) is a mine of fascinating and very readable information.

CHECKING WHO YOU'RE WORKING FOR – WHO BENEFITS?

You

Knowing exactly who and what you are working for can give you a renewed understanding of and pride in your work. It also enables you to safeguard your rights, and to be clear about company policies which affect your work.

Other people

A shared knowledge and understanding of who your employers are can lead to co-operation, mutual concern and solidarity between employees.

The environment

When you know what your employer's environmental and social policies are (or aren't), you can make your voice heard to get things improved.

YOUR WORKING ENVIRONMENT

THE FACTS

If you go out to work, is the place where you earn your living conducive to your health and well-being, or do you long to get out of it as soon as you can to find somewhere more comfortable? Occupational health experts believe that more than a third of all illness in Britain is job-related; the main factors include working with toxic chemicals, avoidable accidents, stress, inadequate lighting and ventilation, and lack of proper training. In one survey of 4,000 office workers, 57 per cent reported sometimes feeling lethargic at work, while more than 40 per cent said that stuffy nose, dry throat and headaches bothered them regularly – for women the figure was over 50 per cent. Similar symptoms are so frequently reported that 'sick building syndrome' is a recognised term among doctors and architects alike.

Six hundred people die at work in Britain every year, and another 300,000 are injured seriously enough to require medical treatment. Accidents due to new and unforeseen circumstances will always be with us, yet the vast majority are caused simply because known hazards are not taken into account, and existing safety guidelines are not followed.

In fact industry guidelines are often kept deliberately lax so as not to compromise profits: this is particularly true of the standards for exposure to toxic chemicals, thought to be responsible for more than a quarter of all occupational illness. Many 'safe' exposure levels have not changed since the 1950s, and there have been a number of cases of the chemical industry ignoring known risks. Dow Chemicals maintained silence on the leukemia risks of benzene for years, and ICI on the carcinogenic effects of the common pesticide and petrol additive ethylene dibromide.

WHAT NEEDS TO CHANGE

More detailed and multidisciplinary research needs to be conducted into occupational health, and the findings acted upon. Standards for exposure to potentially dangerous materials should be set at levels where workers' health is not put at risk, as in countries like Sweden. Occupational health and safety standards should be strictly enforced and monitored.

WHAT YOU CAN DO

- Make sure that you know the health and safety guidelines relevant to your place of work, and that they are adhered to.
- Many businesses have somebody who is responsible for safety. If you need to know more your trade union will probably be able to help, and the Royal Society for the Prevention of Accidents produces a wide range of literature.
- Sick building syndrome is more prevalent in workplaces with artificial lighting and ventilation so, if you can, ensure that you work by natural light in a naturally ventilated room.
- If the windows are ones that open, keep one ajar whenever the weather allows, and ensure that the heating is not turned up too high – this is one of the main causes of dry eyes and itchy throats.
- Take great care with chemicals, using them as little as possible.

The Health and Safety Executive produces a great deal of free literature, including a report on sick building syndrome. Mike Birkin and Brian Price's *C For Chemicals* (Green Print, 1989) is a good introduction to a wide range of domestic, industrial and agricultural chemicals.

CHECKING YOUR WORKING ENVIRONMENT – WHO BENEFITS?

You

Your health will certainly benefit if the place where you work is conducive to employees' well-being. Research has shown that 'healthy' buildings also help to reduce stress and conflict, and even the prevalence of heavy smoking at work.

Other people

If you are responsible for the health and safety of other people at work, they will benefit from a safe, clean and attractive work environment.

The environment

Many environmentalists believe that the dirty practices of British industry, particularly of the chemical industry, are the most important single cause of environmental pollution, putting rivers, seas, soils and wildlife at risk.

CO-OPERATION

THE FACTS

Working co-operatively means that we are much more likely to work in a way which benefits us all, because we can share both the risks and the rewards of a project. A co-operative is an organisation in which all the participants have a financial and organisational stake, and which operates for the benefit of all its members. In modern times the idea was first tried out in the Pennine valleys of Lancashire in the 1840s – you can still visit the Pioneers Museum in Rochdale – but it wasn't until the 1970s that the workers' co-operative movement really began to flourish in Britain.

In 1976 there were 105 workers' co-operatives employing 600 people. Today there are more than 1,500, with a membership of nearly 12,000, and new co-op registrations exceed the number of co-ops closing down by 21 each month. As well as workers' co-operatives, the number of community businesses and community-managed work spaces is growing too, giving workers a real stake in the economic life of their community. Although some business analysts see co-ops as 'pretend businesses', the fact is that a co-op is nearly twice as likely to survive its first two years in business as a limited company. Business confidence in co-ops is so strong that at the time of the stock market crash of October 1987 the Industrial Co-Ownership Fund raised £500,000 of capital within weeks of a share flotation. In a 1988 survey, 59 per cent of co-ops thought they would be doing 'significantly better' in the following year; an equivalent Confederation of British Industry survey of mainstream industry found that only 41 per cent of businesses were that confident.

WHAT NEEDS TO CHANGE

Information about forming co-operatives should be more widely available. The experience of workplace democracy, participation and social ownership gained from co-operative working needs to be analysed, and the results made widely available to worker and community groups. Experimental and flexible ways of working should be encouraged and supported by central and local government.

WHAT YOU CAN DO

- Subscribe to the *Co-operation Catalogue*, a mail order catalogue through which you can buy the products of more than 20 co-ops, from jewellery and cosmetics to books and coffee.
- If you are working, examine the ways in which you are involved with real decision-making at work, and think about ways in which you might become more involved.
- If you are working in a partnership or small business where you know each other well, look into the possibility of registering yourselves as a co-operative. The Co-operative Development Agency (CDA) and the Industrial Co-Ownership Movement will be able to supply details; the CDA's booklet *How To Set Up A Co-operative Business* provides a good introduction.

One way of supporting the co-operative movement is to put business in the direction of co-ops. The Open University's Co-operatives Research Unit produces a directory of co-ops in Britain, and a *Directory of Women's Co-operatives* can be obtained from Everywoman.

CO-OPERATION – WHO BENEFITS?

You

Though working co-operatively can be hard work, you and your work can be matched to each other in the way you want. The business will belong to you and grow with you, and your work can be adapted to your individual needs.

Other people

Co-operative working provides a real opportunity for sharing both the ups and downs of working life with the people you work with. Those who cannot work a 9 to 5 day, like women with children and people with disabilities, often find that co-operative working gives them the flexibility they need.

The environment

People who care about individual needs are usually aware of environmental issues too, and many co-ops provide a range of environment-friendly goods and services.

FAIR TRADING

THE FACTS

Most of the Third World's export earnings – 81 per cent in 1986 – come from raw materials. For many countries, the export of just one or two products accounts for a very high proportion of their usable income. Coffee alone accounts for more than 60 per cent of exports from Burundi, Colombia, Ethiopia and Uganda. Cotton represents 50 per cent of Sudan's foreign sales and cocoa over 70 per cent of Ghana's. The vast bulk of this trade is controlled by multinational companies. The world's 500 largest corporations together have sales equivalent to 23.6 per cent of the total world economy. Only 22 of the world's 229 countries have a larger national income than Exxon, the world's largest corporation. In the food business, Nestlé, Unilever and General Foods between them have factories in more than 80 countries worldwide, with collective sales of more than $60 billion a year.

This buying power leaves individual farmers and workers in a weak position, especially those in the Third World. Not only do the big companies demand efficiency and profits, we the consumers demand the cheapest possible products. As a result producers suffer, especially when there are worldwide gluts and prices fall steeply, as did sugar prices between 1980 and 1982.

There is, however, another way of trading with the Third World. There are now more than 40 alternative trading organisations in 17 countries, offering Third World producers direct access to Western markets; together these organisations have a turnover of £25 million a year. Britain's largest 'fair trade' company, Traidcraft, now has more than a quarter of a million customers, and sells a wide range of products from clothes to coffee.

WHAT NEEDS TO CHANGE

We need to become aware that our buying is only part of an international trade network. We need to know how companies work with Third World suppliers, so we can take this into account when we decide which ones to buy from. Fair trade organisations should be supported, and shops and supermarkets encouraged to stock fair trade products.

WHAT YOU CAN DO

- Look out for fair trade products, especially coffee and tea, in your local wholefood shop.
- Write to Traidcraft for their catalogue: it contains a wide range of mail order items, or you may discover that you are not far from a representative who can deliver your orders.
- Other fair trade organisations producing mail order catalogues include OXFAM, AA Enterprises, Twin Trading and Equal Exchange.

Many of us are woefully ignorant about the Third World and the conditions experienced by the people who produce much of what we consume. Paul Harrison's books, *Inside the Third World* (Penguin, 1982) and *The Greening of Africa* (Paladin, 1987), are good ones to start with, while Richard North's *The Real Cost* (Chatto and Windus, 1986) is a useful product-by-product guide to the implications of our buying behaviour. *Third World Review* (Hodder and Stoughton, 1987) lets the Third World speak for itself, and a subscription to the excellent magazines *New Consumer* and *New Internationalist* will help you keep up to date.

FAIR TRADING – WHO BENEFITS?

You

Fair trading gives you more understanding of the world economy and closer contact with the producers of what you buy. Many items (like clothing) will save you money as well as providing a reasonable return for the manufacturer.

Other people

You will be helping to provide a guaranteed income for Third World workers, many of whom are coming together to form co-operatives and are rediscovering enjoyment and fulfilment in their work.

The environment

Most of the products traded through fair trade networks are ecologically sound, produced by small efficient enterprises using local resources, and thus minimising land abuse and pollution.

BEING AWARE OF ADVERTS

THE FACTS

Over £2.5 billion is spent on advertising in Britain every year, which means that between 2 and 3 per cent of the price you pay for the goods you buy – £325 a year for the average household – goes towards publicity and promotion. Is the investment worth it, or does it make things unnecessarily expensive while having little impact on the prospective purchaser? Recent research suggests that, from an early age, people learn to distrust and ignore advertising, even though they might find it entertaining. A majority of eight-year-olds in one survey knew that 'adverts were trying to sell you things', and that more than half the adverts they saw 'weren't telling the truth'. A 1986 study showed that despite heavy advertising bombardment in the run-up to Christmas, children still wanted almost exactly the same presents in December as they had wanted in September.

In green terms, advertising which gives people the information they need is entirely justified. An increasing amount of advertising, however, is unsolicited, disfigures the environment and uses resources which become instant waste. In Britain we have legislation and industry guidelines which attempt to keep advertisements 'legal, decent, honest and truthful', but we have very little to protect the consumer from unsolicited and unwanted intrusions on their privacy.

One function of advertising is to sell us things, but it also provides models for how manufacturers would like us to be. As one critic has pointed out, 'people are made to identify themselves with what they consume'. If we are to use scarce resources in a more aware way, we need to be clear about how we react to the images in the advertisements we see all around us.

WHAT NEEDS TO CHANGE

Existing legislation and codes of practice concerning advertising and direct selling need to be enforced, with clear and understandable procedures for people to use when they feel they have been misled, cheated or harassed. The law about large advertisements should be enforced to prevent hoardings and signs intruding into the environment. People should be given a choice as to whether or not they receive unsolicited advertising.

WHAT YOU CAN DO

- If you are receiving catalogues and promotional material that you don't want, write and ask the company to stop – they must do this by law.
- Tell them to take your name off all associated lists too; this particularly applies to the largest mail order companies, which between them have 40 million names and addresses – two-thirds of the British population – on their computers.
- Write to the Mailing Preference Service, and ask for a card to fill in saying that you don't want to receive direct mail.
- Tell your bank, building society and credit card companies that you don't want advertising sent with your statement.
- If you feel that you have been misled by an advertisement, tell your local trading standards department or write to the Advertising Standards Authority.

The *Which? Handbook of Consumer Law* (Hodder and Stoughton, 1986) explains the various codes of practice relating to advertising, while Judith Williamson's *Decoding Advertisements* (Marion Boyars, 1978) is a fascinating study of what adverts are really all about.

BEING AWARE OF ADVERTS – WHO BENEFITS?

You
Understanding what advertising is for and what it does helps you to choose for yourself from the various available options. Being more discriminating will almost certainly save you money and anxiety.

Other people
Talking to children about advertising helps them to distinguish between real and fantasy worlds, and to find out what they really want.

The environment
Carefully chosen and sited signs can enhance the environment instead of disfiguring it, both in our cities and in the countryside. Reducing the amount of unsolicited and unwanted advertising saves paper, trees, energy and litter.

INVESTING IN A FUTURE WE WANT

THE FACTS

Ethical investment is booming. Nearly 15 per cent of all the private money invested in the USA is subject to the investor's conditions that it shall not be used to further the business plans of companies whose policies are socially and environmentally damaging. The exact criteria of different ethical funds vary, but most do their best – given the information available to them – to avoid investment in such fields as armaments, nuclear power, gambling, alcohol, tobacco, firms with direct interests in South Africa, and those giving large political donations.

The year 1987 saw the launch of at least six new British ethical funds, in addition to the handful that were already established. A sum in the order of £3 billion is now invested with British ethical funds, at least three of which out-performed the ordinary share index in 1987, thus ensuring that those who put their money where their conscience was also benefited in more conventional terms.

In order to find out what your investment is supporting (whether it be in shares or a deposit account with a bank or building society) it is important to have accurate information about companies' activities and social and environmental policies. Connections between companies need to be understood, such as the fact that Thorn-EMI, a market leader in recorded music and owners of the HMV chain of record shops, are also one of the country's largest defence contractors. American consumer groups, aided by freedom of information laws, have led the way in exploring such connections and there are now several British organisations looking at these important topics.

WHAT NEEDS TO CHANGE

We need free access to information about companies' social and environmental activities and policies. Businesses have to realise that consumers' social and environmental concerns must be taken seriously, and that platitudes and token shifts are not enough. People with money – an important and powerful resource – need to know what their money is being used for, so that they can make informed investment choices.

WHAT YOU CAN DO

- Not many people would consider themselves to be real 'investors'. Many people, however, invest small sums in financial institutions like banks and building societies, so ask what policies your bank or building society has on ethical investment issues.
- Try to think of 'investment' in its widest sense of putting resources into a project to help it to grow, whether it be a nest egg for your retirement, a tree in the garden, money given to charity and community projects, or the raising of your own children.

If you have money for which you want a reasonable return and you would also like to put it to good use, make your first investment a copy of Sue Ward's *Socially Responsible Investment* (Directory of Social Change, 1986). Another useful book is *Choosing an Ethical Fund*, published by the Ethical Investment Research and Information Service (EIRIS). *The Ethical Consumer* and *New Consumer* are useful bi-monthly magazines with in-depth studies of companies and products, while the Ecology Building Society provides a full building society service with a green perspective.

INVESTING IN A FUTURE WE WANT – WHO BENEFITS?

You

Socially responsible investment means knowing that your resources are being used for good rather than destructive purposes. You may find that the same organisations could be useful to you if you ever need to borrow money for a green-tinted project.

Other people

Your ethical investment provides essential resources for people who are planning socially and environmentally sound projects, and starves anti-social and environmentally destructive activities of funds.

The environment

Refusing to invest in environmentally destructive activities stops money from going into such projects, without which the destruction cannot continue.

EVERY LITTLE HELPS

Nothing is guaranteed to bring about environmental disaster faster than everyone in the world believing that, whatever they do, it won't make any difference. Everything we do makes a difference. Every decision we make about how we live our lives, whether momentous or seemingly insignificant, works either towards the greening of the planet, or against it.

Realising that we have that individual responsibility can easily tip us into panic or inaction, but that too is a decision we must make as consciously as we can. In order to care for ourselves and for the Earth we must choose not to panic, and we must choose to act. Unless we are actively *for* a green future, then greyness will surely prevail.

Recognising that every little thing we do has environmental implications and repercussions can be frightening. Recently the papers have regularly carried letters saying things like: 'First it was salmonella in eggs, then hormones in bacon; then we were told that decaffeinated coffee caused cancer, and now my toast has pesticide residues in it. What can I eat for breakfast?' It seems that nothing can protect us from the damage caused by decades of human carelessness.

Yet, in a strange way, the understanding of environmental connectedness can be liberating too, because it shows that you can nearly always choose an environment-friendly course of action rather than an environment-destructive one. The worried letter-writer might now be moved to buy organic bread and genuinely free-range eggs, thus protecting herself and encouraging a shift in food production techniques.

As we approach the last decade of the twentieth century there is a growing awareness of the importance of personal commitment within the wider greening process, of changing our day-to-day habits to take the Earth into account. Members of the recently established Ark Trust, for example, are asked to show their commitment to environmental protection by taking the Ark Pledge. This is a personal commitment to use unleaded petrol instead of leaded, use environment-friendly household products, save energy in the home, recycle household rubbish, eat less meat and insist on organic produce.

This may seem a lot to commit yourself to all at once, but greening starts at an even more mundane level. Never let yourself believe that one bit of litter thrown out of the car window, or one drink bought in a can rather than a re-usable bottle, isn't going to make a difference. Occasionally we all make unecological choices (Jonathon Porritt was once spotted in the hamburger bar at Paddington Station), and every decision must be taken in the light of the prevailing circumstances. Yet, even if the circumstances justify the lapse, it still makes a difference. You don't need to feel guilty or self-judgemental – absolute purists can be real bores – but you can't duck your responsibility.

You may sometimes think that the mess we are in is somebody else's fault, and they should do something about cleaning it up. They probably think the same. In reality it is up to all of us to do something. Even though what you do to help the environment may seem small and insignificant, imagine what a difference it would make if everyone in the country did it. The change has to start somewhere, and it might as well be with you.

FINDING THE FACTS

The food poisoning scares that rocked Britain in late 1988 and early 1989 may have caused many people a good deal of uncertainty and anxiety, but for those who had taken the trouble to find out where their food comes from and how it was produced, they came as no surprise. The most surprising thing was that the problems associated with animal welfare and food hygiene had been kept under wraps for so long.

The dangers of a possible salmonella epidemic were first raised in 1967. Throughout the 1970s and '80s organisations like Animal Aid and Chickens' Lib campaigned for better animal welfare. By June 1988, when the London Food Commission published its book on food adulteration, all the details of the predicted epidemic were there for anybody to read. Why was anyone therefore surprised or confused when Edwina Currie made her famous announcement in December 1988?

Much of the information problem arises because people with vested interests keep things hushed up and juggle the statistics. The size and the scale of the effects on Britain of the Chernobyl fallout are a case in point, where those most seriously affected were only told about possible safety precautions long after the most acute danger had passed. How often have we been told that there was a leak, a spillage, an accident involving radiation, or toxic chemicals, or pesticides, yet there was no danger whatsoever to the public?

Many people are surprised to hear that those with the vested interests are not the only experts. They are often not even the best experts. Much detailed information about environmental and public health hazards comes from independent groups and organisations, active on a wide range of issues. Some of the most important information about coastal pollution comes from Greenpeace and the Marine Conservation Society. The researchers at the London Hazards Centre know as much about the dangers of wood treatments as anybody, and the Network for Alternative Technology and Technology Assessment are the experts on wind energy. The people at New Consumer can tell you as much as any city analyst about the ethics of large corporations, and nobody knows more about the environmental impact of chlorofluorocarbons than Friends of the Earth. None of this information is secret, and it is so detailed and comprehensive that civil servants often trust it more than they do government and business sources.

The spectre of 'official secrets' hangs heavily over certain areas of information, notably defence issues. Yet the problem with finding accurate and useful information is usually not so much that anyone wants to keep it hidden, as not knowing where to find it. Where green issues are concerned, you will find many useful suggestions in the 'What you can do' sections of *How To Be Green*. Other useful sourcebooks include *Green Pages* and the *Friends of the Earth Handbook*. If you are still stuck and can't think who to ask, try writing to Friends of the Earth. Even if they can't help you, they will almost certainly be able to point you in the right direction.

It is part of every politician's media training that people are always impressed by facts. Thus it should be part of every budding green's training to be able to counter irrelevant and inaccurate facts with pertinent and accurate ones. To take just one important green issue, you can usually stop a nuclear proponent dead in their tracks by knowing a handful of startling facts, such as:

- In real terms, nuclear electricity costs 60 per cent more than coal-fired electricity (Colin Sweet, *The Price of Nuclear Power*, Heinemann, 1983).
- Nuclear power stations supply 16 per cent of our electricity, but we could save 25 per cent of our energy consumption by

using simple energy conservation measures (Network for Alternative Technology and Technology Assessment, 1988).

- Britain's existing nuclear power stations were designed and built to produce a certain amount of electricity, but they have so far only managed to generate 52 per cent of that design capacity (Philip Davies, *Magnox: The Reckoning*, Friends of the Earth, 1988).

- Most of Britain's reactors are designed to withstand an earthquake with a force of 0.15g; Britain's strongest earthquake was 0.4g. Wreckage from the Lockerbie 747 crash fell within 6 miles (9.5 km) of the Chapelcross Magnox station; had the cockpit section hit the station we may well have had a disaster similar to Chernobyl (*The Observer*, January 1989).

- A recent Gallup poll shows that 83 per cent of Britons are opposed to building new nuclear power stations (Worldwatch Paper 75, 1987).

- The nuclear industry expert Rosalie Bertell has said that 'there is no known way to prevent the escape of radioactive gases from nuclear waste repositories' (*No Immediate Danger*, The Women's Press, 1985).

- No new nuclear power stations have been ordered in the USA since 1979 (Worldwatch Paper 75, 1987).

Accurate and pertinent information is true power.

MAKING THE CONNECTIONS

When ecologist Barry Commoner wrote *The Closing Circle* (one of the classics of green thinking) in 1971, he included a very simple formulation of the basic 'laws of ecology'. They are so clear and straightforward that it is well worth memorising them:

- Everything must go somewhere.
- Nature knows best.
- There's no such thing as a free lunch.
- Everything is connected with everything else.

The first law is the one to do with pollution. Whenever we throw something away it doesn't just disappear. Whether we put it in the bin, throw it out of the window or dump it in the middle of the ocean, we must live with the repercussions. Our planet is finite; a 'closed system'. Wherever we put our 'rubbish' it will continue to haunt us, just like the boxes of junk under the stairs.

The second law warns us that we thwart and destroy nature at our peril, and that nature has been evolving excellent life-support systems for millions of years longer than human beings have.

The third law makes it clear that everything we consume has an environmental and social cost. Though we might like to imagine that the luxuries of life simply appear before us without any provenance, it is a costly delusion. Up to now most people in Britain have been able to consume as they do at the expense of ignoring the continuing decline of their own health, that of their surroundings, and the chronic ill-health of the Third World. Today, however, the legacy of profligacy and pollution is hard to ignore.

Of the four laws, the last is the key and the one that helps us most to understand the others. Everything is connected to everything else. This is the philosophy and practice of holism, or holistic thinking, which says that you can never make complete sense of anything unless you take into account all its circumstances and complex interconnections.

Holistic thinking has a hard time in a culture which wants quick, simple answers. Radioactive waste? Bury it. Sore throat? Dose it with antibiotics. Traffic jam? Build a new road. Such 'solutions' may deal with superficial symptoms, but they rarely take into account any of the underlying causes of the problems of the modern world, because they refuse to see the connections between things. The burying of radioactive waste doesn't take into account the wasteful way in which we use energy. The antibiotics won't take away the stress and pollution upsetting the membranes of the throat. The plans for the new road won't question the social and environmental problems associated with the continuing rise in car ownership.

The quickfire 'who's-to-blame?' approach of the media doesn't help either. Politicians and industry representatives each have two minutes to put their arguments, which inevitably emerge as simplistic whitewashes. There is also considerable political and commercial advantage in a policy of divide and rule, where different aspects of important issues are deliberately compartmentalised in order to discourage the public from asking difficult questions. Thus, the remit of public health officials to look after drinking water quality is carefully separated from the responsibilities of the agriculture department to keep pesticides and fertilisers from polluting streams and reservoirs. Where two government departments have opposing loyalties, as with health and agriculture over issues of food hygiene, or energy and environment over nuclear energy policy, the resulting confusion is entertaining but profoundly worrying.

Even apparently quite separate issues can be seen to influence each other. The risk to children's health from lead-painted toys is intimately linked with working conditions in Third World factories. The future of a threatened Amazon tribe may depend largely on the programming policy of a British television executive and the response of a concerned audience – and will you still have the programme in mind when you go to buy a new hardwood front door from the DIY shop?

One of the apparent problems of holistic thinking is that whatever you start to look at or think about, a holistic perspective always involves going further and deeper. Whenever you consider the interconnectedness of things, any issue is always only part of a bigger issue. That's just the way the world is. Putting things in little boxes and refusing to look at connections will inevitably blinker your understanding and limit the possibilities open to you.

Making connections doesn't mean you have to think about everything all the time. In fact it can be very stimulating and liberating to discover links that you hadn't noticed before. Such links can often provide simple and elegant answers to seemingly intractable problems.

SAYING WHAT YOU THINK

Ecologists and conservationists have been warning us about most of the green issues currently in the news for at least 20 years, yet those who stood up and said what they thought were more often than not branded as spoilsports, alarmists and loonies. There is still a lot of that sort of reaction about, but things are changing very quickly. Recent market research shows that a majority of consumers are now concerned about environmental and health issues relating to what they buy. Every news programme these days includes at least a couple of green topics. Green issues have reached the whole spectrum of daily papers, women's magazines, teenage magazines, even *The Reader's Digest* and the *Radio Times*.

Yet Britons are easily embarrassed. We are not generally renowned for embracing our beliefs passionately, rushing out to tell our friends and neighbours about the exciting discoveries we have made, standing up in public and saying what we think. We don't find it easy to admit in public that we're trying something a bit different, that we'd prefer a herb tea to a coffee, that we've decided to boycott South African fruit. We're all entitled to our embarrassment, but as being green becomes increasingly acceptable, choosing to display your greenness openly becomes easier and easier. Most people are now genuinely interested to know about green issues, and the herb tea and the non-South-African fruit may well be the opportunity to introduce your friends to green ideas.

When it comes to real communication, the most important ideas in the world can only be effectively passed on by one person talking to another. Public speeches and the reading of books play an important part in the dissemination of new ideas, but one-to-one conversation and the sharing of individual experience is what makes those ideas real to people, linking the concepts directly with their everyday lives.

It is therefore up to each of us to share our new green insights. We won't get very far by ramming them down other people's throats and insisting that they listen to us, but we needn't avoid the topics that concern us simply out of a fear that they are not 'safe'. Those of us who believe that green issues are now at the top of the political and economic agenda must ensure that we don't keep our beliefs to ourselves.

GETTING THE MESSAGE ACROSS

The single biggest obstacle to things changing for the better is the people who say, 'Nothing can be done; it's always been like that and nothing will ever change it now.' As you will have seen in this book, there are many ways in which you can improve the environment on your own. But the greening of Britain must go further than that, so you will need to think of effective ways to get the green message across to those for whom inertia and passivity have become second nature. There are two important aspects to getting the message across effectively: what you say, and how you say it.

It helps if what you say is as accurate (see page 211) and as clear as possible. Whether your audience is your next-door neighbour, the readers of the local paper or the members of your women's group, you are more likely to get a positive response if you are sure of your facts and can explain your argument clearly and concisely.

How you explain things is just as important as what you say. Nobody will listen to your argument, however sound it may be, if they think you are attacking or criticising them. Remember that your point of view is just that, and that other people have their own points of view. Even if you think another person's perspective is faulty, you can still learn a lot from them, especially if they have experience of the subject in question. At one recent meeting I was being rather scathing about the indifference of farmers to the damage being done by pesticides and artificial fertilisers. When challenged by a hill-farmer who was still using chemicals but was interested in organic techniques, I realised that I had been overly critical, and asked him to tell us about his plans. The audience learned a lot more from him about the practical problems faced by farmers than they did from me.

Though you may in the process have to confront your reticence about making your views known, there are many ways of getting the green message across to a wider public. One fairly easy way is a letter to the paper. A letter to a national newspaper or magazine may stand a slim chance of being published, but a local paper will almost always publish a letter which is short, clear, relevant, factual and witty.

Another thing you can do is let it be known that you would be willing to talk to local groups about green issues. Women's Institutes, Rotaries, church groups and schools are nearly always on the lookout for people who can talk knowledgeably about topics of current interest. You don't have to be overly ambitious to begin with: you can decide how many people you feel able to cope with and what you want to talk about. If you feel shy and diffident about speaking in public but would still like to do it, you could consider learning some assertiveness skills: Redwood is a national network of assertiveness skills teachers which will be able to tell you if there are classes near you.

With the present interest in environmental topics, local radio stations are also looking for people who can speak clearly and knowledgeably about green issues. They often have to go to national 'experts', but if there is someone in the area who can tie the general topic in with some specific local examples they are usually delighted. They pay you too.

These are some of the channels for getting across information about green issues, but many people get involved in environmental concerns when something important in their local area is threatened and a campaign is launched. It may be a road scheme, or the council wanting to fell trees, or the electricity board wanting to string high-tension cables across your back yard. This is when you start writing to your councillor and your MP (see pages 219–221), getting together with other people who object, calling public meetings and putting together petitions.

Think carefully before you start campaigning. Work out how much effort you want to put into it, what you want to achieve, and how that end result might best be brought about. Don't take on more than you can realistically handle, but try not to be overwhelmed into taking no action at all.

There is a good short introduction to environmental campaigning at the end of the *Friends of the Earth Handbook* (Optima, 1987), but for the full inside story you will need Des Wilson's *Pressure: The A–Z of Campaigning in Britain* (Heinemann, 1984). *Holding Your Ground* by Angela King and Sue Clifford (Temple Smith, 1985) is a comprehensive handbook about how you can protect the things you care about in your locality. And, if you can handle the commercial sponsorship involved, the Shell Better Britain Campaign has produced a very useful – and free – guide to local environmental action, called simply *Getting Help* (1988).

YOU AND YOUR COUNCIL

Despite the trend towards centralisation of policy making in Britain, local authorities make many of the decisions which affect our daily lives. They also decide a large number of policies which affect the health of our local environment. The amount of information readily available to the public about the activities and policies of local councils varies enormously: some produce excellent information packs, others duplicated leaflets, others nothing at all. In order to understand the policies which affect your well-being and that of your surroundings, it is well worth knowing how local authorities work and how you can make your voice heard within them.

First, we need a very quick summary of local government in Britain. (A fuller up-to-date description can be found in the latest edition of *Whitaker's Almanac*, which you will find on the reference shelves of any public library.)

Britain is divided into 66 large areas, counties in England and Wales and regions in Scotland, in turn comprising 448 districts. The systems in each of the four countries – England, Wales, Scotland and Northern Ireland – are slightly different, but apart from Northern Ireland, where the district councils look after all local government responsibilities, the division of functions between county (or regional) and district ('borough' in some areas, notably London) councils is usually like this:

- County or regional councils look after large-scale planning, transport, police, fire services, education, social services, recreation, museums, libraries, consumer protection and refuse disposal.
- District or borough councils look after local planning, housing, building regulations, environmental health, refuse collection and crematoria.

At the local level in many rural areas, parish councils (community councils in Wales and Scotland) look after things like village halls, allotments and playgrounds.

The elected representatives (the actual 'council') decide general policy and will involve themselves in major decisions. As well as the full council, there will also be committees of councillors meeting regularly to deal with specific issues like planning and housing. Most of the day-to-day work of regional and district councils, however, is delegated to the council's officials – when people talk about 'the council' they often mean the council's employees rather than the elected representatives. Most councils have set up 'management teams', consisting of the council's chief executive and chief officers, to co-ordinate the implementation of council policy.

The information or public relations departments of the councils covering the area where you live will almost certainly be able to supply you with literature explaining how they operate and who to contact for specific information. If you are interested in finding out more, your local public library will probably carry the minutes of most council meetings, and many meetings are open to the public. It is also worth getting to know individual councillors and officials: again, your local library will have all the details of names and addresses.

Some important local public services are not looked after by your council. Sewerage and water supply are looked after by the regional water authorities, and personal health is the responsibility of the regional, district and local health authorities.

Other important documents which you will find in your library are the 'structure', district and local plans affecting your area; if you are sufficiently interested, you will also be able to buy copies of these plans from the planning department. The structure plan explains what the county or regional council has in mind in terms of 'strategic' things like main roads, major housing developments and nature conservation areas. The district and local plans make the structure plan ideas more specific. These are where you will be able to find out if the land next to your house is zoned for industrial development, or whether the nearby wood is covered by a tree preservation order.

If you find things in the plan that you don't like the look of, or if there is any other council policy you want to question, then don't hesitate to write, either to the relevant department, or to your local councillor, or both. Though they may be under considerable pressure of work, your council is there to serve you and look after your interests.

GOING TO THE TOP

There is nothing more frustrating than waiting for weeks for the answer to an important enquiry, hanging around in anonymous official waiting rooms, or staying at home in the hope that someone somewhere believes in the importance of returning phone calls. When your patience runs out, or when you think it will be quicker to bypass the endless buck-passing of unhelpful minions, this is the time to go straight to the top – to the managing director, to the chief officer, to the editor, to the people at *Watchdog* or *That's Life*, to your MP.

Many people who want some action taken, or the answer to an important question, give up at the first setback. I could cynically – but accurately – suggest that many systems are set up precisely to discourage you. But don't give up. Try again. Perseverance is the key to good research and effective campaigning. Here are a few guidelines:

- When you write or ring with your enquiry, be courteous, clear and friendly, but also quite firm. Don't be fobbed off with excuses like 'Nobody here knows anything about that' or 'That's not our responsibility'. If you are ringing and the person answering can't help, make sure that you ask them who might be able to help you.

- Keep copies of letters (both yours and theirs), and a full record of phone calls and visits.
- Keep going until you get what you want, or as close to it as you think you're going to get. If you have the energy to start a campaign or a line of research, you almost certainly have the energy to see it through. Tell yourself that you have the right to be heard and respected. It was this sort of faith that persuaded a 12-year-old schoolgirl to write to Mikhail Gorbachev to say how much she wanted world peace. She got her personal reply.
- Follow up unanswered letters with another letter (enclosing a copy of the first) or a phone call, and make sure that you respond quickly if they need further information – usually I find it easiest to deal with it straight away, so I don't have to keep remembering to do it.
- Make it clear that they have a vested interest in being helpful by reminding them that you are a voter/customer/taxpayer. If the going gets difficult, you can always add at the bottom 'Copy sent to trading standards department/my MP/*Watchdog*/the *Guardian*/the *Express*', but politeness and perseverance will usually make this unnecessary.

One 'top' from which you will always get a reply is your (or any other) MP, since they know it is an important part of their job to keep in touch with the electorate. Be warned, however: nearly all MPs have secretaries with word-processors programmed to spew forth party-line platitudes on a wide range of issues. If you want to avoid a reply which simply sandwiches together a series of bland pre-prepared paragraphs, your letter will need to be to the point and very specific. The likelihood is that it will then be passed to the appropriate ministry to be answered.

On the other hand, MPs take their correspondence seriously for another reason. While one letter on a subject can be written off as representing a fringe interest, two similar letters represent genuine concern. Five letters (reflecting in the MP's mind the views of several thousand voters) may well influence their thinking on that subject, especially if they are fairly neutral on an issue. Even leading politicians are not immune from Damascus-road-like conversions to green causes.

Writing to those who have power – and insisting on replies – is one good way of making yourself heard. Signing petitions is another. Asking pertinent questions during election campaigns is yet another. An excellent way to become involved and informed is to join one or more of the national campaigning groups listed on pages 223–229.

Another thing you might think about is joining the Green Party. The Green Party represents the political aspect of the green movement in Britain, offering people the opportunity to put their votes where their beliefs are. Green Party members believe that concern for environmental issues – in the widest sense – must be reflected in political will, and that while other political parties are developing 'add-on' green policies, it is important to have a party which sees green issues as being the basis upon which all other policy areas are formulated. Though the Green Party is still small, it is by no means a fringe party. Over 90 Green Party councillors sit on local councils, and the Green Party contested every seat in the 1989 European elections, gaining a remarkable 14.9 per cent of the vote. Green Party MPs already sit in the parliaments of 11 European countries.

While many green issues can be tackled at the household and community levels, there are some where only concerted effort at the highest levels will have any real effect. One such issue is the nuclear debate, both in terms of nuclear energy and the threat of nuclear war. Here you stand the best chance of influencing national and international policy by joining an active campaigning organisation. You could join Friends of the Earth or SCRAM, both of which produce very good literature about the risks of nuclear energy generation. Or you could join CND or the Peace Pledge Union, both working for the abolition of nuclear weapons, and both very much in the political eye.

If you feel strongly about nuclear issues, there are still things you can do as an individual using non-violent direct action, such as the Consumers Against Nuclear Energy campaign for withholding the proportion of your electricity bill which pays for nuclear power, or joining one of the half-dozen peace camps outside nuclear-capable military establishments. These activities, however, will appeal to or be possible only for very few people. The rest of us must influence the decision-makers in other ways.

Whatever you choose to do once you have read this book, the course of action most likely to lead to environmental disaster is to do nothing, to carry on as though nothing is amiss. Things are very definitely amiss. But though it is still a long way off, a faint green light is now glimmering at the end of the tunnel.

ORGANISATIONS AND SUPPLIERS

This list includes all the organisations and suppliers mentioned in the main text, as well as a few others.

HOME CONSERVATION

The energy equation

Energy Efficiency Office, Department of Energy, Thames Bank South, Millbank, London SW1T 4QJ

SCRAM, 11 Forth Street, Edinburgh EH1 3LE

Home insulation

National Cavity Insulation Association Ltd

External Wall Insulation Association

Draught Proofing Advisory Association Ltd

National Association of Loft Insulation Contractors

all the above c/o Corporate Public Relations Ltd, PO Box 12, Haslemere, Surrey GU27 3AN

Heating your home efficiently

ECSC Ltd, 99 Midland Road, London NW1 2AH

The Solar Trade Assocation, Brackenhurst, Greenham Common South, Newbury RG15 8HH

Labour savers or millstones?

Consumers' Association, 14 Buckingham Street, London WC2N 6DS (publishers of *Which?* magazine)

SPRING-GREENING

Recycling useful bits and pieces

Resource, Avon Environmental Centre, Junction Road, Brislington, Bristol BS4 3JP

Tools for Self-Reliance Ltd, Netley Marsh Workshop, Netley Marsh, Southampton SO4 2GY

Squeaky clean or ecoclean?

Ecover, Mouse Lane, Steyning, West Sussex BN4 3DF

Faith Products Ltd, Unit 5, Kay Street, Bury, Lancashire BL9 6BU (manufacturers of Clear Spring products)

Household pest control

London Hazards Centre, 3rd Floor, Headland House, 308 Gray's Inn Road, London WC1X 8DS

Beauty without cruelty

British Union for the Abolition of Vivisection, 16a Crane Grove, London N7 8LB

The Vegan Society, 33–35 George Street, Oxford OX1 2AY

Safety in the home

Royal Society for the Prevention of Accidents, Cannon House, The Priory Queensway, Birmingham B4 6BS

ABOUT THE HOUSE

Furniture

Community Furniture Network, 1a Oldham Street, Hyde, Cheshire SK14 1LJ

Friends of the Earth, Projects Unit, 26–28 Underwood Street, London N1 7JQ

Good wood

Friends of the Earth, Rainforest Department, 26–28 Underwood Street, London N1 7JQ

Doing it yourself

Royal Society for the Prevention of Accidents, Cannon House, The Priory Queensway, Birmingham B4 6BS

Noise

Noise Abatement Society, PO Box 8, Bromley, Kent BR2 0UM

Appropriate pets

League for the Introduction of Canine Control, PO Box 326, London NW5 3LE

Royal Society for the Prevention of Cruelty to Animals, The Causeway, Horsham, West Sussex RH12 1HG

Beautiful and really useful gifts

Greenpeace, 30–31 Islington Green, London N1 8BR

The Woodland Trust, Autumn Park, Dysart Road, Grantham, Lincolnshire NG31 6LL

Friends of the Earth Trading, 26–28 Underwood Street, London N1 7JQ

Campaign for Nuclear Disarmament, 22–24 Underwood Street, London N1 7JG

Co-operation (Marketing) Ltd, 34 Islington Green, London N1 8DU (mail order goods from co-operative businesses)

AA Enterprises, PO Box 533, London N19 4SS (mail order goods from southern African front-line states)

Traidcraft plc, Kingsway, Gateshead, Tyne and Wear NE11 0NE

Oxfam, Oxfam House, 274 Banbury Road, Oxford OX2 7DZ

GARDENING

Your piece of land

Friends of the Earth, 26–28 Underwood Street, London N1 7JQ

Recycling organic material

Blackwall Products, Unit 4, Riverside Industrial Estate, 150 River Way, London SE10 0BE (manufacturers of compost makers using recycled plastic barrels)

Wildlife in the garden

Suffolk Herbs, Sawyers Farm, Little Cornyards, Sudbury, Suffolk CO10 0NY (suppliers of wildflower seeds)

The Seed Bank and Exchange, Cowcombe Farm, Gipsy Lane, Chalford, Stroud, Gloucestershire GL6 8HP (exchange of and information about wildflower seeds)

Royal Society for the Protection of Birds, The Lodge, Sandy, Bedfordshire, SG19 2DL

Urban Wildlife Group, 131–133 Sherlock Street, Birmingham B5 6NB

Organic gardening

Henry Doubleday Research Association, National Centre for Organic Gardening, Ryton-on-Dunsmore, Coventry CV8 3LG

The Soil Association Ltd, 86–88 Colston Street, Bristol BS1 5BB

Producing your own food

Henry Doubleday Research Association, National Centre for Organic Gardening, Ryton-on-Dunsmore, Coventry CV8 3LG

FOOD

Organic produce

The Soil Association Ltd, 86–88 Colston Street, Bristol BS1 5BB

Working Weekends on Organic Farms, 19 Bradford Road, Lewes, Sussex BN7 1RB

Food additives

The London Food Commission, 88 Old Street, London EC1V 9AR

Food Additives Campaign Team, Room W, 25 Horsell Road, London N5 1XL

Understanding alcohol

Alcoholics Anonymous (GB) Ltd, PO Box 1, Stonebow House, Stonebow, York YO1 2NJ

Tea and coffee

OXFAM, Oxfam House, 274 Banbury Road, Oxford OX2 7DZ

Traidcraft plc, Kingsway, Gateshead, Tyne and Wear NE11 0NE

Twin Trading, 345 Goswell Road, London EC1V 7JT (coffee only)

Eating less meat

The Vegetarian Society, Parkdale, Dunham Road, Altrincham, Cheshire WA14 4QG

The Vegan Society, 33–35 George Street, Oxford OX1 2AY

Finding healthy meat

Compassion in World Farming, 20 Lavant Street, Petersfield, Hampshire, GU32 3EW

Pure Meat Company, Coombe Court Farm, Moretonhampstead, Devon TQ13 8QD

Red House Farm, Spalford Lane, North Scarle, Lincoln LN6 9HB

Real Meat Company, East Hill Farm, Heytesbury, Warminster, Wiltshire BA12 0HR

Eggs from happy hens

Free-Range Egg Association, 37 Tanza Road, London NW3 2UA

Chickens' Lib, PO Box 2, Holmfirth, Huddersfield HD7 1QT

The South African connection

Anti-Apartheid Movement, 13 Mandela Street, London NW1 0DW

AA Enterprises, PO Box 533, London N19 4SS

Amnesty International, 99–119 Rosebery Avenue, London EC1R 4RE

PACKING UP

Overcoming the throwaway mentality

Friends of the Earth, 26–28 Underwood Street, London N1 7JQ

Resource, Avon Environmental Centre, Junction Road, Brislington, Bristol BS4 3JP

Bags of waste

Industry Council for Packaging and the Environment, Premier House, 10 Greycoat Place, London SW1P 1SB

Separating rubbish

The Warmer Campaign, 83 Mount Ephraim, Tunbridge Wells, Kent TN4 8BS

Waste Watch, NCVO, 26 Bedford Square, London WC1B 3HU

Keeping cans under control

The Can Makers, 36 Grosvenor Gardens, London SW1W 0ED

Bottle banks

British Glass, Northumberland Road, Sheffield S10 2UA

Aerosols

Friends of the Earth, 26–28 Underwood Street, London N1 7JQ

Recycling your paper

Friends of the Earth, Recycling Department, 26–28 Underwood Street, London N1 7JQ

Charities Aid Foundation (Publications), 48 Pembury Road, Tonbridge, Kent TN9 2JD

Using recycled paper

Forestsaver, Freepost, PO Box 1, Portishead BS20 9BR

Greenscene Co-operative Ltd, 123 Fore Street, Exeter EX4 3JQ

Friends of the Earth Birmingham, 54–57 Allison Street, Digbeth, Birmingham B5 5TH

Traidcraft plc, Kingsway, Gateshead, Tyne and Wear NE11 0NE

Recycling Information Service, Friends of the Earth, 26–28 Underwood Street, London N1 7JQ

Paperback, Bow Triangle Business Centre, Unit 2, Eleanor Street, London E3 4NP

Conservation Papers, 228 London Road, Reading, Berkshire RG6 1AH

Earthwrite Co-operative Ltd, Unit 1b, Carlisle House, Carlisle Street East, Sheffield S4 7QN

Disposability

Women's Environmental Network, 287 City Road, London EC1V 1LA

Litter consciousness

The Tidy Britain Group, The Pier, Wigan WN3 4EX

COUNTRYSIDE

Respecting the countryside

The Countryside Commission, John Dower House, Crescent Place, Cheltenham, Gloucestershire GL50 3RA

Countryside campaigning

Royal Society for Nature Conservation, The Green, Nettleham, Lincoln LN2 2NR

Friends of the Earth Countryside Campaign, 26–28 Underwood Street, London N1 7JQ

Council for the Protection of Rural England, Warwick House, 25–27 Buckingham Palace Road, London SW1W 0PP

Council for the Protection of Rural Wales, Ty Gwyn, 31 High Street, Welshpool, Powys SY21 7JP

Association for the Protection of Rural Scotland, 14a Napier Road, Edinburgh EH10 5AY

The importance of trees

Men of the Trees, Turners Hill Road, Crawley Down, Crawley, West Sussex RH10 4HL

The Woodland Trust, Autumn Park, Dysart Road, Grantham, Lincolnshire NG31 6LL

Green holidays

British Trust for Conservation Volunteers, 36 St Mary's Street, Wallingford, Oxfordshire OX10 0EU

Field Studies Council, Preston Montford, Montford Bridge, Shrewsbury SY4 1HW

CHILDREN

Planned parenthood

Population Concern, 231 Tottenham Court Road, London W1P 9AE

The green baby

Association for Improvements in the Maternity Services, Goose Green Barn, Much Hoole, Preston, Lancashire PR4 4TD

National Childbirth Trust, Alexandra House, Oldham Terrace, London W3 6NH

La Leche League, BM 3424, London WC1N 3XX

The Whole Thing Catalogue, PO Box 100, Altrincham, Cheshire WA4 5FZ (suppliers of Biobottoms)

Play and playthings

Play Matters, 68 Churchway, London NW1 1LT

Letterbox Library, 8 Bradbury Street, London N16 8JN

Children and food

Hyperactive Children's Support Group, 71 Whyke Lane, Chichester, Sussex PO19 2LD

Sharing nature with children

Watch Trust for Environmental Education, 22 The Green, Nettleham, Lincoln LN2 2NR

Young People's Trust for the Environment and Nature Conservation, 95 Woodbridge Road, Guildford, Surrey GU1 4PY

Learning: a lifelong process

Green Teacher, Llys Awel, 22 Heol Pentrerheydn, Machynlleth, Powys SY20 8DN

Libertarian Education, The Cottage, The Green, Leire, Leicestershire LE17 5HL

Workers' Educational Institute, Temple House, 9 Upper Berkeley Street, London W1H 8BY

HEALTH

Holistic health

British Holistic Medical Association, 179 Gloucester Place, London NW1 6DX

Institute for Complementary Medicine, 21 Portland Place, London W1N 3AF

(the two leading organisations for practitioners of holistic healing techniques)

British Union for the Abolition of Vivisection, 16a Crane Grove, London N7 8LB

Allergic Reactions

Action Against Allergy, 43 The Downs, London SW20 8HG

National Society for Research into Allergy, PO Box 45, Hinckley, Leicestershire LE10 1JY

Diets and supplements

Institute for Optimum Nutrition, 5 Jerdan Place, London SW6 1BE

Green Farm Nutrition Centre, Burwash Common, East Sussex TN19 7LX

Avoiding the big smoke

Action on Smoking and Health, 5–11 Mortimer Street, London W1N 7RH

Watching stress levels

Relaxation for Living, 29 Burwood Park Road, Walton-on-Thames, Surrey KT12 5LH

Centre for Autogenic Training, Positive Health Centre, 101 Harley Street, London W1N 1DF

Exercise

Health Education Authority, Hamilton House, Mabledon Place, London WC1H 9TX

Sports Council, 16 Upper Woburn Place, London WC1H 0QP

Violence and non-violence

Childline, Freepost 1111, London EC4B 4BB (Tel: 0800 1111 – the call is free)

London Rape Crisis Centre, PO Box 69, London WC1X 9NJ (Tel: 01 837 1600 – can give information about other rape crisis numbers in Britain; in an emergency women may reverse the charges)

Peace within yourself

Open Centres, Avils Farm, Lower Stanton, Chippenham, Wiltshire SN14 6DA

Meditation Group for the New Age, Sundial House, Nevill Court, Tunbridge Wells, Kent, TN4 8NJ

CLOTHES

Natural fibres

Natural Fibres, 2 Springfield Lane, Smeeton Westerby, Leicester LE8 0QW

Cotton On, 29 North Clifton Street, Lytham FY8 5HW

Denny Andrews, Clock House Workshop, Coleshill, near Swindon SN6 7PT

Nightingales Ltd, 23 Union Street, Barnet, Hertfordshire EN5 4HY

Lynx, PO Box 509, Dunmow, Essex CM6 1UH (London shop at 79 Long Acre, Covent Garden)

Buying clothes direct

OXFAM, Oxfam House, 274 Banbury Road, Oxford OX2 7DZ

Traidcraft plc, Kingsway, Gateshead, Tyne and Wear NE11 0NE

Rural Development Commission, 141 Castle Street, Salisbury, Wiltshire SP1 3TP

Wales Craft Council Ltd (Cyngor Crefft Cymru Cyf), 20 Severn Street, Welshpool, Powys SY21 7AD

Scottish Development Agency, Craft Division, Rosebery House, Haymarket Terrace, Edinburgh EH12 5EZ

Clothes care

Ecover, Mouse Lane, Steyning, West Sussex BN4 3DF

Faith Products Ltd, Unit 5, Kay Street, Bury, Lancashire BL9 6BU (manufacturers of Clear Spring products)

TRANSPORT

Is your journey really necessary?

Transport 2000, Walkden House, 10 Melton Street, London NW1 2EJ

Using your legs

Pedestrians Association, 1 Wandsworth Road, London SW8 2LJ

Transport 2000, Walkden House, 10 Melton Street, London NW1 2EJ

Friends of the Earth, 26–28 Underwood Street, London N1 7JQ

How about the bike?

Royal Society for the Prevention of Accidents, Cannon House, The Priory Queensway, Birmingham B4 6BS

Cyclists' Touring Club, 69 Meadrow, Godalming, Surrey GU7 3HS

Friends of the Earth Cycling Campaign, 26–28 Underwood Street, London N1 7JQ

Lead-free petrol

Campaign for Lead-Free Air, 3 Endsleigh Street, London WC1H 0DD

Society of Motor Manufacturers and Traders, Forbes House, Halkin Street, London SW1X 7DS

Catalytic converters

Johnson Matthey Catalytic Systems Division, Orchard Road, Royston, Hertfordshire, SG8 5HE

Helping public transport to serve you

National Express, 4 Vicarage Road, Edgbaston, Birmingham B15 3ES

Transport 2000, Walkden House, 10 Melton Street, London NW1 2EJ

Railway Development Society, 15 Clapham Road, Lowestoft, Suffolk NR32 1RQ

Community Transport Association, Highbank, Halton Street, Cheshire SK14 2NY

WORK AND MONEY

Checking who you're working for

New Consumer, 52 Elswick Road, Newcastle upon Tyne NE4 6JH

Your working environment

Royal Society for the Prevention of Accidents, Cannon House, The Priory Queensway, Birmingham B4 6BS

Health and Safety Executive, Baynards House, 1 Chepstow Place, Westbourne Grove, London W2 4TF

Co-operation

Co-operation (Marketing) Ltd, 34 Islington Green, London N1 8DU

Co-operative Development Agency, Broadmead House, 21 Panton Street, London SW1Y 4DR

Industrial Co-Ownership Movement, 7/8 The Corn Exchange, Leeds LS1 7BP

Co-operatives Research Unit, Faculty of Technology, Open University, Walton Hall, Milton Keynes MK7 6AA

Everywoman Ltd, 34a Islington Green, London N1 8DU

Fair Trading

Traidcraft plc, Kingsway, Gateshead, Tyne and Wear NE11 0NE

OXFAM, Oxfam House, 274 Banbury Road, Oxford, OX2 7DZ

AA Enterprises, PO Box 533, London N19 4SS

Twin Trading, 345 Goswell Road, London EC1V 7JT

Equal Exchange, 29 Nicolson Square, Edinburgh EH8 9BX

New Internationalist, 120–126 Lavender Avenue, Mitcham, Surrey CR4 3HP

Being aware of adverts

Mailing Preference Service, Freepost 22, London W1E 7EZ

Advertising Standards Authority, 2–16 Torrington Place, London WC1E 7HN

Investing in a future we want

The Ethical Investment Research and Information Service, 401 Bondway Business Centre, 71 Bondway, London SW8 1SQ

The Ethical Consumer, 100 Gretney Walk, Moss Side, Manchester M15 5ND

New Consumer, 52 Elswick Road, Newcastle-upon-Tyne, NE4 6JH

The Ecology Building Society, 8 Main Street, Crosshills, Keighley, West Yorkshire BD20 8TB

PRESS FOR ACTION

Every little helps

Ark Trust, 498–500 Harrow Road, London W9 3QA

Finding the facts

Friends of the Earth, 26–28 Underwood Street, London N1 7JQ

Getting the message across

Redwood, 83 Fordwych Road, London NW2 3TL

Shell Better Britain Campaign, Red House, Hill Lane, Great Barr, Birmingham B43 6LZ

Going to the top

The Green Party, 10 Station Parade, Balham High Road, London SW12 9AZ

Scottish Green Party, 11 Forth Street, Edinburgh EH1 3LE

Friends of the Earth, 26–28 Underwood Street, London N1 7JQ

SCRAM, 11 Forth Street, Edinburgh EH1 3LE

Campaign for Nuclear Disarmament, 22–24 Underwood Street, London N1 7JG

Peace Pledge Union, 6 Endsleigh Street, London WC1H 0DX

Consumers Against Nuclear Energy, PO Box 697, London NW1 8YQ

ECO-FAX

These pages are designed for you to fill in the addresses and/or telephone numbers you may need in order to notify, complain or enquire about green concerns. You may like to photocopy the filled-in pages and pin them by the telephone. Start filling it in now: you never know when you might need it in a hurry!

Community/Parish Council ....

Local Authority (borough/district/council/region):

Environmental Health Department ....

Water and Sewerage Department ....

Planning Department ....

  Rights of Way Officer ....

Transport Department ....

Trading Standards Department ....

Water Authority Pollution Officer ....

Police .... (999 in an emergency)

Railway station ....

Bus station ....

Citizens Advice Bureau ....

Local library ....

Local Health Council ....

Health Centre ....

Hospital .... (999 in an emergency)

Natural Health Centre ....

  Practitioners ....

....

Institute for Complementary Medicine information number:
01 636 9543

Local radio ....

Regional television ....

Local newspaper/s ....

	National	Local
Friends of the Earth, 26–28 Underwood Street, London N1 7JQ	01 490 1555	....
Greenpeace, 30–31 Islington Green, London N1 8XE	01 354 5100	....
Council for the Protection of Rural England, 25–27 Buckingham Palace Road, London SW1W 0PP	01 976 6433	....
Green Party, 10 Station Parade, Balham High Road, London SW12 9AZ	01 673 0045	....
Royal Society for Nature Conservation/WATCH, The Green, Nettleham, Lincoln LN2 2NR	0522 752326	....
Nature Conservancy Council, Northminster House, Northminster Road, Peterborough, Cambridgeshire PE1 1UA	0733 40345	....
Royal Society for the Prevention of Cruelty to Animals, The Causeway, Horsham, West Sussex RH12 1HG	0403 64181	....
Royal Society for the Protection of Birds, The Lodge, Sandy, Bedfordshire SG19 2DL	0767 80551	....
Traidcraft, Kingsway, Gateshead, Tyne and Wear NE11 0NE	091 487 3191	....

MP .... House of Commons, London SW1A 0AA

MEP .... Centre Européen, Kirchberg, Luxembourg

Department of the Environment, 2 Marsham Street, London SW1P 3EB, 01 276 3000

Ministry of Defence (low-flying military aircraft complaints), DSBc, Main Building, Whitehall, London SW1A 2HB

Advisory Committee on Pollution of the Sea (pollution incidents), 3 Endsleigh Street, London WC1H 0DD, 01 388 2117

Health and Safety Executive, Baynards House, 1 Chepstow Place, Westbourne Grove, London W2 4TF, 01 229 3456

A BASIC GREEN LIBRARY

Information and stimulation are vital if we are to transform our values and lifestyles to take account of green insights. The media are all now beginning to cover the issues regularly and in depth, and an increasing number of bookshops are recognising the need for a section on 'environment' or 'green politics'.

Here is a selection of books which should give you plenty to think about and lots of ideas for further action. The first five are in my opinion the most practical; the three which follow look at the issues in more depth. As well as (or instead of) buying the books from this selection that you want for yourself, order them from your public library – that way you'll make sure that the ideas reach as wide an audience as possible!

For a comprehensive catalogue of books on green issues, send an A4 stamped addressed envelope to Books for a Change, 52 Charing Cross Road, London WC2H 0BB, asking for their *Green Catalogue*.

The Friends of the Earth Handbook
Optima, 1987
An accessible introduction to environmental issues, and to what can be done to limit environmental damage. The appendix on campaigning is particularly good, and the cartoons by Chris Winn are very funny.

The Coming of the Greens
Jonathon Porritt and David Winner
Fontana, 1988
A book which traces the recent burgeoning of interest in green issues and green politics; very readable and stimulating, with contributions from a galaxy of green-tinted celebrities from Ken Livingstone to Fay Weldon and Julie Christie.

The Green Consumer Guide
John Elkington and Julia Hailes
Gollancz, 1988
The book that launched the term 'green consumer' into everyday parlance: an excellent source of information about the environmental implications of buying and using everything from herbs to holidays. It doesn't, however, grasp the nettle of voluntary simplicity: it relies on 'safer' rather than 'less'.

Home Ecology
Karen Christensen
Arlington, 1989
A more domestic and chatty, but no less hard-hitting, guide to all the things you can do in your personal life to ensure the well-being of your family and your environment. Unlike *The Green Consumer Guide*, Karen Christensen isn't afraid to ask the really difficult questions, and to suggest practical answers.

Green Pages: A Directory of Natural Products,
Services, Resources and Ideas
John Button
Optima, 1988
More than 300 magazine-style large-format pages, on green recycled paper, providing the background to a wide range of green concerns from recycled paper to self-help therapy. Lots of names and addresses, book reviews and quotations: 'Every home should have one' said the Friends of the Earth reviewer.

Seeing Green
Jonathon Porritt
Blackwell, 1984
Despite getting a bit long in the tooth, this is still the best available introduction to green ideas and politics. Jonathon Porritt, the green spokesperson whom politicians have come to learn means business, is fluent, fearless and inspiring.

A Green Manifesto
Sandy Irvine and Alec Ponton
Optima, 1988
An effective antidote to critics who say that green politics is all hot air and empty promises, *A Green Manifesto* offers a clear, refreshing look at the challenges of the 1990s, showing that ecological principles do offer a practical way forward.

Blueprint for a Green Planet
John Seymour and Herbert Girardet
Dorling Kindersley, 1987
Calling itself 'a handbook of positive measures and realistic alternatives', *Blueprint* puts a wide range of green concerns into an international context, and includes many helpful illustrations.

ABOUT FRIENDS OF THE EARTH

Friends of the Earth (FoE) was established in 1971 to campaign for a better environment. It has a network of over 270 local groups and over 100,000 supporters. FoE's main campaign areas are: energy, air pollution, agriculture and countryside, tropical rain-forests, cities for people, water pollution and toxics, and recycling. FoE works with any party or organisation interested in furthering green ideas, and recent successes include mobilising people to persuade aerosol and fast food companies to move to CFC-free products, enforcing EC laws on drinking water quality in Britain, and the tightening of pesticide legislation. In addition to its active campaigning, FoE is seen by the public, industry and the government as an important source of environmental information.

Membership of FoE puts you in touch with other local members, and brings you a regular mailing of environmental information, including the magazine *Earth Matters*. FoE also has an active youth organisation called Earth Action. If you would like to join FoE, all you need to do is fill in the membership form on the next page, add a cheque, and send it off. Do it now.

To: Friends of the Earth (Memberships), Freepost, Melksham, Wiltshire SN12 7BR

Having read about you in *How To Be Green*, I would like to be a Friend of the Earth. Please enrol me as a member and send me FoE's quarterly magazine, *Earth Matters*.

Name ....

Address ....

....

Postcode .... Phone ....

I enclose a cheque for £......... (payable to Friends of the Earth), or please debit my Access/Visa/Mastercard account with my subscription of £ ....

Card number ☐☐☐☐☐☐☐☐☐☐☐☐☐☐☐☐

Signature .... Expiry date ....

I also include a donation of ....

1989/1990 subscription rates: ordinary: £12

           unwaged: £5

           overseas: £20

           life: £250

Friends of the Earth urgently needs your regular support to enable the organisation to reduce office costs and plan for long-term success, and would be delighted if you were to make a monthly standing order. If you would like a standing order form, please write to the above address.

LAAD

About the author

John Button's involvement with green concerns goes back over 20 years when, as a student, he helped establish an ecology study group with David Bellamy. In the 1970s he founded Friends of the Earth's most northerly local group in the Shetland Islands, and became the publisher at the famous Findhorn Foundation. More recently he has become actively involved in green politics, standing as a candidate in the 1989 European elections.

An author, journalist, lecturer and group leader, he is currently consultant editor of *New Consumer* magazine and writes a monthly column in *Environment Now*. His other books include *A Dictionary of Green Ideas*, *Green Pages* and *The Green Guide to England*. He has two teenage daughters, and lives in a small seaside town in Galloway.